Letters from the Peninsula
1808-1812

Lt-General William Warre, C.B., K.T.S.

Letters from the Peninsula 1808-1812

The Correspondence of an Anglo-Portuguese Staff
Officer during His Service in the Peninsular War

William Warre
Edited by Edmond Warre

LEONAUR

Letters from the Peninsula 1808-1812
The Correspondence of an Anglo-Portuguese Staff Officer during His Service in the Peninsular War
by William Warre
edited by Edmond Warre

First published under the title
Letters from the Peninsula 1808-1812

Leonaur is an imprint of Oakpast Ltd

Copyright in this form © 2019 Oakpast Ltd

ISBN: 978-1-78282-832-7 (hardcover)
ISBN: 978-1-78282-833-4 (softcover)

http://www.leonaur.com

Contents

Preface

Some years before his death in 1875, my father entrusted to me a packet containing letters written by his eldest brother, my uncle, Sir William Warre, from the Peninsula during his service there from 1808 to 1812.

The packet was not opened by me until the year 1908.

The letters, on perusal, seemed to be of interest, as giving a graphic description of the life and opinions of an officer serving on the staff during the Peninsular War, and, in particular, of one immediately concerned in the organisation of the Portuguese Army.

Moreover, the letters, which are written on the spot and without reserve, being chiefly addressed to his father or mother, seem to reflect in some measure, as regards the campaign, and as to home politics, to which there are plentiful allusions, the conversation and opinions of the Headquarters' Staff at the time; and further, the intimate acquaintance of the writer with the Portuguese character, and with the methods of the Portuguese Government, enhances the illustration of the difficulties which had to be overcome in the effort of Great Britain to save her ally from the crushing yoke of French imperial despotism.

Mr James Warre of Oporto, the father of Sir William Warre, was a man of great ability, and of influence both in Portugal and at home. He was a partner in the firm of Warre & Co., which was at the time one of the leading commercial houses in Oporto—an old firm, established in the seventeenth century—with which, however, the family connection was severed at the death of Sir William Warre's brother George, in the year 1850.

The letters themselves, considering the circumstances under which they were written, are very fairly legible; but in places there are *lacunae* which are sometimes difficult to fill up. The orthography is not at all consistent—often old-fashioned, sometimes faulty. I have corrected it in some places, but in many have left it as in the original.

I cannot claim to have any particular knowledge of military history, and, as regards the brief introductions to the several chapters, wish to acknowledge *in limine* my indebtedness to Napier's great work, to Professor Oman's three most interesting volumes, which bring the story of the war down to 1810, and to Sir Herbert Maxwell's *Life of the Duke of Wellington*.

I am indebted also to my cousin, Mr George Warre, for help in translating the Portuguese words and phrases that occur in the letters.

My thanks are also due to my cousin, Mrs Wm. Rathbone, for kindly allowing me to use several of the collection of family letters in her possession, extracts from which help to fill up some of the gaps in the correspondence.

Lastly, I must acknowledge my debt of gratitude to my friend and publisher, Mr John Murray, for his most valuable help in many ways. Without his assistance, the map which illustrates the volume could not have been constructed.

Edmond Warre.

Finchampstead, 1909.

CHRONOLOGICAL TABLE
OF EVENTS

	1807.	
Nov.		French Conquest of Portugal.
Nov.	30.	Junot occupies Lisbon.
		Portuguese Royal Family fly to Brazil.
	1808.	
May.		Napoleon makes Joseph Buonaparte King of Spain.
		Outbreak of Spanish insurrection.
June.		French invade Valencia and Andalusia.
		Siege of Saragossa.
July	14.	Battle of Medina del Rio Seco.
„	20.	Capitulation of Baylen.
Aug.	1-4.	Landing of British army in Portugal.
„	17.	Combat of Roliça.
„	21.	Battle of Vimiero.
„	30.	Convention of Cintra.
Oct.		Napoleon's invasion of Spain.
Oct.	6.	Sir John Moore takes command of British troops in Portugal.
Nov.	13.	Moore at Salamanca.
„	23.	Battle of Tudela. Spaniards defeated.
Dec.	4.	Napoleon arrives at Madrid.
„	15.	Soult with 15,000 men at Saldaña.
„	20.	Moore reaches Mayorga ; junction with Baird.
„	21.	Combat of Sahagun.
„	22.	Napoleon's pursuit of Moore begins.
„	23.	Avanilla, near Sahagun, 5½ leagues from Saldaña, half-past 5 P.M.—orders to march on Saldaña, 6 P.M. ; news received about 7 P.M. of Napoleon's advance ; Moore resolves on and orders retreat.
„	28.	Benavente.
„	29.	Astorga.
„	31.	Bembibre.
		Napoleon leaves the pursuit to Soult and returns to France.

1809.

Jan.	Retreat of Sir John Moore's army continued.
Jan. 2.	Bembibre.
,, 3.	Villa Franca.
,, 6.	Rearguard finds army at Lugo in position.
,, 8-9.	Lugo evacuated.
,, 9-10.	Betanzos.
,, 11.	Corunna—no transports.
,, 14.	Transports arrive.
,, 16.	Battle of Corunna.
,, 17.	Embarkation completed.
,, 18.	H.M.S. *Barfleur* sails from Corunna.
,, 23.	Arrives Plymouth.
Feb. 20.	Fall of Saragossa.
Feb. (end).	Beresford appointed to command Portuguese army.
March (early).	Beresford arrives at Lisbon.
March 10-20.	Soult's operations in Portugal ; capture of Oporto.
,, 29.	Battle of Medellin—Spaniards defeated.
April 22.	Sir A. Wellesley arrives in Lisbon.
May 12-22.	Oporto retaken ; Soult's retreat to Orense and Lugo.
June.	Advance of British army from Abrantes.
July 27-28.	Battle of Talavera.
Aug. 4.	Wellesley retires on Badajos.
Oct. 18.	Battle of Tamames—French defeated.
Nov. 19.	Battle of Ocaña—Spaniards defeated.
,, 29.	Battle of Alba de Tormes—Spaniards defeated.

1810.

Jan.	Lord Wellington retires into Portugal.
Jan. and Feb.	The French invade Andalusia.
Feb. 1.	King Joseph enters Seville.
	Siege of Cadiz.
,, 12.	Badajos summoned by Mortier.
March to April 22.	Siege of Astorga.
May to July 9.	Siege of Ciudad Rodrigo.
July 24.	Combat of the Coa.
July to Aug. 27.	Siege of Almeida.
Sept. 16.	Masséna advances into Portugal.
,, 27.	Battle of Bussaco.
Oct. 1-9.	Wellington retires within the lines of Torres Vedras.
Oct. to Nov.	Masséna before the lines.
Nov. 14.	Masséna retreats to Santarem.
Dec. 21.	Soult moves northward to support Masséna.

Memoir of William Warre

William Warre, the subject of this *Memoir*, was the eldest son of James Warre of Oporto, and Eleanor, *née* Greg, his wife. He was born at Oporto, 15th April 1784, and spent most of his childhood there. He was sent to Harrow, but seems to have left early, and to have been placed in the office of Messrs Warre & Co., of which his uncle, William Warre, was the senior partner, in order that he might learn the business which both his uncle and his father desired him to follow.

But his own strong wish was to be a soldier, and, as it turned out, a piece of mischief achieved that which arguments and entreaties had failed to obtain. One day in the office, when letters had to be got ready for the mail, the duty of sealing them, in which, after the fashion of the day much wax, red or black, was consumed, devolved upon the young clerk, who, observing that the pigtail of Pedro Alves, the Portuguese member of the firm, had lapped over to his side of the desk, while the old gentleman was enjoying a peaceful post-prandial slumber, felt moved to play a practical joke, which had momentous consequences. He poured the red wax upon the ribbon of the pigtail, fastening it to the desk, sealed it with the seal of the firm, and fled. Great was the wrath that ensued. No apologies could be accepted. It was the end of his commercial career.

He was then sent to a private tutor at Bonn to learn foreign languages, and to prepare for the army. On the breaking out of the war between France and Austria, he and another fellow-student joined the Austrians, and went out, as they said, to see the fun. As luck would have it, they were taken prisoners in a skirmish, and were brought before General Custine, who commanded the French force in the neighbourhood. Custine, seeing that they were English and mere boys, scolded them and told them that it was very lucky for them that Marshal Davoust had not arrived to take over the command, "for," said he,

13

"he would have hanged you without mercy on the nearest tree. Now go back to your books and your tutor, and don't meddle with affairs which do not concern you."

Shortly after this William Warre was sent back to England, and on the 5th November 1803, when he was 19 years of age, received his commission in the 52nd Light Infantry, then under the command of Sir John Moore. He served with the 52nd till 25th April 1805, when he was promoted Lieutenant in the 98th, which was then in Canada. He did not, however, proceed thither, having purchased promotion as Captain in the 23rd Dragoons.

He served with this regiment in Ireland until the summer of 1807, when he was sent to the Royal Military College, then established at High Wycombe, to study for Staff employment.

In 1808 General Ferguson selected him as A.D.C., and took him with him to Portugal. There he was present at the combat of Roliça, and at the Battle of Vimeiro, both of which are described in his letters. His health gave way under the hardships of this campaign, and he was detained ill at Lisbon for several months. His knowledge of the Portuguese language enhanced the value of his services, and after his recovery, General Ferguson having returned to England, he was attached by General Beresford to his personal staff, and served with him as his principal A.D.C. until the year 1812.

Captain Warre took part in Sir John Moore's retreat and, with General Beresford, was the last to embark after the Battle of Corunna, 16th January 1809.

In March 1809, Beresford, with the rank of Field-Marshal, was placed in chief command of the Portuguese Army, and employed Captain Warre, his A.D.C., in the organisation of the national troops. He entered the Portuguese service and was promoted therein to the rank of Major, and appointed first A.D.C. to the Field-Marshal.

After the passage of the Douro, May 1809, Major Warre was sent forward by Beresford to raise the armed peasantry in the province of Minho, with a view to harassing the French forces under Marshal Soult, which were then in full retreat. He succeeded in getting the peasantry to dismantle the bridges of Ponte Nova and the Saltador, but could not get them to destroy their own means of communication. Had this been done the French Army was lost. The delay, however, caused by the necessity of forcing and repairing the bridges, cost the French the loss of many men and horses, (see *Oman*, vol. ii.), and of most of the spoil they were carrying off from Oporto. Unfortunately, the letters in which these operations were described are wanting. But for the rest of the long campaign up to the Battle of Salamanca, with the exception of Talavera, when he was with Beresford in Portugal, and of Albuera, and Bussaco, from which he was absent through illness, his letters are fairly consecutive comments of an actor in the events which occurred during that period of heroic struggle.

On 30th May 1811 he was promoted by brevet to the rank of Major in the English Army, and to that of Lieutenant-Colonel in the Portuguese Army. At the last siege of Badajos, he was the senior staff officer at the summons of Fort Christobal, and had the honour of taking prisoners the Generals Philippon and Weyland, who surrendered their swords to him.

In the Battle of Salamanca, 1812, he was with his chief, Marshal Beresford, when the latter was severely wounded, and, as narrated in the letters, carried him into the town, nursed him through his illness, and went with him to Lisbon.

In 1813 Major Warre was promoted to the rank of Lieutenant-Colonel in the English Army, and resigned his commission in the Portuguese Army. He received from the King of Portugal medals for his conduct at Vimeiro, at the siege and assault of Ciudad Rodrigo, and for the two sieges of Badajos, also a medal for the four campaigns. He was also made a Knight of the Order of the Tower and Sword, and of the Order of St Bento d'Avis.

In 1813 he was sent to the Cape of Good Hope, where he was appointed Q.M.G., a post which he held till 1819.

In November 1812 he had married Selina, youngest daughter of Christopher Maling of West Herrington and Hillton, in the county of Durham. By her he had a family of three sons and two daughters. His youngest son, Henry, born 1819 at the Cape, was afterwards General Sir Henry Warre, K.C.B. His wife died 3rd February 1821.

In November 1820 he returned to England, and in 1821, by reason of ill-health, went on half-pay.

In May 1823 he was appointed A.Q.M.G. in Ireland, and in 1826 was transferred to a similar appointment in England. In 1826-1827 he served on the staff of the army sent to Lisbon under the command of Sir William Clinton, G.C.B.

On 22nd July 1830 he became a full Colonel. He served again on the Staff in Ireland till 1836, when he was appointed to the command at Chatham. He held this appointment till his promotion to the rank of Major-General 23rd November 1841. It was during his command that the Review took place which is immortalised by Dickens in *Pickwick*. He was made C.B., and was Knighted in 1839. In 1842 he was placed in command of the North-Western District. Subsequently he was transferred to the Northern District, with his Headquarters at York. Reference is made to him in the letters of Queen Victoria (vol. i.).

He gave up the command at York in the year 1851, and, liking the place and neighbourhood, remained there in a residence which he rented at Bishopthorpe. His health broke down in 1852, and in the following year he died, and was buried in the churchyard at Bishopthorpe. The church has since been pulled down, and the churchyard, which is adjacent to the gardens of the Archiepiscopal Palace, closed. His tomb is on the south side of the old graveyard, and bears the following inscription:—

SACRED TO THE MEMORY
OF
LIEUTENANT-GENERAL SIR WILLIAM WARRE
C.B., K.T.S., K.C., ST BENTO D'AVIS
COLONEL OF THE 94TH REGIMENT
DIED AT YORK, 26TH JULY 1853, AGED 69 YEARS.

CHAPTER 1

1808

In June 1808 the British Government determined to send assistance to the Spaniards, who had risen in revolt against the French domination in the Peninsula.

Spain, which had been an enemy, was now regarded as a friend.

In the previous year, an expedition under General Whitelock had been despatched to invade the Spanish Colonies in America, with disastrous results. In 1808 a force of about 9000 men was already assembled in Ireland, with a view to renewing this attempt under a more competent general. But in the altered circumstances the destination of these troops was changed, and they were placed under the command of Lieut.-General Sir Arthur Wellesley, with orders to proceed to Portugal and to co-operate with the Spaniards and Portuguese in attacking the French.

Beside the troops ready to embark in Ireland there were two brigades—Anstruther's and Acland's, quartered at Harwich and Ramsgate respectively—available for immediate service abroad. These were added to Wellesley's command. And in addition to these there were at this time about 5000 men, under General Spencer, observing Cadiz, who could join the expedition on Portuguese soil. Lastly, there was a force of about 10,000 men under Sir John Moore, who had been sent to the Baltic to co-operate with the Swedes, a task which proved impracticable. These were on their way home, and were ordered to Portugal, though some time elapsed before they could join their comrades in the Peninsula.

Major-General Ferguson, with his *aides-de-camp*, Capt. Warre and Capt. Mellish, embarked at Portsmouth in H.M.S. *Resistance*—Capt. Adam—in May; but their destination at that time was quite uncertain, though General Ferguson, nominally at least, belonged to the force under General Spencer's command. After some further delay, owing to contrary winds, the *Resistance* arrived at Cork, where Sir Arthur Wellesley on 7th June assumed the command of the troops assembled. The news of the Spanish insurrection had already reached England, and although quite uncertain as yet as to their future movements, everyone seems to have taken it for granted that they were to sail at once. As it turned out, they had many weeks to wait before the actual start took place.

The six letters written in May and June, though not belonging properly to the letters from the Peninsula, have been included in the series, as giving an account not altogether uninteresting of the kind of life led while waiting for orders to sail, the needs and necessities recorded, and the ideas generally entertained by the writer as set forth in his correspondence. The difficulties respecting the soldier servant, whom he was so anxious to take with him, have an almost tragic interest in view of the ultimate fate of the man, which is afterwards described in the letters.

Not without interest also are the sidelights occasionally thrown upon the jealousy with which colonels of regiments regarded the taking of officers from service with the regiment for staff employment, and the indications of the necessity of influence in high quarters to obtain any appointment of the kind. But more than all is the evidence of the enthusiasm which pervaded all ranks—enthusiasm for a glorious cause, which was no less than the liberation of Europe from the domination of the tyrant, who had trampled right and justice underfoot, and was without gainsaying England's bitterest and deadliest foe.

LETTERS

Portsmouth, May 22, 1808.

Here we are, my dearest Father, after a very hasty journey and pleasant, as constant rain and a complete overturn about ½ a mile short of Kingston, from which Capt. Mellish and myself escaped quite safe, except a few trifling bruises and a sprained thumb I got, which renders my writing somewhat difficult— with these exceptions it was as pleasant as could be to me, leaving all those dearest to me in the world.

We have just got all our baggage, and go on board ourselves this evening. Capt. Adam appears to be a very fine gentlemanly young man, and much inclined to show us every civility.

We shall sail as soon as the wind is fair, and are much hurried.

Should my things arrive this evening they will be in time, otherwise I fear not. Nothing can be kinder than the general. I think myself every moment more fortunate in going with him. Pray get some advice about Rankin. I shall send him on shore at Cork, if I can, and have no answer from Seymour. (Lt.-Col. 23rd Dragoons.) If I am not able to send him on shore, the advice I want you to get is, how to get him leave to go, as if he were not gone but to Cork. Pray write. It may find me on board the *Resistance*, Cork. I will write every opportunity. May God bless and preserve you all and give you every happiness, is the constant prayer of your affectionate son,

Wm. Warre.

H.M.S. Resistance,
St Helens, May 24th, 1808.

Many thanks, my dear Father, for your letter of yesterday, and the books and wine, about which I have just written to Messrs Smith and Atkins, directing them, if we are sailed, to send it to care of Markland at Gibraltar. Here we are with the wind as foul as it can blow, and too hard to put to sea. We shall sail the first opportunity, and are not a little anxious to get off. Nothing can exceed the general's and Capt. Adam's kindness. We are as comfortable as on shore, and as happy as possible.

We have not the least idea of our destination. Reports I never believe. If the general does not know, it is not likely any newspaper can. I received my books and wine safe, for which accept my thanks. The books, at all events, I could not read if I had them not. They are therefore as well with me, and God knows how long we may be on board or away.

I am glad you intend to call on the duke. It is as well; and pray do not forget to assure Ld. Mostyn of my gratitude and sense of his kindness towards me. I have written, or rather I wrote the day I left town to Seymour, but should I not get his answer at Cork, must send Rankin on shore; and to go without a servant is very inconvenient indeed. Therefore, I think, if you could hire me a steady, honest servant, it would be worthwhile his coming to Cork to me; or the general thinks it would be better to ask General Calvert, by *empenho* (desire) to send me an order to Cork for him to accompany me at all events.

Adieu; we are ordered off by signal. May God preserve and bless you all, is the constant prayer of your affectionate son,

Wm. Warre.

Cove, June 8, 1808.

My Dearest Father,

Till yesterday, on Sir A. Wellesley's arrival at Cork to take the command, our sailing was so uncertain, that I did not write to you, for other news, except that we are all well, from hence I had none to tell. We now expect to sail the day after tomorrow, Sunday, if the wind is fair. The glorious accounts from Spain have hurried us off, and I believe there is now no doubt that that is our destination, but what part we know not. The Rendezvous is Tangier bay, in case of parting company, which looks like Cadiz (this *entre nous*).

We are exceedingly anxious to get away, after six weeks' delay. The army are in the highest spirits; indeed, the cause we are engaged in is the noblest a soldier could wish, and to support the liberties and independence of a country so lately our enemy. To forget all animosity and cordially join against the common enemy of Europe, the would-be tyrant of the world, is worthy of the British name; and a soldier's heart must be cold indeed that would not warm with enthusiasm in such a cause. I am not one of the most sanguine; you know my opinion of armed mobs, though in this, from the accounts we have received, there is an appearance of system and order that promises well. May God assist the Right. It may be the crisis of the tyrant's power. If he fails now, it may open the eyes of Europe.

I will write by every opportunity and let you know how we are going on, and the news, and a line when we sail. The general's best thanks for your present of maps. They are most acceptable to him. He is gone with Adam and Mellish to Cork to dine with the mayor, or dine in public in honour of Sir Arthur. I was asked, but having a good deal to do, and not fancying a crowd, have sent an excuse. We have been very gay here ever since we arrived, but long to be off.

How unfortunate we were not to be with Spencer at landing at Cadiz. There will be yet something I hope to be done. Boney will not easily give up his point, and a more beautiful army never embarked, for its size, from any place. We have been joined by 45th, 4 troops 20 Lt. Dns., and 2 companies artillery, besides a very large staff, and are to be by the 36th Regt. The troops are very healthy, in all about 9650 men.

I have not heard further about remaining in the 23rd. Seymour has allowed me to take Rankin, if I can get a man to exchange. Stuart is trying to get me one from the 9th Foot, but they are all so high in spirits at going on service, I fear of his getting one. I think we shall certainly sail on Sunday, if possible. Write to me, in case we should go to Porto, direct Gibraltar, and tell me if I can do anything there; depend on my punctuality and exertions. Such a thing might happen as going in there. Our party is much augmented on-board *Resistance*. Generals Craufurd and Fane 1 *a.-de-c.* or 2, 1 brigade-major, and a civil secretary. It will not be so pleasant as hitherto. Patience, it is a million times better than a transport.

From your ever affectionate son,

Wm. Warre.

Pray desire Hawkes Piccadilly to send me a hat and feather, the same *shape exactly* as the last, by 1st opportunity; my old one is gone to pieces. *Adieu.*

Cove, June 17, 1808.

My Dear Father,

I have to thank you for your kind letter on the 11th inst, and for that you wrote to Genl. Payne, in which you have said everything that can be said. I am much afraid he is offended with my carrying my point in spite of him.

It is however of consequence my remaining in the regiment, as more captains are quitting it I hear, and I have therefore this day written to Greenwood's with the enclosed paper of exchange signed, of which letter you have an extract annexed. It may do good, and cannot do any harm.

Seymour, I think, will do what he can for me; his letters are as friendly as possible, though he will not allow me to take Rankin, which is very annoying, particularly now that I have bought a horse, nor do I know what to do for a servant here. There is no such thing, and as all the troops are now embarked, and we may be ordered to sail every hour, I have no time to write for one. I should therefore be much obliged to you, if you would enquire about some honest, trusty man, who must understand horses, and send him out to join me at Gibraltar.

Agree about wages, clothes, etc., and send him out to join me at Gibraltar, or off Cadiz, as soon as a conveyance offers. To be on service without a trusty servant will be exceedingly unpleasant. We know nothing further of our destination or plans. We have been here amusing ourselves in perfect idleness, though very gayly. We yesterday dined on board Ld. Thomond's yacht, and went in the evening to a play, acted by the officers of the *Resistance*, for the poor of Cove. It was exceedingly crowded, and went off very well. I have bought a nice little hack, a mare, the only thing of the kind I could get for the price, 30 guineas Irish, for which I drew yesterday on you. They ask 50, 60, 70, for nice hacks, and the genl. and Mellish have been obliged to pay it. I got mine from an artillery officer, through a friend of mine, and am very lucky. I also further drew upon you for £20 British to Mr Mayhew, of which Mellish has half and is to pay me in the money of the country we go to.

I hope we shall now leave this very soon. All the regts. are embarked, and we only wait for orders. I will write as soon as they arrive. I rejoice to hear that dear Tom was safe at Stockholm, and daily expected. God send him safe, dear fellow. It would have been great happiness to have seen him before I sailed, but I shall now be satisfied with hearing of his safe arrival. Give him my kindest love and welcome home. (Thomas Warre, second son of James Warre, a merchant in St Petersburg, escaped from Russia to Sweden after war had been declared against England.) Pray assure Lord Rosslyn when you see him of my high sense of his Lordship's goodness, and that if I must quit the 23rd, I shall feel highly gratified by being in his regiment. Pray get my uncle to get the duchess to speak to Gordon about the exchange. As things are now, it is really a very hard case that I must give up my chance of advancement because I am anxious to learn experience of my profession, and it has disgusted me not a little. In the midst of this idleness, such is the confusion and hurry that we can scarcely settle to anything. Report says we are going to Spain. I am working hard at Spanish, as is Mellish, who is a very clever fellow.

Stuart, my old friend, embarked today. His regiment marched in, in the finest order, and got great credit. He desires to be most kindly remembered, as does the general. I believe General Hill, who commanded at Fermoy when I was there, goes with us in the *Resistance*. He is a very pleasant, mild man, and much liked. He commands here till the arrival of the commander-in-chief, Sir A. Wellesley, I believe certainly; but whether he will come here, or we join him at sea, is not known.

Wm. Warre.

EXTRACT OF MY LETTER TO GREENWOOD & COX.

June 17, 1808.

The objection to my accompanying Major General Ferguson (the number of captns. then on the staff from the regt.) being now removed by Captn. F's exchange, I hope H.R. Highness and Major-General Payne will be pleased to allow me to remain in the 23rd, to which, independent of the number of steps I shall lose by the exchange, I am much attached, and shall only quit from my great desire of acquiring experience in my profession on actual service, of which I saw but little prospect in the regt. at present. Any emolument I can receive from my staff situation, I can assure H.R.H., is not an object, my only wish being to render myself, as far as lays in my power, useful in the service, however great the loss I may suffer by entering another regt. as younger captain from one in which I am so high up.

I have the honour to request you will lay this before H.R.H., at the same time assuring him of my willingness to fulfil the conditions under which he was pleased to allow me to accompany Major-Genl. Ferguson, by exchanging into any regt. of dragoons H.R.H. may think proper. I have the honour, etc., etc.

I have desired them to write to me what answer the duke gives.

Cove, June 22, 1808.

My Dearest Father,

I have this morning received your kind letter of the 16th, and am very much obliged to you for the maps, which will be most acceptable, as I have hunted all over Cork without finding anything of the kind, and I think there is little doubt of Spain's being our destination in the first place. I shall offer them to the general, but I fear he will not be prevailed on to accept them. He is always ready to oblige or give anything away himself, but would not take a pen from anyone, if he thought he deprived him of it. I shall note carefully what you say respecting . . . though on his score of fortune, I think you have been misinformed. He is not amiable in his manners, but very clever, and though very good friends, we are not likely ever to be very intimate or confidential. A sort of outward cordiality must seem to exist, placed as we are together in situation.

I am most sincerely rejoiced that Douglas is coming to join us. For him I have really a very warm regard, and should Johnstone succeed, shall have with me two of my greatest friends. Our general has nothing to do with the present Expedition. He belongs to Spencer, and is ordered to proceed by the first safe conveyance (a man-of-war) but, should one not offer, to remain in the *Resistance*; this *entre nous*. He has applied, but none offers, and I think there is very little doubt of our all having the same destination. He is naturally very anxious to join his brigade at his post off Cadiz, but we should all quit the *Resistance* with very great regret. Nothing can be more pleasant than our situation with so excellent a fellow as Adam.

I was in great hopes of hearing of dear Tom's safe arrival, and hope still to have that happiness before we sail. Enclosed I send him a few lines welcome home. They but faintly express a brother's feelings at his escape, and return, after so long an absence, to the bosom of his family.

All the troops are embarked, and certainly finer, as far as they go, never were seen. We now only wait for orders and Sir A. Wellesley, who is expected today, and will I hope bring some further orders for Genl. Ferguson. As to Rankin, I have written to Seymour to allow him to exchange into the 9th Foot. Stuart has been so good as to promise to get one of his men to do so, and I trust the general, who, by the bye, it was that wrote, will have an answer.

I have no answer to my letter about buying his discharge, which I fear will not be allowed. It will be abominably unpleasant to embark with a horse and no servant. As to Payne nothing but the steps and prospects I have in his regiment would induce me to remain in it, though Seymour's letters are highly kind and flattering. Payne considering dispassionately, has but little right to be angry at my using all my endeavours to get a very advantageous situation, although in spite of him; nor can I rate my services so low, as to suppose they are a matter of indifference

to my regiment, particularly considering the sacrifices I offered
to make on my return to England. His not answering your letter is want of good breeding. Seymour's letter to him, however,
perhaps makes him hesitate.

We have been endeavouring to establish a ball here this evening for the relief of the poor distressed wives of the soldiers,
but it is a very bad day and I fear we shall have but thin at-
tendance. I have been much troubled with the toothache, and
yesterday had the unruly member drawn with much difficulty,
and today my face is very sore and swelled; but, as I was one
of the chief instigators of this ball, I must go, though not at all
in the humour for it. *Adieu*, my dearest father. Ever your most
affectionate son,

Wm. Warre.

The genl. thanks you for your kind messages, and desires to be
most kindly remembered.

Cove, June 27, 1808.

My Dearest Mother,

Even had I not this morning received your most kind and affectionate letter by Douglas with the locket, it was my intention to have written a few lines, nor have I time for much more,
as we dine at a Mr Frankland's some way in the country, and
I have a good deal of writing on hand. Accept my best thanks
for the letter and locket which shall never quit me, though you
know I did not want it as a souvenir. I wish it was the Talisman,
so famous in the *Arabian Nights*, that conveyed its possessor in
an instant wherever he wished. I should often visit the happy
circle at Hendon.

We really know no more of our destination than you do, except
that we all belong to the same, and are to join General Spencer
at Gibraltar, which is a great satisfaction. Hitherto we have been
longing for an opportunity to get out to him, not knowing but
this expedition might have quite a different destination.

We have a large list of the staff, among which are many friends
of mine. Sir A. Wellesley, Lieut.-Genl. commands in chief, and
under him are Major-Genls. Spencer, Hill, Ferguson, Br- Genls.
Fane, Crawford, Nightingale. Col. Torrens is Mily. Secretary, and
a long list of Staff-officers, which I need not trouble you with
reading. Genls. Fane and Crawford go in the *Resistance* with

us, which will take away greatly in point of room. The latter and his brigade-major I know very well, the former not at all, though I hear he is a very good man. I could have dispensed with him very well, as they just turn us poor *ADCs* out of our snug berths, and strangers will prevent that pleasant gaiety and freedom we have enjoyed hitherto.

It is very uncertain when we shall sail. We are waiting for the *Donegal* 74, Capt. Malcolm, and *Crocodile* frigate, and for some transports, with artillery and cavalry, and some empty ones to thin those now here, which are very much crowded, though hitherto quite healthy. The additional room allowed looks like a longer voyage than we expected, though cavalry and our taking horses seems to contradict this idea. I am rather for going to Spain. It is a noble service assisting a nation fighting for its independence, and it is impossible to say what a brave people fighting for liberty, and actuated at the same time by resentment for great injuries, and a bigoted attachment to ancient customs may do, if properly supported. At all events, our assisting to the utmost of our power the mother country will greatly facilitate our establishing the independence of America, whither I hope will be our ultimate destination.

Sir A. W. is a very good officer, and much esteemed, and I trust we have neither a Whitelock or Gower amongst us. I have not been very well today—I expect from the effects of bad water—and so liable to catch cold, that the general has made me put on flannel, and I find myself better since I have ordered a dozen of waistcoats of it at Cork.

We had a gay ball here on Friday, in a storehouse fitted up with flags, for the relief of the distressed soldiers' wives. We had a good many people, and collected about £50 free of expenses, little enough among so many objects. I have had a good deal of trouble, but who would grudge it in such a cause? Tomorrow there is a ball for the poor wounded Dutchmen taken in the Guelder land. I have never seen greater objects. Poor fellows! they fought very bravely, but knew nothing of their business. Our frigate only lost one killed and one wounded, and they 60 in both. (See James's *Naval History*, vol. iv., May 19, 1808, *Guelderland*, Dutch 36-gun frigate taken by the *Virginie*.) I went to see them, and the genl. has sent the officer refreshments and wine.

He is an excellent man. His purse is always open to distress, even too much. He is, I fear, often imposed upon. I am much pleased for many reasons, you may suppose, with Mr Adamson's kindness. Pray thank him most kindly from me. As for Moll, I shall be much affronted if he talks of paying for her. He must accept her as a very small proof of my friendship and very high regard for him, to say nothing of his kindness to me and my gratitude for it. I hope Hardy will suit dear Emily, and she will have him as a present from her affectionate brother. I shall be able to afford not to sell him, if we have a long voyage, and think she will like him with greater pleasure as a present from me. I was rejoiced to see my friend Douglas, he is gone in to Cork today and returns tomorrow. . . .

I am anxiously waiting to hear of dear Tom's arrival. Write to me the moment he does. We are not likely to sail for some time,

     Yrs., etc.,

                        Wm. W.

Chapter 2

1808 Continued

After long delay the expedition under Lieut. General Sir Arthur Wellesley sailed from Cork on 12th July. Meanwhile the Government had altered its mind as to the command of the army, and, after Sir Arthur Wellesley had sailed, entrusted the command of the whole force to Sir Hew Dalrymple. Under him were, in order of seniority, Sir Harry Burrard, Sir John Moore, Sir Arthur Wellesley, who thus, after his arrival in Portugal, found himself as the junior lt.-general only fourth in command.

On 26th July the fleet reached Porto Roads, and on 1st August and the following days, the troops were landed at Figueira, in Mondego Bay, not without difficulty, owing to the surf, which from the open Atlantic beats with violence on the unprotected coast.

It was not till 9th August that the army was able to move forward. Difficulties as to transport were almost insuperable, and some guns had to be left behind. Wellesley had determined to take the coast road, wishing to pick up on his way towards Lisbon the brigades of Anstruther and Acland which had sailed on July 19th, but had not yet arrived. His impression was that Junot, the French marshal, had 10,000 troops under his command, but he had underestimated these, which amounted in reality to about 26,000; though it was true that Junot had detached about 7000 under Loison to quell the insurrection in the Alemtejo.

On hearing of the landing in Mondego Bay, Junot hastily recalled Loison, with orders to join De la Borde, who, with 5000 men, was sent forward to observe and check the British Army, till a concentration of the French forces could take place. Loison, however, whose force had a long and weary march, was delayed at Santarem, and, on the day of Roliça, was full fifteen miles away from the scene of the fight. De la Borde, who left Lisbon on August 6th, advanced as far as Alcobaça, but fell back on a position he had selected near Roliça. On August 16th the forces came into contact, and on the 17th was fought the first combat of the Peninsular War, which takes its name from Roliça. The action is described in the letter from Lourinhao. Wellesley after the action moved on still by the coast-line, neglecting Loison and allowing him unmolested to join Junot at Cereal. He was anxious to pick up Acland and Anstruther, who were reported off Peniche. They landed at Porto Novo, at the mouth of the little River Maceira, 12 miles south of Roliça.

Meanwhile Junot, after many delays, had moved by Villa Franca on Torres Vedras. It was not until the 20th that he learnt for certain that the British force was keeping the coast road. On the evening of the 20th he was ten miles south of Vimiero, where the British Army lay covering the disembarkation of the two brigades. During the night the French Army marched, and at dawn on the 21st found itself close under the British position. Followed on that day the Battle of Vimiero, which is graphically described in the letters.

The victory was won; but to the disgust of the army, and afterwards of the whole British Nation, it was shorn of its glory, and possible advantages, by the command of Sir Harry Burrard, who landed in the course of the morning of the 21st, superseding Sir Arthur Wellesley, and forbidding all pursuit. Burrard himself was shortly superseded by Sir Hew Dalrymple, and the result which ensued, in the Convention of Cintra, is too well known to need comment here.

After the Battle of Vimiero, William Warre was laid up with an attack of enteric fever, which brought him to death's door. He recovered slowly, and by the month of October was sufficiently well to see active service again as *A.D.C.* to General Beresford, who commanded a brigade in the army of which Sir John Moore was the C.-in-C. General Ferguson had not, as he had expected, returned from England.

LETTERS

Porto Roads, July 25, 1808.

My Dear Father,

We arrived this morning off this place, which was the appointed rendezvous. I have not been able to communicate with the shore yet, and it is very uncertain whether I shall be able to see my friends there, or land at all. I have just heard a frigate is going to England, and the boat is waiting to take my letter, so I

29

have only time to say we are all well. I think we are to land at Lisbon and attack Junot. This is my idea, but nothing is known. To express my feelings at seeing the spot of my birth, the place in which I spent some of the happiest days of my life, would be impossible, or how tantalised at not being able to communicate. Should we land, you shall hear further and by first opportunity. At present they are calling for my letter.

Your ever-affectionate son,

Wm. Warre.

I have opened this to say that I have a message from the commodore, saying he is sorry it will not be possible for me to land, as they only wait for Sir A. Wellesley's return from shore to make sail. They are making dispositions for the anchoring of the fleet and landing. Spencer is to join us. I am much disappointed at not landing or communicating with shore.

A Deos,

Com as may ores saudades.

("With greatest regrets," or, as we should say, "With much love.")

Monday evening, July 25th, 1808.
Off Ovar.

Dearest Father,

The enclosed is a second time returned to me, and as the *Peacock's* boat, by whom it is to go, is delayed a few minutes, I have opened it to tell you we are making all sail for Figueira, where we are to land tomorrow morning in order, I understand, to cut off a French corps marching to Lisbon to Junot's assistance, and then to march to Lisbon and try his mettle. I cannot imagine what corps is meant, as the annexed is the official account of their disposition in Spain (minus 18,000 said to be killed in Spain, and some must have been in Portugal), *viz.* (?9000) at St Sebastian, 6000 Pamplona, 15,000 Barcelona, closely besieged by the patriots in great force, 10,000 Burgos, 2000 Vittoria, 50,000 Madrid and adjacent country, 16,000 Lisbon, said to be now reduced to 12,000. I have no accounts of the state of the country. We made sail to the southward immediately, and not a single boat came on board. *Adieu.*

I will write after our landing, if opportunity offers. The most anxious moment I ever felt was seeing Porto and not being

30

able either to write or go near. Every house I could see looked beautiful to me who felt how happy I had been there.

Camp Lavos, Nr. Figueira,
Aug. 8, 1808.

My Dearest Mother,

I have seized the opportunity of a few leisure moments to write a few lines just to tell you I am quite well, though a good deal fagged and burnt by being constantly exposed to the sun, and the exertions, which my knowledge of the language, and our situation, render indispensable; though I feel the sincerest pleasure in being in any way useful to my country or the service, and fully recompensed by it for every fatigue.

We disembarked the first of this month. It took three days to land the whole army, and had we been opposed from the land I am positive we could never have effected it, so great is the surf both on the coast and the bar. However, thank God, the whole army landed without any loss but a horse or two, and now occupy a position at this place, or rather with our left to the village and right to the sea, where we have been waiting for the arrival of General Spencer and his corps, who arrived, and have been landing yesterday and today, I trust without any loss, though the surf is very heavy.

We advance to attack Monsr. Junot the day after tomorrow; the advance guard, under Genl. Fane, tomorrow. It is several days' march. The severest part of the business is in these infamous roads and scorching sun, which with the large train of artillery and baggage will oblige us to move very slow. Junot has in all about 14,000 men, but he cannot long resist, being about to be completely surrounded by us, about 13,000 to 15,000 in all, from the North, and by a corps of about 6000 Portuguese; and from the North bank of the Tagus, from Badajos, by a corps of 10,000 men from General Castanhos' army in Spain, I hear, the bravest fine fellows possible, as is their general, and indeed the whole of the Spaniards in arms. Nothing can exceed their courage and enmity to the French. Hitherto their conduct has been most noble, and their praise in everybody's mouth. Andalusia is clear of French. Dupont and his army capitulated to be sent to France with his arms, a curious concession from the Spaniards, who are so much in want of them.

Three armies of French have been taken or destroyed, and Castanhos is in full march towards Madrid, and every hope entertained of his success. 8000 of the French who had surrendered were massacred by the Spanish peasantry, so great is their animosity. All this is positive information. Castanhos has 45,000 men, 4000 of which excellent cavalry, and about 23,000 regulars. He is a very mild man, but a fine fellow as ever was. Whittingham was in the action with Castanhos; his conduct most gallant, and his praise universal in the army. He is appointed a colonel in the Spanish service, as a proof of the esteem he is held in. The Portuguese have about 28,000 men in all the kingdom, in arms of all descriptions, all badly armed, and I fear not so enthusiastic in the cause (though they boast much) as their neighbours the Spaniards. As to what the English papers say, do not believe a word of it. I never read such a parcel of nonsense. General Ferguson's staff here occupy an old fellow's house, where we are comfortable enough, from Mrs Wm. Archer of Figueira's attention in sending us out everything we can want. Otherwise I know not what we should have done, as Figueira is 4½ miles off, and not a thing eatable or drinkable (besides the rations) nearer. We are up in the morning at 3 a.m., and, what with visiting the outposts, or line, and guards, 7 or 8 hours a day on horse or mule back, so that we are quite ready to lie down 3 in a small room (for which luxury we are not a little envied), at nine o'clock, and sleep as sound as on the finest down beds in the world, but for turning out now and then in the night, to interpret or some other trifle (from nobody speaking the language but me in the brigade), which now consists of the 66th, 40th, 71st Highlanders, all tried regiments on service, and longing to meet these so much vaunted Frenchmen.

From your ever most affectionate son,

Wm. Warre.

The general desires kindest remembrances. He is the best man almost I ever met.

Lourinhao, 12 miles from Peniche (South),
August 19, 1808.

I have just time to tell you I am well and quite safe. We had a very sharp action the day before yesterday, at a strong position at Roliça, near Obidos. The French were strongly posted at first in the plain, and then retired to a mountain almost inaccessible. But what could resist the gallantry of our brave fellows? They clambered up exposed to a tremendous fire, and drove them for several miles, killing a great many and taking two pieces of cannon. Our army lost about 500 men in killed and wounded, and a very large proportion of officers. The 29th Regt. suffered most, and lost 19 Officers killed and wounded, the Col. (Lake) among the former. The 9th also suffered, and my poor friend Stuart badly, I fear mortally, wounded. Capt. Bradford of 3rd Guards, and a Lieut. R. Dawson, (45th Reg., carrying the King's colours), killed, a fine gallant fellow. Our brigade having been sent to turn the right, arrived rather late, and were scarcely engaged. We lost a few men—5 or 6—and poor Capt. Geary of the artillery, after firing 4 shots at the enemy in most masterly style.

The French fought most gallantly, and their retreat does honour to their military character. They were inferior to us greatly in numbers. First commanded by Laborde, who it is said is badly wounded, and then by Junot, who arrived from Lisbon, though his column did not get up in time. Their loss from every account is nearly 1000. General orders today thank 9th, 29th, 5th, and Rifle corps for noble conduct. Though obliged at times to climb on hands and feet, nothing could restrain their impetuosity. Poor Stuart fell calling to his officers to see that his young regt. did their duty, and not to mind him. Poor, dear friend, I fear he cannot live. We marched to this place yesterday to cover the landing of the troops under Genl. Anstruther, and have just received orders to advance towards Lisbon.

The French retreated, all night of the action, by the new road. I wish we had pursued them, but feel every confidence in Sir A. W.

Hitherto we have had a most harassing march in the sun, and suffered much from the heat, though all healthy and in high spirits. We shall give the French a good dressing wherever we meet them, and in 3 or 4 days shall be in Lisbon victorious ....

Vimiero, August 22nd, 1808.

My Beloved Parents,

Since I wrote to you a few days ago by Col. Brown we have had a most glorious and memorable day for England. The French attacked us yesterday in our position with their whole force, near 15,000 men. The attack was expected at daybreak, and would have been so, had they not been delayed by the roads. We had laid by our arms about 2 hours, after turning out before daybreak as usual, when the 40th, part of General Ferguson's brigade, had their picquet driven in, and beat to arms.

Our noble general, of whose gallantry and conduct it is almost impossible to give an idea, was soon on the mountain, our quarters being about ½ mile off in a small town, Vimiero. From thence we could perceive the enemy advancing to attack the centre of the army, and a strong column marching to turn the hill on which the general's brigade was, with cavalry and artillery; but as they had to make a considerable round, we had full time to prepare.

Sir A. W. (who commanded, Sir H. Burrard not having landed) ordered up several brigades, and made the most masterly disposition. The centre of the army, from which we were divided by a deep valley, was soon attacked with great vigour, but they received such a check, that we had soon the glory of seeing the French staggered and then relax in their attack. At this time General Ferguson's brigade, and those under General Spencer, who commanded this wing, were briskly attacked, but our noble general in about ½ hour after the fire commenced ordered his brigade to charge, leading himself in a manner beyond all praise (it is enough, too, that the commander-in-chief considers him to have most contributed to the completest victory that could be obtained without cavalry to follow it up).

The French gave way, and were followed with three cheers by the whole brigade. A part rallied, but the 36th and 71st charged them with an irresistible impetuosity, led on by our brave general, and drove them from their guns, of which they took four, with as many tumbrils. The victory was now certain, though they again rallied once more, and were again dispersed by the 71st. Our artillery completed the triumph of this glorious day. To speak of the conduct of anybody would in me seem presumptuous. Every soldier seemed a hero. The fire for some time was tremendous, and the field strewed with our brave fellows in charging the guns. My horse, a beautiful, nice creature, I had received but a few days before from Porto, which cost me 38 *moidores*, was shot in several places and fell dead. I got on an-

34

other belonging to a dragoon, but so tired he could not move; and when I had the cloak shot away from before me, I thought it high time to dismount and join the 36th, who were advancing, and with them I had the honour to remain during the rest of the action.

The loss of the French is very great, upward of 1200 killed and wounded left on the field, besides prisoners. Our army lost about 500 in killed and wounded, and a good many officers. The only one you know is little Ewart, shot through the leg, not dangerously, I hope. The French Army was commanded by Junot, Laborde, Loison, Chariot, Brennier. The two latter were taken with a great many officers, and thirteen pieces of cannon. We could adore Ferguson for his bravery and skill and coolness in a fire like hail about him. His orderly, a very fine trooper of the 20th Drns., was shot close to me, and I fear cannot live. My poor friend Stuart of the 9th died two days ago, after the fight at Roliça, universally lamented—to me a loss I have not yet recovered. I was much attached to him. I have not time to write any more particulars. I am very much fatigued, having been yesterday till past 5 p.m. collecting the wounded English and French, and conducting them to a place of safety from the Portuguese cowards, who won't fight a sixteenth of a Frenchman with arms, but plunder and murder the wounded, poor wretches. Had I time I could tell you such things of these countrymen of mine, (William Warre was born in Portugal), that you would not wonder at my despising them and having unpleasantly changed my opinion of their character,

I am very happy to tell you none of our Staff were killed. I have suffered a good deal all night and today from a bowel complaint, but am better. I wish we had advanced today and followed up our victory, without giving them time to rally from a check they are so little used to.

Adieu; God bless you all. Kindest love to them, from your most affectionate son,

Wm. Warre.

Buenos Ayres, Lisbon,
17 Sept. 1808.

My Dearest Friends,
I should be most ungrateful did I let another opportunity pass

of thanking you for your very kind letters of 25 July, 1st Aug., 3 Sept., which latter I received yesterday, and am, believe me, most sensible to the praise and approbation of friends so infinitely dear to me.

You will long before this have heard of the dreadful illness and narrow escape I have had since the action, the extreme weakness occasioned by which alone prevented my writing to you and my uncle William by the *Donegal*, who went home as one of the escort to the Russian Fleet. I never suffered so much in my life as during those 14 days I was at the worst, though the fever left me on the 4th or 5th day for a time. I had very slender hopes I should ever again see my beloved family and friends. I have now been on shore a week, and so much recovered and gaining so much strength that I am able to take a walk every day a short way, and am getting my flesh again, though still very thin, the disorder having left me a perfect skeleton. I even yesterday paid a visit to some friends of the Barnardo Bettrao's, and sat there a considerable time. To the friar (Frè Barnardo), one of the family, I am indebted for the most friendly attention and kindness. He has been most anxious to procure me every comfort and supply every want I could have in my situation.

I think of going to Cintra next week for a few days, for change of air and quiet. As soon as I am able to undertake the journey, I shall go to Porto, as Genl. Ferguson is going to England for a short time on particular family business. I have determined to remain behind, as I consider myself bound to join my regt. should I return to England, and have great doubts whether they would allow me to return, which would be provoking, if there was anything to be done, and I am the more inclined to do this, as from the government of this country having written to beg my worthy kind friend in the Albany to come over, I have great hopes of embracing him once more at Maçarellos.

I feel great *saudades* (regrets) notwithstanding, at being obliged to postpone the happiness of seeing you all, after such a narrow escape, but trust the time is at all events not very far distant, and that we shall yet talk over dangers past with additional accounts to tell and battles to fight over, for I hope they will not leave so fine an army idle at such a time

You ask me for some account of the battle. I will give it you nearly in the same words as I have written to my friends and

Uncle William. After having had all the fag and labour, it is hard not to have been able to partake in the least of the exultation and joy of the victory, or enter into the rejoicings of this place, for eight days illuminated, and every heart elated at the French having left it. The last division embarked two days ago, but have not sailed. The 1st and 2nd, I believe, have.

The natives have murdered every straggler or unfortunate Frenchman they met behind the column, and, but for very strong English guards and patrols, would destroy every person who supported them, and their houses. It is cowardly in them now, but when we hear of the ferocious cruelties and insolence, of the system of robbery and plunder and murder, almost incredible had we not seen such proofs of it, we cannot wonder at the fury of this naturally passionate and revengeful people.

Now to the battle. We had received information on the evening of the 20th that the enemy intended to attack us next morning, but this was generally discredited. We were as usual every morning under arms an hour before daybreak, and remained after daybreak longer than usual, when, not perceiving anything of the enemy, the troops were dismissed, and Genl. Ferguson and his staff again retired to our straw at a house about ½ a mile from camp at the town of Vimiero.

About 8 I was woke by a serjeant, who told me our picquets of the 40th on the left were driven in and the enemy advancing. I ran to tell Genl. Ferguson, and we were soon on horseback and on the hill on the left, from whence we had a full view of the French Army, on its march to attack us in two strong columns. The strongest and principal attack was on our centre, and the other against the hill, and left of our position, which was separated from the centre by a deep valley covered with vineyards, occupied by our light troops, and to the top of which Genl. Ferguson ordered his brigade to advance to await their attack.

Sir A. Wellesley arrived soon after, as I had been sent to tell him of the attack, and perceiving the intention of the enemy, ordered Genl. Bowes' and Genl. Ackland's brigades to support Genl. Ferguson's; and made his dispositions in the most cool and masterly style, as from our commanding situation we could see all the movements of the French and of our own army. Our light troops in the centre, consisting of the 60th 5th Batt. (Riflemen) and 95 Rifle Corps, supported by the 50th, were by this warmly engaged and with various success, though they behaved most nobly; but were at last forced to retire before the French column, who advanced with the utmost confidence to the attack, expecting, as we have since heard, that we should have given way immediately, but were so warmly received that they retired.

They made several attacks, and endeavoured to turn both flanks of the centre, but were received on their left by the 97th, who charged them and drove them through a wood, and on their right by the 52nd 2nd batt. and 50th, and 43rd 2 batt., who defeated them also, though very unequal in numbers, and very hard pressed by the French columns.

The enemy suffered so much that they soon retired in confusion. Our artillery was excellently well served, and they were pursued by our handful of cavalry of the 20 dgns. and some Portuguese dgns., but who, venturing too eagerly in pursuit, the French rallied, and our people extricated themselves with great difficulty, losing a great many officers and men, among the rest Col. Taylor killed.

While part of this was going on, we were spectators of the fight from the hill, and the account I gave of the rest of what passed in the centre is from what I can collect. The column that was to attack us had a round to make, and did not arrive till long after the centre was engaged. They advanced in column—cavalry, infantry, artillery—with great confidence, and were well received by our light troops. As soon as they were within reach Genl. Ferguson ordered his brigade to charge them, which was done with all the intrepidity and courage of British soldiers, and the enemy retired before us, keeping up a sharp fire.

A part of them rallied, but Genl. Ferguson hurrahed the 36th, a very weak though fine regt. to charge, which was done in great style three successive times, till, as they were very much thinned, and in some disorder from the rapid advance, I was sent back to hasten the support which was far behind, the gallant little Regiment forming to rally again under cover of a hedge of American aloes though much pressed. I just returned in time to join the 71st, who were charging 6 pieces of the enemy's cannon that were retiring, and the fire at this time from the enemy was really tremendous.

The enemy attempted to rally and advanced with drums beating, but the 71st charged them so manfully that they retired in confusion, and the retreat became general.

Thus, ended this glorious day, in which the valour and intrepidity of our gallant fellows was most conspicuous. Their appearance would have made a stone feel in such a cause. As to Genl. Ferguson, all I could say would not be half what he deserved in praise. His gallantry and judgement decided the day on the left. My only astonishment and that of everybody else is how he escaped. He was always in advance in the hottest fire animating everybody by his noble example. I have not seen any return of the killed and wounded.

The general idea is that we lost about 500 or 600 men, about as many as in the affairs of the 16th and 17th, when we lost a great many officers, our fellows storming an almost perpendicular rock in face of the enemy, who own they were never more astonished. I there lost my dear friend Stuart of the 9th, one of my oldest and greatest friends. It appears odd to weep in the midst of an action, but I was so shocked by the sudden change of a friendly shake of the hand about two hours before, (when our brigade parted from them with Genl. Bowes to turn the enemy's flank), and his dying in great pain, exclaiming to his officers to see that his young regt. did their duty, that the tears ran down my face like a child's. The 29th had 15 officers killed, wounded, and prisoners in that affair.

The loss of the French in the first affairs must have been from 800 to 1000 in killed and wounded, on the 21st near 4000 in killed, wounded, and prisoners. Our artillery, which was extremely well served, did great execution, particularly the new shells filled with musket balls invented by Major Shrapnell. The action was over before 2 p.m., and I was left the whole evening to collect the wounded French, and save them from being massacred by the natives, who plundered everyone they could. I remained till evening on this harassing and affecting duty, contemplating all the miseries and tortures war can inflict on human nature in all shapes. To this, added to the anxiety and fatigue I had previously undergone in the sun, and being very unwell before, I attribute the severe illness, which has prevented my partaking in the general joy and exultation at our success, but from which I am recovering very fast.

I was much surprised to see D'Aeth, who is a charming fellow.

He is going to Porto in the *Eclipse*, to which he is appointed acting commander. I have given him some letters, which I hope will make it pleasant to him; but I was much more astonished to see Wm. Archibald, whom I thought in the *Warrior* with Spranger. He came and dined with me, and comes tomorrow to breakfast to take this and some other letters on board a ship that is to sail for England. He is very well, he says, and very happy in his ship and captn., but I think he looks very pale and thin. He is very much grown. It is some years since I saw him and I should scarcely have known him again.

I must mention to you two instances of noble conduct in and among many others I had an opportunity of observing. These are of the two cousins M'Kays of the 71st. One of them was piper to the regt., a remarkably handsome fine fellow, and was playing to the men while advancing to charge, when he was wounded badly in the lower part of the belly and fell. He recovered himself almost immediately and continued to play on the ground till quite exhausted. I afterwards saw him in a hovel, where we collected the wounded, surrounded by them, both French and English. I shook him by the hand and told him I was very sorry to see so fine a fellow so badly hurt; he answered, "Indeed, Captain, I fear I am done for, but there are some of these poor fellows, pointing to the French, who are very bad indeed." The other a corporal had taken the French general, Brennier prisoner, who offered him his watch and money, but M'Kay told him to keep his money, he would have need of it, and took neither. A rare instance of forbearance in any soldier in action.

I have written till I am so tired, I fear I cannot write more. I will if possible, in the morning, but I wish at all events you would send my dearest Mother this letter as it gives so much detail, and, having written so long a one to my Uncle William, I cannot write another account and know she will like to hear all these particulars. If I do not write tomorrow I will by the very first ship that goes.

Sept. 18th.—I am very much better today, so much that I intend going into Lisbon in a carriage.

Yrs. affecly.,

W. Warre.

Direct to me, care of any resident here to forward it by enquiry where I am. I know none but Portuguese.

Lisbon, Sept 29, 1808.

My Dear Father,

I wrote a few lines by General Ferguson who went home in the *Plover*, and by the same ship were also, I believe, forwarded two long letters with some details of the action, which you will of course see.

The indignation expressed in all the English papers at the capitulation made subsequent to that is scarce equal to what has been felt by every individual of the army, whose glory and the gratitude of their countrymen (their best reward) has been so completely frittered away. This in a political point of view is the least of its evils. The consequences of sending to France 25,000 to join Buonaparte in his reconquering Spain and Portugal, men who have marched, and countermarched all over the country, may still be most disastrous, for I never can imagine that the struggle of these countries, (I should rather say Spain, for this country is not in a state to do anything for itself), is more than begun. The tyrant will not so easily give up his point, but will march all his disposable force, and best generals against her, unless indeed some unforeseen diversion in the north, or on the Continent, put some weight in the balance, in favour of Spain.

As the French retreat and approach France, they come nearer their supplies, etc., properly their base of operation. While in separate armies the gallant Spaniards could by numbers surround and cut off their supplies and communications, and by enthusiasm and impetuosity overcome them. But the case is far different, when a regular army is collected and within reach of its supplies, nor have we of late heard of any material success of the Spaniards. I do not mean by this, that a nation like Spain urged by such motives for enthusiasm and revenge is not able, if unanimous, to gain at last and maintain its independence, but that it must be at the expense of many thousand lives, of proofs of the greatest fortitude and constancy, not, if, as they are doing in this country, they totally neglect their army, who instead of learning the very elements of their duty, of which they are totally ignorant, are employed in rejoicings and illuminations, or talking big of actions and valour, who never saw a shot fired. I live almost constantly with Portuguese, and have had a great deal of conversation with them. Some of the most enlightened foresee the consequences of the government as now established, and the utter ruin of the country. They speak sensibly on the subject, and affect to feel its situation, but no one steps forward to point out the defects.

The regency as appointed by the prince in the midst of hurry and confusion, was as lame a government as could well be, mostly all old superannuated generals, who had never seen an enemy, or lawyers, who if they knew anything of the jurisprudence of their country, are entirely ignorant of politics and finance. Pedro de Mello is supposed to understand the interior regulation of the country, its police, and resources in men, etc., but little of finance. He has been very properly removed for his conduct during the stay of the French, as were Principe al Castro, Conde de St Payo, and the Marquez de Abrantes, the latter being a prisoner in France. To supply these, they have chosen the Bishop of Porto, and the Marquez das Minas, a very young man, of whom I hear that he has no other merit than that he wears a very gay uniform and a very long feather. Thus, in a country, whose finances are in such a deplorable condition that they have been obliged to pay the Police Guard out of the funds voluntarily raised for the support of the army on its march, they have not chosen one man who has the least practice or knowledge in that branch, nor have they attempted to improve the state of their army.

Their decrees since they came into power are as puerile and weak as might be expected. In short, all classes call out against the want of vigour and the ignorance of their rulers, though themselves wrapped up in the most unaccountable apathy and egotism.

I am getting my strength and health very fast.

I removed last week from the lodgings I was in to the house of a Senhor Manoel Maçedo, who married Lucas Siabra's daughter. Nothing can exceed his kindness and attention. We were going for billets in the town, but having been introduced to us by Frè Bernardo Bettrao (by us I mean also Major Wilson 97th, who was wounded on the 21st, and we have been ever since together) he called and insisted upon our coming to his house, and would take no apology, assuring us that we should go and dine and live where we pleased. But since we have been in his house, he not only feeds us but any friend who comes to see us. He is a man of very large property, but only lately married. He is very much attached to everything that is English. He has lived a great deal in Brazil and shewed me some curious accounts of the natives of the interior, and a plan he proposed for their civilization, very well written and with wonderful liberality and tolerance for a Portuguese.

Frè Bernardo Bettrao has been most friendly and constant in his attention, and introduced me to several of my uncle's friends, who have been very attentive, particularly Lucas Siabra, the Lieutenant-General of the Police, to whose house we are at all times welcome. Society in Lisbon, or amusements, there are none. The opera is closed for want of funds, and in private families, that is the few that are in Lisbon, people meet of an evening, sometimes with great formality, but the change, and distrust of difference of opinion, while the French were here, and petty intrigues, evidently cast a gloom over every Portuguese.

In the town, but for the strong English guards and picquets, the mob would have murdered, and destroyed the houses of everybody connected with the French, and even now, if a French deserter, or spy (for I am informed many have been detected) is found, the cry of "*Hè Francez*" is enough, unless some English are near, to have him murdered without mercy, and many have been murdered.

I intend setting out from this for Porto about the end of next week, with Frè Bernardo. We shall travel slow as I wish to see Coimbra, and am not yet equal to long journeys, though quite wonderfully recovered, considering how ill I was. I will write as soon as I arrive there and have seen how things are going on. I am very anxious to hear from some of my dear friends. Except a letter of the 3rd from Hardy I have not a line from home, though all my friends have heard since, and therefore suppose my letters are wandering about Lisbon. I have made every enquiry for them. Having been so little out, nobody knows where I am to be found, and I fear they are lost, if any came. In future pray direct to the care of Senhor Carlos Oniel or any of your correspondents, who will easily find me out. I called yesterday on Madame Mantzoro. She received me with great politeness and attention, and desired me to remember her most kindly to you and my uncle. She and all the family are well.

If the 23rd have sailed, or are to sail, and that Genl. Ferguson should not return, or be employed elsewhere, pray send me out the things I wrote for, and also in addition a white dragoon sword-belt which is in George Street; and from Hoby, who had my measure, two pairs of long Regent boots, but these only if 23rd should embark, and the general not be employed, as if he is, I should hope he would wish to have me with him anywhere. I long to see him back here. In his absence I am quite *desamparado* (unsupported). *Adieu*, my dear Father. Daily in my own quiet hermitage, . . .

When I think of my own native land,
In a moment I seem to be there;
But alas! recollection at hand,
Soon hurries me back to despair;

"to despair" is too strong, but certainly to great *saudades*. Pray remember me to all my friends also in the village, and believe me ever, yr. most affectionate and dutiful son,

Wm. Warre.

PS.—Lane the tailor having sent me a coat I cannot wear, it is so tight, and with buff lining, I have written to him for the last he shall ever make for me, though he alone has my measure, and I will thank you to send it to me to this place, as soon as possible, as I have not a coat to wear of an evening, owing to this disappointment. Pray direct your next to Porto, as I shall most probably be there for the next month or 6 weeks, unless something unexpected happens. We have sent 8000 men to Elvas and several regiments into cantonments at Abrantes, Santarem, Almeida, etc., etc., which does not look like the armies moving at present into Spain—to re-embark, there are but few transports. 4000 *dons* were to sail today for Barcelona.

CHAPTER 3

1808-9

Between the 29th of September and the 23rd of December 1808 no letters have been preserved in this collection. But in the interval, much had happened.

After the Convention of Cintra, the French evacuated Portugal, though slowly. It was not until the second week of October that the last of them were embarked. The exasperation of the Portuguese against them, as well as against the Convention, was great, and it was with difficulty in some cases that they were protected from the fury of the populace in Lisbon and in Oporto.

In the month of October, Sir John Moore took over the command of the British Army. He found to his hand a fine body of troops, but an absolute want of organisation as regards transport and commissariat. It was a full month before he was able to move, and even then, want of knowledge of the roads led to the sending round of the artillery with Sir John Hope by a circuitous route, causing many days' delay. During the whole of this time, great pressure was brought to bear on him, urging him to advance towards Madrid to the support of the patriot armies in Spain.

On 11th November he entered Spain, and reached Salamanca on the 13th, but it was not till 23rd November that his army was concentrated. A force under Sir David Baird, which had been landed at Corunna, was ordered to move through Galicia and to effect a junction with him, which, however, owing to counter orders which were in turn countermanded, did not take place till nearly a month later.

Meanwhile, Napoleon, set free for the moment from complications in Central Europe by the Treaty of Erfurth, was pouring reinforcements amounting to 200,000 men into the Peninsula.

The Spaniards, defeated utterly at Burgos (10th November), at Espinosa (11th November), and at Tudela (23rd November), were now practically without any organised force in the field, and it seemed as if Sir John Moore would find himself in the presence of overwhelming French forces. Fortunately for the British Army, Napoleon, who arrived at Madrid on 4th December, was unaware of the position of Moore at Salamanca, and believed that the English were in full retreat for Lisbon.

On 13th December, an intercepted dispatch revealed to Moore the distribution of the French forces, and more especially the isolated position of Soult with 16,000 men at Saldaña. Accordingly, he determined to move north to Mayorga, where on 20th December he was joined by Baird. On 21st December, the combat of Sahagun occurred, the most brilliant exploit on the part of the British cavalry during the whole war. (*Vide Oman*, vol. i.)

On the evening of 23rd December, when the army was just starting to attack Soult at Saldaña, Moore received the news that Napoleon had turned north from Madrid and was hastening with all his forces to overwhelm him.

The letter of William Warre dated 23rd December, 5.30 p.m., is singular in noting the exact time at which the orders were given to march against Soult at Saldaña. Among the letters it is unique in its tone, as if the writer was oppressed with a presentiment that he was marching to his death. It reflects in some measure the feeling which had been current in the army owing to the period of uncertainty and disappointment through which it had been passing. Within half an hour of the time at which the letter was written, Moore had received the news of Napoleon's advance. The columns which had marched to attack Soult were ordered to return to Sahagun, and within twelve hours the celebrated retreat on Corunna had begun. The next letter belongs to 1809.

The new year saw the army of Sir John Moore toiling through the snows of the highlands of Galicia on its disastrous retreat to Corunna, of the miseries of which a glimpse is given in letter of 4th January 1809 from near Lugo.

Then came the Battle of Corunna, and the tragic death of the commander of the army in the moment of victory. General Beresford's brigade covered the embarkation. The general and his *A.D.C.* were the last men to get into the boats.

They arrived safely at Plymouth in H.M.S. *Barfleur* on 23rd January. But the stay at home was not to be for long.

Before the end of February, Beresford, who understood and spoke

Portuguese, was appointed Commander-in-Chief of the Portuguese Army. He retained the services of Captain Warre as his A.D.C. They arrived in Lisbon early in March.

The work before him was the organisation of the Portuguese forces, a task of no little magnitude and difficulty, to which there is abundant reference in the letters.

Sir A. Wellesley arrived in Lisbon towards the end of April, and, within a short time, important movements were on foot. The French under Marshal Soult had moved southwards from Galicia, and in March had taken Oporto.

Before the end of May, Sir A. Wellesley had retaken Oporto, and Soult had been driven northward, leaving his baggage and artillery and his sick behind him, into the wilds of Galicia.

There followed, after an interval, the summer campaign, which ended with the Battle of Talavera. After this, owing to the behaviour of the Spaniards, the British Army retired on Badajos, and went into cantonments.

The Portuguese Army, which had not taken any part in the Talavera campaign, was meantime growing steadily in numbers and discipline.

In October the Spaniards gained a victory at Tamames, but in November suffered two disastrous defeats at Ocaña and Alba de Tormes.

Peace had now been made between France and Austria, and the French paused while awaiting the reinforcements which were pouring into the Peninsula preparatory to an attack on Portugal, and the attempt to drive the British Army to the sea.

During this year Captain Warre was fully occupied with the work of organising the Portuguese forces, translating drill books, visiting and inspecting various corps, and other necessary work. His time was much disturbed by two anxieties. His servant Rankin, of whom he had thought well (see Letter of 23rd December 1808), turned out to be a rogue and a thief. He was tried by court martial and shot, in accordance with the severity of martial law which was prevalent at the time.

His elder sister, Clara, who was a Roman Catholic, had taken the veil and was a nun in the convent at Lamego. On the invasion of Portugal by the French from the north, the question of how she could be removed into a place of safety exercised her brother's mind greatly. The French were notorious for their ill-treatment of convents and other ecclesiastical establishments. But the difficulties in the way of her removal, added to her own desire to stay with the rest of the nuns, were insuperable.

Fortunately, after Soult retired from Oporto, they were not molested, and the good lady lived on to a good old age in the convent at Lamego.

The letters to his father with regard to expenses, which the latter deemed excessive, illustrate the financial difficulties with which a good many officers serving in the field and their families must have been troubled during those years of strife and bad business.

A note on the back of the last letter of the year seems to indicate the nature of a reply to application for clothing for the Portuguese troops made to some English firm.

LETTERS

Avanilla, Nr. Sahagun
(5½ leagues from Saldanha),
Dec. 23, 1808, ½-past 5 p.m.

Though, as you will suppose, my beloved parents, not a little hurried, I cannot leave this place to march towards the enemy at Saldanha, without a few lines, which although I am sure not necessary to convince you how much I feel, or how grateful for all the affection, love, and kindness I have ever received, will I am sure be a gratification in case of the worst. Should I fall, my dearest friends, do not grieve for me. It has been the fate of many and much finer fellows than I am, and I fall in a just and glorious cause, trusting to my God and my Saviour to forgive me and have mercy on my soul. I do not know of any crime that I have committed, that should make me fear death, but we are all liable to err. At all events I have not disgraced myself or my family. That would be worse than a hundred deaths, or to lose your affection.

The French are at Saldanha, 5¾ leagues from this. We march at 6 this evening to arrive at daybreak, not much over-matched in numbers. I have not a doubt of the issue of the contest. Our cavalry have hitherto behaved most gallantly and taken in all from 500 to 800 men, great booty, and 26 officers.

Rankin has served me very faithfully and honestly, particularly during my severe illness. I would like him to have his discharge bought, and £10 to take him home. We shall have a cold march tonight, but shall be warm when we see these so vaunted robbers. The Last Bugle sounds. *Adieu*, may every happiness attend my dearest parents. Do not regret, I conjure you, the loss of an

individual in so glorious a cause. Your ever attached and affecte.
son,

Wm. Warre.

My heavy baggage is at Lisbon at Senhor Manoel de Maçedos,
68 Rua das Tunas.

Sobrado, between Lugo and St Jago,
Jany. 4, 1809.

My Dearest Father,

I have only time to say I am quite well, thank God. We have
been rather harassed lately, having retreated from Sahagun to
this place sometimes by night and forced marches, which have
nearly knocked up all our men. We have not halted for 22 days,
and marched in that time near 70 leagues. For myself I have
fared very well compared to officers not on the Staff and men.
I suppose no men ever did more, or any army, some even officers barefoot.

We are now ordered this instant to return to Lugo, which has
disappointed our hopes of returning home. For this country
we can do nothing. They will do nothing for themselves. Never
have a nation been more infamously deceived than the English
about this country. The people are willing, I believe, but neither
army, officers, clothes or anything necessary; and I fear many
traitors. We have not seen, since we have been in the country,
a symptom of organisation, or, till lately, even a recruit. Nothing can be more really despicable than their army, and in want
of everything; though in abundance—Such miserable arrangement! In short, I have no hopes of any success, and am not a
little annoyed at our return.

I had intended to go to Porto, and had leave if we quitted the
country. I might be of use to my family, particularly my dear
uncle, in getting his things away. My name would, I know, and
some firmness be required. Clara could not remain in Portugal. From some French officers, prisoners to us, I know priests,
nuns, and friars, would not be spared. Write to me implicitly
your wishes on this head. I dare any trouble or risk, you know,
for any of my family. Also send your instructions as to my conduct at Porto, and if your letter is likely to reach me in time,
whether I shall go there or no. I can get leave, I know, and intended going from St Jago.

Kindest love to my beloved mother, brothers and sisters, and to my uncles. I have never had an opportunity even of writing to say I am well, and am uncertain whether you will ever receive this. Pray write to me. I have no greater happiness than your letters. I have only received yrs. of 24th Dec. in postscript to my uncle's, and one before (date I cannot recollect), also one from Genl. Ferguson, whom I shall be most happy to see, though I rejoice that he has escaped this winter campaign. I never wish to serve another, particularly for such a morose uncivil set, who will only talk. *Adieu*, may God bless you all, and may I soon have the happiness of embracing you. Remember me most kindly to the Adamsons, and believe me, ever most affectionately yours in the greatest haste,

W. W.

P.S.—Everything should be moved from Porto, I think. I will write by first opportunity.
Our cavalry have distinguished themselves. This letter in perfect confidence from yrs.

W. W.

We have had tremendous weather, particularly during our march over the mountains. As long as I have health, however, I do not care for myself, though I am not yet really hardened enough to misery and wretchedness, not to be unhappy at contemplating the miseries of war in our men and the wretched inhabitants of the country. May our beloved country never be a scene of warfare. Better half of its men should die on the beach.

Barfleur, at Sea,
Jany. 18, 1809.

My Dearest Friends,

I have just time to say I am quite well, and happy in the prospect of soon seeing all my beloved friends, after our disastrous and most harassing retreat from Lugo. We arrived at Coruna and found no transports, they arrived a few days after, but before we could embark the French attacked us on the 16th, with all their force, in our most disadvantageous position. They were repulsed by a valour which only English troops can possess, though exposed to a tremendous commanding fire of cannon. Poor Sir John Moore was killed. Sir David Baird lost his arm. Our loss in killed and wounded is very great, though not so much as that of the enemy.

Our brigade, which was in the town to cover the embarkation, moved to cover a road to the right of the position, but were not attacked, or engaged at all, as was expected. We were therefore contemplators only of the gallant and astonishing firmness of our comrades. The 50th and the 42nd suffered most.

During the night most of our army embarked. Genl. Beresford's brigade covered the embarkation, having retired into the works of the town. The French approached in the morning close to us. We gave them a warm reception with our 24 prs. assisted by the Spaniards, who on this occasion behaved very well. The enemy fired on our transports most, and several went on shore and were lost in the confusion. Our situation was most critical all the next day and night, till we embarked the whole, about one in the morning.

Fortunately, the enemy did not fire on the town, and suffered us to embark, (or were totally ignorant of it), without annoying us. We were very weak, just enough to man the works, and dreaded an assault, the boats being able to take only 500 at a time, and weather very bad. However, we not only got ourselves but most of the wounded in safety, though all most overcome with fatigue.

Adieu, in hopes of soon seeing you, My dearest parents. Kindest love to all my friends, from your most affectionate son,

Wm. Warre.

(Note, in Henry Warre's writing, "*Received 24th Jany. at night.*")

Plymouth, Jany. 23, 1809.

At last, my dearest mother, I have the happiness to tell you of our safe arrival at this place. I wrote a few lines in a great hurry from off Coruña, which I hope you received. I long to reach town, and shall set off as soon as possible in a chaise, with Col. Douglas of Wycombe. We go by Bath, where we shall shake the Hardies by the hand, and in 4 days shall, I hope, embrace all my beloved family. I am very far from well, and most in need of rest. A constant bowel complaint, occasioned by fatigue and being constantly wet, has pulled me down very much. I am a mere skeleton, but rest and the happiness of seeing all that is dearest to me will soon, I think, recover me.

To describe our anxiety, and what we went through at Coruña

the last day and night, is not easy. Suffice it to say, we had (but for Mr Samuel How) been left behind, and now instead of being in our dear native country, should have been marching prisoners to France. The thought even now makes me shudder. Nearly exhausted and harassed to death, we were in a bad state to undertake such a journey. We, however, were more fortunate and brought off all our sick and wounded except very few.

Don't forget our last conversation. I have indulged in it in my most distressing moments. What a spur it has been to exertion I leave you to guess.

Adieu; kindest love to my dear father, Emily, Uncle Wm., etc., etc., etc., from, dearest mother, Your most truly affectionate

Wm. Warre.

P.S.—Pray buy me some worsted socks very long in the feet, I am almost naked as to foot, having worn my present pair at least ten days.

Lisbon, March 3, 1809.

My Dearest Father,

We arrived here yesterday, safe and well, after a very pleasant voyage of 8 days. The Portuguese are in high spirits, and promise well. They have had some skirmishing on the Minho, and repulsed the French, whose numbers we know nothing certain of. Of course, these accounts are much exaggerated, but if they can be made to think they can resist, and stand fire, it is a great point. As to our own destination I as yet know nothing. The Portuguese Army is on the frontier towards Monte Rey. I suppose we shall join them. Romana is near there, and, I hear, has collected a considerable force, and is in spirits as is the Marquez de Valliadacen, who is with them. It is, it seems, the general opinion that the French under Thornier, about 10,000 men, will endeavour to penetrate by the Minho, and that the Portuguese are determined to give them fight. By the last accounts from the frontier not a Frenchman had passed it. Something may yet be done.

The Spaniards under Cuesta and the Duke of Infantado have advanced towards the border of the Sierra Morena nearest Madrid, and at least our official accounts tell us that they speak with confidence, and are in high spirits. Romana wants nothing but ammunition, which has been sent, and we spoke at sea and brought into this with us a Spanish schooner with 105,000 dollars for the Asturians, who has proceeded.

Everything that I hear confirms my opinion that our retreat from Spain, etc., etc., etc., was inconsiderate, and I fear will place us in rather a disgraceful light. This *entre nous*. The French after they entered Coruña acknowledged having lost 1000 men killed on the 16th, and of course more than as many wounded. They spoke highly of the bravery of our men. This we have from the general's Italian servants, whom we left there, and who were in Gurèa's house when Laborde took up his quarters there. This I believe certain, that Buonaparte has returned to Paris, and taken his Imperial Guards with him.

The Brest fleet 16 S. L. and 3 frigates is out. We were becalmed off Cape Finisterre only a few hours before they came up bringing the breeze. It was a narrow escape. Yesterday Sir John Duckworth was off here with 11 S. L. and 2 frigates, and was joined from here by 2 S. L., the *Norge* and *Conqueror*, and is in pursuit of them. God send he may come up with them. The issue is not doubtful.

So much for public news. I send on mere reports, though I do not entirely vouch for the whole being true. The Portuguese are very anxious for Sir Arthur Wellesley. They think he would do everything that is possible. Nothing can exceed the high idea they have of him, and they are right.

I am very sorry to tell you that I hear Alvez had not shipped any of your wines, and had near 340 pipes on hand. They complain of want of instructions from you, but could, I believe, if he had exerted himself, have got freight for most. Ignorant as I am of business, and particularly of the instructions you may have given him, I feel great delicacy in writing and giving any orders. He never, I think, can have received my letter from Coruna. Croft certainly did not. I shall write to him by tomorrow post, desiring him to give me an account of how your affairs are, at the same time taking upon myself to desire him, if not contrary to any instructions he may have received from you, to charter at all events a vessel to ship off all your wines (if he can get one), but to wait for convoy unless the business presses very much. Though things look brighter than I expected, the fate of war is so uncertain, and the odds are against us, so that I think no time should be lost.

I should have chartered a vessel here, but on consulting with our worthy friend James Butler, he seems not to think it worth-while till I hear from Alvez, and there is no English ship at present in this port. I have felt much distressed at this apparent want of foresight, but suppose the last packet must have brought him your instructions. Nothing can be kinder than the interest that Wm. Naylor and Butler take in your concerns, but with great delicacy. It was said on change at Porto that several pack-ets only brought 2 letters from my uncle to John Benito, which caused a smile.

I write this to you, my dearest friend, because these sort of smiles, I fear, do much harm in business. This I heard from other quarters. Croft is here, but I have not yet met him. My heavy baggage, which was left here, I will send by the *Amazon* to Eng-land. I write this by the *Peacock* sloop of war, though in great haste. I am quite well. I have so many things to do and think of that I hope I shall not have time to be sick. I will write again by the first opportunity. In meantime may God bless and pre-serve you all. Give my kindest and warmest love to my dearest mother, etc., etc., and from yr. ever most affectionate son,

Wm. Warre.

The weather is most delightful though very warm. The change from England is very striking. *Adieu.*

I hope the wines I ordered from Spain, have or will be sent.

Lisbon, April 1, 1809.

My Dearest Father,

In addition to what I wrote to my mother by this conveyance, the *Diligent* gun brig, which has been delayed by the bar, I have merely time to communicate the very disastrous news of the taking of Porto by the French. We have as yet received no particulars, and only know that the bishop, and one British of-ficer, Captn. Arenschild of artillery, the G. Legion, were arrived at Coimbra.

From the complete state of insubordination of the populace of that city, this event we have for some time foreseen, and in the state of indiscipline and insubordination of the Portuguese Army, any assistance we could have sent would have, I much fear, only added to our loss, as they would have been also hur-ried away by, and as intractable as, the mob, who, cruel and san-guinary to an excess against themselves or prisoners, are always timid and cowardly. They have assassinated many people there, amongst others Oliveira the former governor, who was in gaol. They also murdered nine or ten French prisoners, and let all the felons loose. Such was their wretched state that they would obey no one, and rendered it highly dangerous to attempt any plan to secure a retreat, in case of accidents, as you would risk being murdered. I therefore fear our loss in men and arms very great, but we have no details.

The mob, some days before, broke into a magazine of arms, which they plundered, and then seized the fort of St Johns, allowing no ship to go out. I have therefore every reason to fear your ship with wine, which was loaded, was unable to get out. The captain had moved over to the other side of the water, which is however within shot. The wines in the lodges, if they have, as I hope, destroyed the bridge, are still safe, for bad as this news is, I have still hopes that Soult and his division are in a bad scrape, and weaker in numbers than generally supposed. The provinces behind him are in a state of insurrection, and I trust Silveira will get into their rear, as he is now disembarrassed by the taking (by him) of the Fort of St Francisco at Chaves, with 870, added to 200 in Chaves, when he before entered, who were sick, upwards of a thousand, and 300 killed. He has also taken more mules, horses, artillery, etc., etc., than were in the place when taken by the French, and his own loss trifling.

Galicia is certainly in a state of complete insurrection and full of enthusiasm and spirit. They have summoned Vigo, and given the French garrison only 24 hours to decide in. Tuy is also surrounded and expected to fall. Thus, the retreat or communications of Soult's corps (of whose numbers we are ignorant, but cannot believe exceed 15,000 men) are pretty well cut off, and, unless supported by the corps, which threatens us by the banks of the Tagus, and at present besieges Ciudad Rodrigo, will, I hope, be destroyed.

We have also a report here today that the Duke of Albuquerque and Cuesta have joined and given Victor a beating, which we give little credit to, as we knew of Victor's precipitate retreat from pursuing Cuesta towards the South, and being followed by that general, whose retreat was a very masterly movement, and I suspect had really drawn the French into a *cul de sac*, which they discovered before it was intended they should, but late enough to enable their rear to be turned. Urbina, it is said, is advancing towards Madrid. If Austria would but declare, everything might yet go well.

Our friend Whittingham has distinguished himself very much, and been thanked in orders by the Spanish general, I am not sure which. He was quite well with the Carolina Army. The people here are quiet at present, though not much pleased with the inactivity of the English force. They are great fools, and know nothing about the matter, though I myself wish our people would make a movement. *Adieu*, in great haste, with kindest love to all at home, ever yr. most affectionate son,

Wm. Warre.
Major P.F., *Aide-de-Camp*.

April 7, 1809.

My Dear Father,

I take the opportunity of Fred Crofts going in the *Amazon* to send you receipts for my staff pay. I also yesterday drew on you, dated 5th inst., to Dr Deane or order £56. 10s. amount of a Spanish horse bought of him, and which by providing me with two horses renders it unnecessary you should be at any trouble about buying me any, as the general having given me one, I have now 3, which is enough.

Croft will tell you all the news and all about me, which it is out of my power to do now myself, as Croft will tell you. We leave this tomorrow for the army at Thomar, which the marshal is going to take command of.

By the *Amazon* I have sent all my heavy baggage, five cases, etc., and some sweetmeats, which pray send to Ferguson to present to Mrs Ferguson with my best respects. I have also sent some chains directed to my Mother, which she will be so good as to distribute as directed. I am most anxious to hear from you and will write myself on the first opportunity.

As I have only time now to beg my kindest love, and assure you I am ever most affectionately yours,

Wm. Warre.

Hdqrs., Thomar,
April 27, 1809.

My Dear Father,

Many thanks for your very affectionate letters of the 10th, 7th,

5th April, which I received all together, and which were most pleasing to me, whose happiness so much depends upon your approval of my conduct.

You will long before this arrives have heard of the melancholy fate of Oporto. It did not in the least surprise me. I was sure it would be taken the moment it was attacked in earnest; the inevitable consequence of insubordination and anarchy. I hope you had ensured your property.

I was of course delighted to use every exertion in my power, and am very much indebted to Mr Villiers for his friendly assistance. Long before the crisis he offered me a transport or more to go round and bring away the property, which I refused in consequence of letters from Pedro Alvez stating that one ship was arrived, and another daily expected, and fearing that the expense of chartering them would be lost. At the same time, I was unaware of how little *resistance* would be made at Braga, and the passes of Salamonde, etc. Since that Mr Villiers wrote, as did also Noble, very strong letters to Capt. Loring of the *Niobe* to render every assistance, but these were too late and have since been returned to me, as also one you wrote to Chiappe with some accounts, which I opened, and have ready to deliver when an opportunity, I trust not very remote, shall enable me, as also those you send me now.

We expect to march immediately to drive that miscreant Soult out of Porto. The general went two days ago to Lisbon to meet Sir A. Wellesley, and as soon as he returns this evening or to-morrow, we shall all advance. I was left here to continue to form the Algarve brigade, the finest in the service, and who march tomorrow morning.

I have every hope that Soult has committed himself by his rapid advance, and since detached corps, one of which 7000 to 8000 have attacked Silveira at Amarante two days successively. He has defended himself bravely as did the Regt. No. 9 (Peña Macor) commanded by Major Patrick, who came over with us, and who is, poor fellow, I fear, badly wounded, after distinguishing himself very much. Silveira expected to be attacked next morning, and will, I fear, not be able to resist, as the militias and *ordenança* had abandoned him.

Victor has called everything to him near Merida, from Salamanca, and even Zamora, which looks as if he was close pressed, and leaves our Eastern frontier unmenaced for the present.

Cuesta has certainly reassembled 20,000 infantry and 5500 horse and has pushed forward his advanced guards. If the Spaniards can reassemble their armies in so short a time after being dispersed, they must in the end destroy the French, unless they receive great succours, which I believe impossible.

My friend Col. D'Urban, who was in the Battle of Medellin, assures me he never saw any troops behave better than the infantry, or worse than the cavalry, of Cuesta's army. And I think this was, as well as the loss of the army, in a great measure owing to Cuesta's bad order of battle, in the extended line without any reserve whatever, his cavalry in the first line advancing with the infantry at their pace, and his having allowed the enemy to pass the bridge of Medellin and deploy before he attacked them. He committed the same fault at Rio Seco, and suffered for it. It appears an infatuation, and as unaccountable as Victor's not attempting to pursue the Spaniards, who fled in confusion, even with his cavalry, which leads me to suppose he must have suffered more than we are aware of.

The enemy have occupied Valença de Tuy without resistance, Vianna, Ponte de Lima, Penafiel, and desolated these unhappy countries. On this side their posts are at Ovar and on the Vouga, and our advance on this side of that river, under Col. Trant. They have constant skirmishes which signify nothing except wasting ammunition. In Porto itself there are not above 800 or 1000 men, and they are organising a Portuguese Legion, for which they have got some men.

I was in a state of the greatest anxiety about poor dear Clara, to whom I had written several letters without receiving an answer, till yesterday, when, by a letter from my worthy friend Bettrao, I heard she with the rest of the ladies had quitted the convent on the news of the approach of the French, and their entering Porto, and had travelled on foot over the mountains to Mesao Frio, and then to Ancede, where she now is with another nun, a friend of hers, with some of Frè Bernardo's relations who have afforded her every protection, and he has written to them to give her every assistance. She was quite well, he tells me. I immediately despatched John Benito by the extra post, with a letter to her and 15 *pieces*, besides an order for 15 more, in case of necessity, desiring him to stay with her as servant, and to remove her as a guard, in case of absolute necessity towards Lisbon, where I intend to place her with Sr. Lucas de Siabra's family, if she is forced to fly, till I can make some proper arrangement.

If danger should not press, she is to stay where she is, till I can get away to see her myself and make other arrangements. At present the chances of war are so uncertain that I think she is better out of the convent, the marked objects of vengeance to these unprincipled invaders. Frè Bernardo, to whom I have sent John Benito, (in whom I have every confidence from his attachment to our family and honesty), will give him the orders he thinks necessary, and he will stay with her as her servant, and in case of removal guard, till I can make any other arrangement. I have got three pretty good horses and therefore, unless you have already sent them, do not think it worthwhile being at the expense of sending out any more.

The Portuguese troops immediately under the instruction of British officers are coming on very well. I could have wished we had been allowed more time, but even now have great hopes of some corps. The men may be made anything we please of, with proper management, and, wherever I have had authority, I have soon settled the little mean jealousies and tricks of the officers, and without, I hope, gaining much ill will. I endeavour to combine inflexible firmness with politeness of manner. I know it is the only way to make these fellows respect you, and the mass of officers is miserable indeed. This, however, will in time be altered. Merit is the great recommendation with the general, not grey hairs and number of years' service, however much to be respected, for these Subalterns, some of whom should be anything but soldiers.

I am very happy to hear the 23rd are coming out to this country, and should like much to join them, if I could with propriety. It is a fine dashing service, but this I fear is impossible, and I begin to learn the necessity of commanding my wishes and feelings. At all events I completely agree with you that it would be folly to quit the dragoons, when I have two years longer to serve as captn., and God knows what changes may occur in that period.

Every officer I have heard speak on the subject is much dissatisfied with the new C. in C, particularly those who most know him; and, setting H. R. Highness's morality aside, he did incalculable good to the army, and I am sure we cannot have a better, at least that I know of, and this is the opinion of, I believe, the majority of the army.

By the new regulations of service, we shall have brigadiers at 60 years of age, and generals in night cap and slippers, prudent and inactive as they formerly were, and as the Portuguese are. It is surprising that people can suppose a man unfit to command, till he has attained an age at which enterprise and activity generally cease. I should not be surprised to see some years hence advertised in the papers of the day restorative cordials for generals taking commands, or patent easy-chairs for foreign service, addressed to the generals of the British Army.

I am much obliged to you for your kind attention to Custine's letter, (see Memoir), and the advance of £10. I would not wish you to commit yourself in cashing his bills to any considerable amount. He was once in Germany very civil to me, and I am happy to be able to repay him. I should have been better satisfied with the *parole d'honneur* of a gentleman, than that of a French officer, which goes very little way in my opinion. He is a prisoner, and in distress, poor fellow. I therefore in moderation will be very happy to afford him some assistance, and I hope he will not deceive the idea I have formed of him.

I have just heard that the 3rd and 4th Heavy Dragoons are arrived and landed at Lisbon.

My boots, etc., will be a valuable acquisition to me, and which, as well as the plans you are so good as to send, are arrived.

Pray give my kindest love to all at home, from, my dearest father, your ever affectionate and dutiful son,

Wm. Warre.

I wrote two days ago to my mother, and suppose the letter will go by the same conveyance as this. *Adieu.*

Lisbon, 13th July, 1809.

My Dear Father,

Though I wrote to you a very long letter by last packet, and am now somewhat pressed for time, I will not delay thanking you for your affectionate letters of 20th of May and 1st of June, which did not reach me till yesterday, having travelled to Porto and back again after me, and in it my Uncle Wm's. very kind letter of 20th May, for which pray thank him with my kindest love, and tell him I will answer very shortly, as also Hardy's, whose entire recovery gives me the sincerest pleasure, and I hope soon to hear that he has got a ship. At a time when so much is doing in all parts of the world, I know it must be irksome to him to be unemployed.

We were to have left this place yesterday to join the army assembled about Guarda, etc., and to advance into Spain as an Army of Observation, but business has prevented the general, and we only set off tomorrow morning, and proceed direct to Guarda, where we shall remain but a few days, I suppose.

Most of the English officers who came over to join the Portuguese Army have accepted the pay. I have however refused it, as I cannot see any credit in serving them for the pittance of pay, particularly when I know they are so poor they cannot pay their own officers. Besides, I consider that receiving pay invalidates in some measure my claims on future promotion in my own service, and in some degree deprives me, I consider, of the right of quitting this when I choose. I am ready, as I told the marshal, to exert myself for the service of this country without being any weight or charge to them. They have certainly some claims to my service from the kindness my family has for a long series of years experienced, and if H.R.H. hereafter chooses to reward me in the end, he can do so, without my being an expense to his government, and, if he does not, I am pretty tolerably indifferent, and shall be satisfied with having done my duty. I certainly very much dislike this service and their mean intrigue and absurd presumption, which shades their good qualities, and would therefore avoid any possible reason for my being kept with it longer than suits my convenience and I consider my duty requires. I hope you therefore will approve of my having declined any emolument for my services.

The conduct of the English Government in refusing the step of rank to those officers who have come out, or, being here appointed, have joined the army, is very extraordinary. They now have only an additional step in the Portuguese, and the pay of both. I am astonished any British officer will come out on these terms.

I will write to you whenever an opportunity occurs. In the meantime, my dearest father, give my kindest love to all at home, and believe me affectionately your dutiful son,

Wm. Warre.

I do not send the certificate of horses lost at Coruña, as we have written home for the printed form, when I shall know how it is to be filled up. *Adieu.*

Lacebo, 10th August, 1809.

My Dear Father,

An unfortunate accident of having dislocated the knuckles of my right hand, and having broke one of the small bones, obliges me to apply to my friend Captn. Souza to serve as an amanuensis. It being now nearly a month since the accident happened, I am afraid you will be very anxious to hear from me. I am in other respects perfectly well, and so far, recovered from this, that I but yesterday returned from travelling night and day to the English Hd. Quarters post and back again. I have not yet, however, quite the use of my hand.

You will long before this have heard of the Battle of Talavera perhaps the most glorious ever gained, if we consider the disproportion of numbers. Not having had the good fortune to be present I can give no further particulars than you will have seen by Sir Arthur's despatch. The attacks were most vigorous and repeated by upwards of 40,000 men in heavy columns, first against the left, then the right, and afterwards along the whole British line which was occupied by about 19,000 men.

Nothing however could overcome the steadiness and gallantry of our troops. After having been engaged the 26th and 27th, the greatest part of the night between the 27th and 28th, and from daybreak till night that day, the enemy was completely repulsed, leaving 11,000 killed and wounded on the field, and the next morning retired 4 leagues to Sebola. Our loss was also very considerable, about 4500 killed and wounded. You will be sorry to hear that the 23rd lost half their men in a charge, and among a great many officers wounded are Capt. Howard badly, Drake *ditto.* He was taken and afterwards released by the enemy, Allen wounded and taken, D. W. Russell slightly, Frankland slightly, Lieut. Anderson badly, and 226 men killed and wounded. I saw Col. Seymour and Dance, who are quite well. The regt. was ordered to charge two columns of the enemy, who were deploying, but who unfortunately had time to form square without there being time for the order being revoked, and they unfortunately persevered in attempting an attack which it was impossible should succeed.

The British Army as usual has been deprived of the fruits of their glorious victory; for Soult, Ney, and Mortier, having penetrated from Castille to Placencia with 34,000 men, added to the impossibility of placing any dependence upon the Spaniards, who during and after the Battle of Talavera had remained, except their artillery, entirely spectators, with 20,000 men, exposing the British Army to finding itself between two fires, besides entirely cutting off its retreat and communications with Portugal, obliged Sir Arthur to retire by the bridge of Arço-bispo to the other side of the Tagus; that of Almaraz was already occupied by the enemy. Cuesta, who was left at Talavera to keep the army of Victor in check, I suppose not feeling very confident in his troops, set off after Sir Arthur, thus abandoning all such of our wounded, who could not crawl along the road, to the enemy, who however, it must be confessed, on all occasions have treated the English prisoners with great humanity.

We have moved forward with the Portuguese Army to occupy the strong passes near this place, and assist, as far as we may be able with our small force of 12,000 men, the British and Spanish Armies, the former of which occupies a position on the South Bank of the Tagus at Almaraz, the latter at Arçobispo. The names of these passes are Perales and Gata and are at four leagues distance from Coria. The French have advanced towards Talavera from Placencia. Our army are in very good spirits, and will, I have no doubt, maintain their character better than their neighbours, in whom, you know, I never had much confidence. I am happy to tell you that Jack Prince is well, also Genl. Fane. Poor Milman is badly wounded, as is Sir W. Sheridan.

I am much obliged to you for the boots and my glass, which I have received, and which I was in great want of.

I will write to you again the moment I am able, and in the meantime I have only to add that I remain, my dear father, with love to all at home, your very affectionate son,

Wm. Warre, A. D. C.

I beg you will believe my hand is really of no consequence and nearly well, nor do I find it a bit the worse for a ride of fifty hours de suite to the British Headquarters and 36 back, and I am otherwise in as good health as I ever was.

Los Hoyos, August 13.

I have been unable to forward this letter before today and have merely to add that my hand is much better. We continue near these passes, though we made the other day a movement to Salteros, but retired again to the same position, and established our headquarters at this place. I believe Soult's, Ney's, etc., army are moving again into Castille by Baños without deigning to take notice of us. The cowardly Spaniards have suffered the enemy to pass the bridge at Arçobispo with very little *resistance*, and now occupy the passes in which I left the British Army, on its right flank.

Every day convinces me more strongly that the fate of these countries depends entirely upon Austria, of which, you may well imagine, we are most anxious for positive accounts. We have had a French bulletin with accounts of an armistice, and other rumours of a peace. But as they have all come from the French, I trust unfounded. I hope you will let all your arrangements, with regard to Portugal, depend upon the successes in Germany.

Yrs. most affectionately,

Wm. Warre.

Salvaterra, August 18, 1809.

My Dearest Mother,

I take the opportunity of being able to write to give you some account of myself and our proceedings. My hand, as you will see by my being able to write, is nearly well, though still weak. I suffered a good deal from it, from not applying the proper remedies, and supposing I had merely dislocated two of my knuckles, for my hand and arm had swelled so much, from travelling day after day in the excessive heat, that it was not till I arrived at the English Headquarters express a month after, and consulted an English surgeon, that I discovered that one of the small bones in the back of the hand was broken. Nature, however, has joined it, and I trust in a few weeks I shall be entirely as strong as ever. It has been a serious inconvenience, particularly when near the enemy, and expecting to be engaged. Except in writing, however, it never has prevented my duty, though I confess sometimes, after a sleepless night, I could almost have cried from pain and vexation.

I dictated a letter to my father from Acebo and Los Hoyos, fearing you would be very anxious at not hearing from me, which I hope has been received. We have now made a forward movement to Moralega in order to straiten the enemy in his foraging. They constantly dislodged a post we had at Coria, where they came for provisions, nor was it in our power to prevent them, and the inhabitants, who had not fled, either from fear or treason, seemed more ready to supply them than us, so much so in every direction, added to the ignorance and want of arrangement in our commissaries, that our troops have suffered greatly from want of provisions, particularly bread.

The selfish unfriendly conduct of the Spaniards high and low, not giving us any hopes of a supply, Marshal Beresford has been forced to retreat towards this place, on his way to Castello Branco, in order to feed his troops, who are in great distress, without even seeing the enemy, or his making the least forward movement towards us, except in small foraging parties, to Coria, near where they have caught a valuable convoy of English hospital stores, I cannot help thinking, in a great measure from the excessive ignorance and want of energy in the purveyor, who was seven days considering whether the French would come there or not.

As to the conduct of the Spaniards, both to the English and this army, it has been most shameful. I shall not enlarge on this disagreeable subject. It is enough to say both armies are very much irritated. They have every wish that we should fight for them, but do not deign to treat us with common civility, or our men, when sick or wounded, with common humanity. They conceal their provisions, drive away their cattle, and when possible escape themselves, leaving either friends or foes to subsist as well as they can, complaining however most loudly and bitterly if a single cabbage is taken without leave. When our men have been starving, they have refused to sell even a loaf, and if they did, at a most exorbitant price. They will rob your very stores almost in your sight, and, though every town and village expects you are to stay for its defence, they will not, except forced, contribute in any way to assist.

This is the complaint, and universal in both English and Portuguese armies, and as for their soldiers fighting, I never thought they would. They never have. The French treat them with the utmost contempt. 5300 and odd brave soldiers of the British were killed or wounded at Talavera without 45,000 Spaniards, who were present, moving in any way to their support; and since, 3000 wounded of these were abandoned by that old brute Cuesta in Talavera, contrary to Sir A. Wellesley's orders or intention, and without any attack on the part of the enemy. This obstinate surly old ignorant fellow is, thank God, removed. He was, to say the best of him, quite superannuated, and so violent and obstinate that everybody feared him but his enemies.

There never was such folly as sending an army into Spain again. The character of the Spaniards is so selfish, jealous, and proud, with all the surliness of Englishmen, and not a spark of their good qualities, that a foreign army in their country must always risk being abandoned. They, besides, will not fight for themselves, and it is impossible England alone can defend them.

This picture is perhaps strong, and I really feel much irritated against them, but I am sure it is the opinion of almost every individual. The inhabitants fly in all directions at the approach of the enemy, and whenever your army comes, they fancy the enemy are coming also. You are therefore unable to procure subsistence, and of course equally so to defend them. The magistrates fly, to avoid the trouble of providing you, as everything is concealed. All the towns we have been in are nearly abandoned, and we have been forced to break into empty houses for a lodging. In short, war in any shape is a horrid scourge to the inhabitants.

We are in very low spirits at the bad accounts from Austria. A peace in that country will decide the fate of these most undoubtedly. We may prolong the war and sacrifice many lives, but I am convinced that it will be to no purpose, and even should Sir A. W., who, it is reported, is to be made commander in chief in Spain, and a most clever fine fellow as ever existed, be able to avert their ultimate destruction, another brilliant victory, or even more, if the tyrant overruns Germany, and Austria falls, cannot alter my opinion, and I shall doubly regret every British life that is lost after that country makes peace.

Poor Whittingham, who is a brigadier in the Spanish service, was shot through the cheek and hurt severely, while endeavouring most gallantly to rally a Spanish regiment of cavalry. He is however doing well. I am much annoyed at not being able to get any account of Harvey. Milman is badly wounded. These are the only officers I have heard of that you know. Fremantle is well.

Castello Branco, August 20th.
We arrived here yesterday, and will, I hope, remain some days to refresh our poor patient half-starved soldiers, and observe the enemy's motions. A strong corps of theirs forced the Pass of Baños defended by Sir R. Wilson and about 3000 men, Portuguese and Spaniards. They resisted the whole day, but had no guns, and were forced to retreat to avoid being surrounded.

It is impossible to judge yet of what the plans of the French can be, particularly this corps, which has re-entered Castile and marched towards Salamanca, leaving 10,000 or 12,000 men at Placencia; nor have I the least idea of what Sir A. Wellesley's intentions are. I over and over again wish I was with his brave army. It is wretched unsatisfactory work being with this; nothing but constant vexation and disgust, particularly of their officers. The men, poor devils, are patient and obedient, *voilà tout*, I think, yet the British officers with the regiments think they would fight. I am convinced this would depend entirely on circumstances, and if they do unfortunately get beaten, I fear they will at any rate not hazard it again. What a different army I was with a year ago! How gloriously employed where with such soldiers! If Austria makes peace, I shall soon have the happiness again of embracing my beloved family, for the game will be soon settled in these countries.

I think the French will move towards Zamora, and threaten Portugal immediately, to draw away our army from this quarter, and Sir A. W., if possible, out of Spain, to protect it.

Adieu, my dearest mother, kindest love to my father, etc., etc., etc., from your ever affectionate son,

Wm. Warre.

You sent me out last year, which I never got, a new *aide-de-camp's* coat. If it is in existence and not lost, pray send it to Lisbon to me, as I sometimes wear it, and do not wish to make another Portuguese, which is very expensive.

Hdqrs., Lisbon, Sept. 6, 1809.
My Dearest Father,
I wrote to my mother from Castello Branco, as soon as my hand which I broke would permit me without inconvenience, which

I hope you have received. My hand is now quite well. We left Castello Branco on the 30th. The greatest part of the army having marched, in different divisions, to occupy cantonments at Abrantes, Thomar, Vizeu, Coimbra, etc., in order to be able to feed them and clothe them, so as to be enabled to take the field again, with some chance of health, as soon as the enemy, who has also retired into cantonments, shall attempt anything. We know they want rest as much as we do, and have divided their corps, Soult at Coria, Placencia, Larza, etc., Marchand at Salamanca, etc., etc., Mortier at Zamora, Toro, etc. This is the army that was in our front. Of that of Victor I know nothing. Nor do I even know where Sir A. Wellesley is.

We quitted Spain (Coria, Placencia, etc.), partly from orders from Sir A. W. partly because we were absolutely starved, and the cursed Spaniards would do nothing for us, concealed all means of subsistence, and fled as fast as approached. The French, who have not the same necessity of temporising as we have, will know how to extract what is left, though we know from deserters that they are very badly off. At Castello Branco also the army would not exist many days longer together, and our commissariat, and even distribution of what little we had was infamous. There was no remedy left but to divide the army into corps, station them where they may be assembled at the shortest notice, and at whatever point we may be attacked, and meantime employ ourselves in getting them clothed and disciplined, of which there is much want after all their exertions. The men, poor fellows, are well enough, very obedient, willing, and patient, but also naturally dirty and careless of their persons, dreadfully sickly, and they have a natural softness, or want of fortitude, which makes them yield immediately without exertion to sickness or fatigue. The officers, for the most part, are detestable, mean, ignorant, and self-sufficient. It is incredible the little mean intrigues, the apathy, and want of military sentiment, Marshal Beresford has had to work against. Nothing but a very severe discipline can overcome these, and which I hope he will follow.

Should however Austria fall, and France turn her whole force this way, I fear the ruin of these countries could but be for a short time delayed, and at the expense of many lives. The events in Germany, as I before wrote, should decide your conduct with regard to this. I merely venture an opinion in a military point of view. I confess in this last campaign I felt not the least wish to see the Portuguese troops engaged. If we had been beat, we were lost, and the state of our men from hunger, fatigue, want of proper clothing, made me feel but slender hopes of the contrary. We were, however, most anxious to afford every assistance in our power by a diversion in favour of our gallant noble countrymen with Sir A. W., and in such light would have regretted no loss, and certainly dared any danger.

We came from Castello Branco to Abrantes in one day by Niza, in a day nearly 20 leagues, or 70 odd English miles. It was dreadfully hot, and I think I never suffered more from fatigue and heat. We left Castello Branco at 12 at night, and I rode my own horse to Niza, where, however, I got a tired post mule, who could only get half way to Gaveon, and made me walk a great part of the way. In consequence it was near 7 p.m. before I got into Abrantes. The rest had arrived at two. We left that next day in a boat for Lisbon at 5 in the morning, and arrived about 6 next morning. It was rather a tiresome voyage, nor can I say much for the beauties of the banks of this famous river. It is also very shallow above Vallados, so that even in an English flat we were constantly on shore. Just about Abrantes, (which the marshal has made very strong) and Santarem, it is pretty enough. Also, near Barcinha and Tancos, where the banks are higher than they are generally.

Rankin has turned out one of the greatest villains I ever met with. He had latterly behaved most infamously, and I had reason to suspect him of stealing, but could bring no absolute proof. I, however, had determined he should join his regt. as soon as I should come near it. However, at Castello Branco I detected him in falsifying a ration return from 2 to 12 rations of bread and wine, adding the 1, and turned him off at Niza to a party of the 23rd. On coming to Lisbon, however, I have discovered that he has robbed not only me of a great many articles of value, but in every place we have been he must have done the same, as on examining his trunk, which, however, a friend of his had re-moved out of my room here, and opened, but had not had time to secrete, I discovered a large amount of banknotes and silver and gold, many stolen articles, among others a spoon belong-ing to this house, a very valuable gold and agate snuffbox; and, though he made me buy him clothes just before we left Lisbon, saying he was quite naked, a large quantity of every kind.

I have sent off to General Crawford who commands at Niza, to have him confined closely, and shall write to Sir A. Wellesley for a court martial on him. I do not so much mind what I have myself lost, however provoking, but am vexed beyond anything at his having plundered everybody wherever we went. Though I have sent up to General Crawford, I have no doubt he has deserted, as he asked me for money at Niza, stole one of my double-barrelled pistols and all my shaving things. As a great part of his money is in English Bank Notes, I should not at all wonder if he had robbed your house. You would be astonished at the rascality that has come out against him since he was detected, and that he should have so long deceived us.

I got a letter from Clara the other day. She was quite well. Should things go worse, I will get an order for her to quit the convent, and act for the best, as circumstances may occur, and as I think you wish.

Sept. 8th.—We are just returned from reviewing the cavalry which has been for some time organising here, that is reducing some regiments to act as dismounted, and from them endeavouring to complete some squadrons of the others effective. They are tolerably equipped, but I think no great things, certainly the worst arm of its kind in Portugal. They will, however, soon be able to march. It has rained incessantly during the 5 hours we have been out, and I suppose the marshal staid in it to accustom them *a nao ter medo a chuva*, (not to be afraid of the rain) though I fear in consequence many will be troubled with *dores de bariga*, (stomach-ache) a disorder we have found very prevalent among the officers going to Spain, and for which we had numberless petitions to go to Caldas, till it became proverbial for not wishing to serve. It is currently reported some of the wretched old crook-kneed horses we ran intend to petition for a like indulgence, fearing their strength will not be sufficient to carry them through the campaign. It should be granted. The 3 eldest cornets of one regt. make up near 180 years age!

Pray give my kindest love to my dear mother, etc., and believe me most truly, my dear father, your very affectionate son,

Wm. Warre.

My Dearest Father,

I have been most truly vexed at not receiving your very affectionate letters of 5th July and 2nd August, annexed with my dear mother's of 10th July, till yesterday, late in the evening. The stupid clerks in the army post-office sent them up to Lord Wellington's army. I have for some time past been very fidgety at not hearing, and three last packets do not bring me a line from anyone, or they also are gone to the English Army while I am in Lisbon.

I am sorry my letter was so expensive. It was Col. Brown's brother's fault, who told me it would go free. With regard to the affairs of this country I have nothing new to communicate, and observe from your letter we are perfectly agreed. Nor shall I say anything further to Pedro Alvez, as you have given him your orders. Just what I intended to have done, had not the French Army retired into cantonments. Only I will apprise him with all possible speed, should any unexpected danger arise.

Also, about Clara, I had already determined to apply for a permission for her to quit the convent, which I will do, and act on it as circumstances may require. I think, however, she is better there as long as she can be so without risk. With regard to Madeira, I am unable on so short consideration to give any opinion. I am told there is a most respectable convent there, but the means of transport, admission, etc., etc., have of course some difficulty. I should also like to bring it about with her so that it should appear rather her own wish than ours, which may be done with a little management. On this subject, however, I will write further when better informed.

You wish to know my situation in the country, etc., etc. It is simply this, I have the rank of major, but neither pay, nor allowances, or fixed regiment. It was intended to have given those who chose it the Portuguese pay, that is those who got no rank, by entering it, in their own service. This I refused, and have already informed you of my reasons, which I hope you approve. However, since I find we are not to get it, as we receive English staff pay, and batt and forage, I received the other day, which, however, they threaten to make me refund, (150 $f.$ for horses), and besides this I neither have nor do receive one farthing from their government, or any besides my English pay.

I could indeed make it out very well on my staff pay, but for my losses in horses. Within these four months I have paid 80 guineas for one horse. He is completely lame and at Pinhel; 50 *do.* for another, left at Lamego, water in his chest. I have been forced to ride a black horse, which the general lent me, the whole campaign, as to buying horses at any price is impossible, except at Lisbon. Here I yesterday bought a mare blind of an eye, though a very nice one, for 40 gns. In this case, as you will suppose, with very expensive dress, I cannot save much towards my majority.

Since Rankin robbed me and was turned off, I have found it impossible to get a servant of any kind who would look after myself and horses, and am at last obliged to hire a *valet de chambre* (to avoid paying 800 *reis per diem* to a *valet de place*, who does nothing). He is highly recommended, has the care of everything, overlooks the stable, and finds himself in everything at 4 *moidores* a month. I shall not however keep him longer, when I can get an English groom.

I will send you the statement of losses at Coruna as soon as I can get an opportunity, and a printed form. The conduct of our government towards the young men who entered the Portuguese service, and have exerted themselves very much, all meritorious young officers, in not giving them the step of rank, in consequence of which most will quit it, at this most critical moment; and their giving rank to men totally out of the army, as brigadiers, to come and command English lt.-cols. and majors, is most extraordinary and disgusting. Beresford's exertions have been constant and unremitting and their excellent effect daily visible, but the government have behaved shamefully to him in many respects.

As to myself, I perfectly agree with you, though I think not quite so *desconfiado* as you suspect. I am much obliged to you for sending the *encommendas* and will write to Porto about them. I will make the *fidalgos* pay, or *nada feito*, (no transaction, nothing done.)

I do not yet know when we quit Lisbon. It of course depends much on the movements of the enemy. You shall hear from me when we do. I believe our army is getting on very well, but, unless government will make the magistrates do their duty, and most severe examples of what deserters are caught, it (will be) impossible to keep them together, while they know that they can return home with impunity when they like. There is also a disgusting delay in getting anything done, when everything should be vigour and activity, and I really sometimes wonder at Beresford's perseverance and patience. A less firm man would have done nothing with them.

We look to Germany with the greatest anxiety. The renewal of hostilities is something, but the consequences are not less a matter of anxiety and fear than their armistice. God prosper them. Their cause is that of Europe.

Adieu. Kindest love to all at home from, dearest friend, your ever affectionate son,

Wm. Warre.

Lisbon, 25th Sept. 1809.

My Dear Father,

I avail myself of my friend Bushes going to England to send you my claims for losses at Corunna, which I will be much obliged to you to endeavour to recover for me from the Board of Claims which I hear is sitting. Van Diest can put you in the way, as also to recover for my horse killed at the Vimiero, which I was informed I had been allowed, at Salamanca, where I gave in my claim, by order of Sir John Moore, and which having done precludes my including it in my losses now; and being at a distance from hdquarters I could never receive it.

I intended to have written a long letter from this to my dear mother by this conveyance, but have so much to do today that it is impossible. We go to St Ubes, Palmela, etc., tomorrow to visit the posts in that country, and I fear before we return, in two or three days, the Packet will have sailed, but she shall hear from me the very first opportunity. We are getting the army clothed and disciplined with all diligence during this quiet interval. The French are, I suppose, doing the same, as all the armies have been for some time in *statu quo.*

We long for a packet. Never was a more anxious moment. I flatter myself with the idea that, if the affairs in Austria were favourable to the French, we should have heard them. Both parties seem to await some decisive news from that quarter, and the Spaniards, I hear, promise fair. I don't believe a word they promise, unless I see more sincerity in them than hitherto.

I have taken no steps as yet about dear Clara. It is needless to alarm her or her friends, till we have more certain intelligence and reason to act, for, whatever I say or do, people draw conclusions from, and judge of the situation of affairs—and above all things we must avoid appearing to despond, or give the thing up. I will, however, shortly inform you of my plans, which I hope you will approve. I am in perfect health and latterly as idle as any private gentleman need to be. I wish we had something active going on, and were in the field again. I always think I like Lisbon best when away, and *vice versâ*. Such is human nature.

Adieu, my dearest father; kindest love to all my dear friends at Hendon and elsewhere, from yours ever most affectionately and dutifully,

Wm. Warre.

Lisbon, 10th October 1809.

My Dear Father,

I have to thank you for your very kind letter of 18th September, and will, you may depend upon it, do everything that my affection can dictate, or yours wish, respecting dear Clara. I am, however, sorry you have written to Pedro Alvez who has sent me your letter, as in these times we cannot be too cautious in giving the slightest reason of mistrust or despondency. I do not by any means consider the danger as so pressing or near as you do, and my dear Father will suppose, I am sure, that if I did, I would not risk the safety of one so dear to me.

At the same time, I cannot see the use of alarming her unnecessarily, particularly as being my sister, take what precautions we may and desire what secrecy we will, it will spread in the country. They will fancy that I, and consequently the marshal, think there is danger to be apprehended. You know the nature of the people, and their malicious propensities are not improved by the unsettled revolutionary state in which they have latterly been.

It is almost impossible I should not have notice of the danger approaching in time to remove her to a place of safety, and subsequently, wherever you may think proper. In the meantime, I have already drawn up a petition to the regency, which I have no doubt they will grant, to remove her to a respectable house in Lisbon. And then if occasion press, I can be at hand to assist her, and we need not at once send her to England with

74

strangers, contrary to what I know also is her wish, unless there was absolute danger. I will write to Pedro Alvez, and wait your further orders. To her I will say nothing till it is time to act, and you may be quite at rest that I will not risk anything, and I think I can depend on the marshal's friendly assistance.

I am much vexed at . . . bill being protested. He is a very brave gallant officer, was much distressed, and I felt happy in relieving him. I would have given him the money, raising it as I could, if that was all, for I admire his conduct as a soldier, but feel much hurt that he should have deceived me, and have written to him as much, and he will pay the money, I have no doubt. Genl. . . . also had 41 fl. which he has not paid, and I have written to him, and sent him the account.

I am I confess much surprised at the manner of your letter with regard to my taking up money at Porto. I went there ill, and had no means of getting a farthing any other way. Expense with servants was inevitable, and when I was forced to pay 40 guineas for a horse unexpectedly, I was unable to remit to Porto, as I told Pedro I should, and desired him not to send the account home till he heard from me. I do not at the same time deny that I spent more than I absolutely need, but it was under particular circumstances, and intended to have been paid by my bat. and forage money, £42 odd I had to receive, which the loss of my horses prevented. Nor did I imagine at all events even with that expense, I exceeded my pay, which I hope you constantly receive in England, as I never receive any here but my staff pay as *A.D.C.*

With regard to my Portuguese Commission, I refused the pay of it for reasons I already stated. From the tenor of your former letters, I was in hopes you would have approved, and most sincerely regret you do not. I have a feeling of dislike to taking the pay of any Sovereign but my own, and, as I am now circumstanced, I merely consider myself as indirectly serving my own king and country, and they have a right to my services, however insignificant, without any further pay or emolument, and shall think myself fully rewarded if Marshal Beresford's exertions are successful, and that we can give the cursed oppressors of Europe a good beating with Portuguese troops. Under certain circumstances I have not a doubt we should. They are perfectly subordinate and their discipline progressively getting into a very good state. I hope they will soon be completely clothed and equipped and as respectable an army under British officers as any.

From Spain we have no news. The French appear to wait accounts from Germany previous to any operation of consequence. The English Army is getting healthy and is in good spirits. I see little of absolute despondency except in some English newspapers, or discontented officers, and most sincerely hope the new Ministry will not discontinue their exertions for the defence of this country, *if affairs go well in Germany*.

The approaching rainy season renders the advance of an enemy into Portugal very difficult, and confines our defence to particular posts. The British Army is, I believe, going into cantonments about Elvas, Badajos, etc., etc. Ours between Abrantes and Coimbra. The former in a very good state of defence commands the Tagus and secures our right, while we are in reach of all the passes of Muradal, etc., and within reach of the Douro if necessary.

The money for the *encommendas* I will remit,, as also drafts for two pipes of wine, sent by your house to Sir David Dundas and Capt. Otter by desire of Col. Delaney and Major Brown, who will forward the bills of loading. I am very much obliged by your kind attention about the *encommendas*; which are much approved, though I think particularly the hat ornaments tawdry, and such as I would not wear, and Souza's sabre of wretched quality and badly finished, which it will be right to tell Hawkes. I am vexed at it, for the prices are for the best.

Rankin, I have had tried by a general court martial for robbery. Never was such a scene of iniquity as I discovered. I fear it will go very hard with him, and am therefore glad that I only prosecuted for what he stole from other people, passing over my own losses.

Pray give my kindest love to all at home, and believe me ever, my dear kind friend and affectionate father, your most sincerely and affectionately,

Wm. Warre.

Pray tell my Uncle Wm. with my love that I have received his *empenho* (recommendation) for corporal of the 6th, and will do what I can for him.

Many thanks, my dearest mother, for your very affectionate letter.

It is still uncertain when we leave Lisbon and must depend on circumstances. I long for a more active life than this, though far from an unpleasant one. We yesterday received a pleasing account of the defeat of a French division of 12,000 men commanded by Genl. Marchand, Ney having, it is said, returned to France. They attacked the Duque del Parque, who was in his position near Tamames, but he completely defeated them after a very sharp action, and took 300 arms, 1 12-pounder, 1 colour. They left 1200 men dead on the field, and were pursued 4 leagues by the Spanish cavalry and light troops, who killed a great many more. Their loss is therefore estimated at 2000 or more, as they retired in great confusion to Salamanca, near 8 leagues. I most sincerely rejoice the Spaniards should have done this by themselves. It will give them confidence, and persuade them that with a little perseverance the invaders can be conquered.

The Spanish cavalry at first ran away, but falling back on their infantry regts. they fired on them and forced them to attack the enemy, when they regained what they had lost in so infamous a manner. The Spanish horse artillery, which is anything but light artillery, was taken in the beginning of the action, but most gallantly retaken by their infantry with the bayonet, and they throughout appear to have behaved with great courage. I am ignorant of their force, but know that they had not been joined by Ballasteros' division, which they expect, and will, I hope, make some use of this victory.

It augurs well in young troops, and I approve greatly of the system of firing on those that misbehave. It is thus the French Revolutionary Army gained such victories at the commencement, when indisciplined and badly officered. The *duque* himself appears to have behaved with great valour and conduct, and to have exposed himself everywhere he thought that his presence might avail. I know him, and I confess am agreeably surprised, for, though very gentlemanly, I had little idea of him as a soldier on a great occasion.

Last night about 10 o'clock, just after I had gone to bed, I was alarmed by a very sharp shock of an earthquake. It lasted several seconds and was generally felt, even in the playhouse, and occasioned some alarm. From the long-continued heat and dry weather it has been expected. But the rain seems now to set in. I hope we shall have no more. My curiosity is completely gratified. It was strong enough to wake me, and lasted sometime after I sat up in my bed, not quite determined what to do. Tonight, we are all going to a very grand ball at Mr Villiers' the envoy, on his going away, universally respected and regretted. I have the highest esteem for him and owe him some gratitude for his kindness to me. A better or kinder man could not be, and he was much esteemed by the natives. Lord Wellesley is expected here, though this is only what I hear as a report. Lord Wellington leaves this tomorrow for the army.

I wrote to dear Emily by the last packet about some friends of mine, most amiable good people, to whom I, as well as every English officer, owe a great deal. I am sure you would like them, and I therefore beg you to second my petition for them to stay with you some time, should they be forced to quit the country, till they can get settled in some degree in England previous to going to Brazil.

With kindest love to all, believe me, my dear mother, Yours affectionately,

Wm. Warre.

The ball was very handsome, and also the supper in grand style, which table many of my Portuguese friends, who dined at No. 3, did not seem to disapprove.

Lisbon, October 26, 1809.

My Dear Father,

As I write to my mother by this conveyance, and tell her all the news, this merely serves to enclose 1st and 2nd of exchange, for some wine shipped by your house at Porto for Capt. Otter by the direction of Major Brown. I have not yet received that from Lt.-Col. Delaney, for a pipe shipped by his order to Sir D. Dundas, but will remit it as soon as I do. I also enclose my final account current with Messrs Armit & Borough, Dublin, and their bill on Hammersley's for the balance, £53. 18s. 8d. Greenwood & Cox must therefore have 5 months' pay of mine in their hands, and I enclose accordingly a bill for £90, which I will thank you to place to my credit.

I observe with the greatest surprise, in a letter from my dear mother, that my expenses at Porto amounted to £500, nor can I imagine it possible, and accordingly write to Pedro Alvez for a statement. I should have thought £100 far beyond the mark exclusive of Genl. . . . account, and . . . bill for 133 dollars, and I really am completely at a loss to account for it. It is true I was in one respect at an unnecessary expense, and gave the servants a present each. Poor devils, they had lost all they had, and told me, except old Domingos, my uncle's allowance to them had ceased, and compassion for their sufferings made me give more than at the time I thought I could afford.

Rankin previous to his execution confessed having robbed me at different times to the amount of £40 or more. Others were perhaps more immediately guilty than this unfortunate fellow but I fear having no other proof than the confessions of a condemned man, it will be impossible to bring them to justice. I have fortunately discovered the most valuable part of the property, and am happy in being able to restore it to its owners. The sum of money found, and which he confessed to have been in great measure mine, the court martial ordered to be given to the fund at Lloyds, as they were ignorant of the right owners.

I have no objection to that, as I could not wish to possess this money after prosecuting him, but should have felt as well pleased to have given it myself. The money for the *encommendas* I will remit as soon as I can collect the whole. . . . I have written to about the protested bill and have no doubt he will pay, though I fear he is still much distressed. Public news of any consequence we have none. Lord Wellington leaves tomorrow for the army; when we go is uncertain. We most anxiously look for news from Austria. It must decide almost everything.

Adieu, my dearest Father; believe me ever yr. affectionate son,

Wm. Warre.

Lisbon, Dec. 1st, 1809.

My Dearest Mother,

Your affectionate son does allow that you never miss an opportunity of doing or saying everything that can contribute to his happiness, and that it is indeed a very agreeable way you have chosen of making up to him for his anxiety at not hearing from home. . . .

Poor Rankin died very penitent. It was the most afflicting scene

I ever witnessed. Could my exertions have saved him, though duty forced me to prosecute him, I would have been happy indeed. I am sorry to tell you his accomplice, and I think instigator to wickedness, has been detected and tried, and will I fear share the same fate. He is a private servant of the general. I hope Ld. Wellington will think one example sufficient, and mitigate his punishment. However, convinced I am that it was an imperious duty to society, who can help feeling much annoyed at the idea of being so instrumental in bringing these poor wretches to justice? Nature pleads sometimes louder than policy and right, and I regret I ever knew anything of the matter.

Our departure from Lisbon has been repeatedly postponed for some reason or other. It was fixed for next Monday, but I believe will not then take place. A tour round the provinces at this wet season will not be a journey of pleasure. But it is absolutely necessary we should know the board on which we are to play our game. We must do our best. The country possesses many great advantages for a defending army and the business may be prolonged. Providence, however, must decide the issue as it pleases, though I certainly think the peace with Austria, and the late total rout (Ocaña) of the Spaniards, augur ill. No considerable reinforcements have yet arrived from France. A very large army must be left in Germany. The season is greatly unfavourable to attack, particularly in this country, which abounds in rivers, in winter impassable, and in difficult passes. All these thoughts leave room for conjecture how long we may remain quiet.

The Spanish Army was completely destroyed and by their own ignorant dispositions, and their obstinacy in persisting in their old system, and if they continue, it will be so, every time they meet the French. Never was there a stronger proof of how unavailing courage and enthusiasm are against discipline and order. Their men are led, and go to the very mouth of certain destruction, by the ignorance of their generals and officers, and these are so bigoted to the system they fancy they know, that nothing but such woeful experience can cure them. I do not wonder the men run away. I wonder much more they ever go so far, knowing as they do the ignorance and often treason of their leaders. I send all the letters open enclosed to you, and beg you will seal and send them.

Dec. 2nd, Monday.—We certainly leave this on Wednesday next for our tour to the northern frontiers and provinces.

I have nothing further to add but my kindest love to my dear Father. I am, etc., etc., from your ever affectionate Son,

Wm. Warre.

P.S.—Prior is going on very well, and desires to be remembered. He is a very good officer and has a good heart, though very weak in some things. I have no doubt he will yet make an excellent member of society.

Thomar, Dec. 31, 1809.

My Dear Father,

I have to thank you for your very kind letters of the 15th Novr. and 20th Decr., the latter this moment received, and, as I have a short leisure, I answer it immediately. Marshal Beresford is gone with Lord Wellington to Torres Novas to see the Algarve Brigade men, and left me to continue my translation of *Instructions for Light Infantry*, a tiresome undertaking, but most necessary, and for the appearance of which I am much hurried. While in Lisbon, Dundas' book was translated under my direction, and has, I am happy to say, already been of essential use, and gained me some credit.

I have considered my account very carefully and am a good deal surprised at the amount. Some expenses were unavoidable from circumstances such as horses and mules. My expenses at Oporto in 1808 were heavy, as, though Genl. Beresford insisted on paying many things, it was impossible for him to be there in my own house without great expense, particularly as I was then living as a guest in his family. The expenses with hams and plumbs were most thoughtless. Indeed, I never dreamt of the expense and thought they were to be paid for by those who ordered them. Genl. Payne has repaid me the $41.510 advanced for him at Porto. Genl. Beresford's $46.085 in 1808 I will enquire about.

In short, my dear Father, the expenses for the last few years I feel are very great, and from the unfortunate turn of business I most sincerely regret it. I am most sensible and feel how happy you would be and always have been when in your power to make me the most liberal allowance, and hope for the future this conviction of your kindness will make me square my expenses to my means. Hitherto, my greatest expenses, horses, I have been most unfortunate in.

I must be well mounted to be able to do the duty with Marshal B. Unfortunately, though I have paid very high prices, all my horses and mules have turned out ill, and even both my last purchases have been unlucky. I bought a mare strongly recommended with the whole of my last Batt. and Forage money, but the day we left Lisbon she very near broke my neck, and falling upon me lamed me for a fortnight, but I am quite well again. The mule also I bought, when leaving Lisbon, for 100 dollars, and appeared so fine a one, has swelled in the legs and I scarce know what I shall do to get my servant on.

I hate being obliged instantly to make excuses, but feel that you have an undoubted right to know why I do not make it out on my staff pay. My regimental pay I intend while I remain in Portugal shall go towards the bills you pay for me, and unless unforeseen accident occurs, hope to make it out on my staff pay, though it will, I know, be with very considerable difficulty, for our expenses are unavoidably not inconsiderable. With regard to the Maçarellos, I have written to my uncle as you wish, and very strongly, and hope you are convinced that I cannot have greater pleasure than meeting them on every occasion.

With regard to dear Clara I intend asking leave in a few days at Coimbra to go to see her, and will write to you from Porto, what arrangements I have made. The patriarch has promised to obtain the leave for her to quit the convent, from the Nuncio, and, you may depend upon it, I will run no risk as to her safety. My friends, the Marquis and Marchioness of Louriçal, have offered to give her an asylum should it be necessary, and I should not wish to have her in a more amiable family, but this is really a very delicate step to take both in regard to her, who has many prejudices to overcome, besides her own, not small ones, as to quitting the convent, and my official situation in this country. I will, however, see how the ground lies, and inform you further from Oporto.

I do not with you consider danger so near or that the French will attack us till the spring. The loss of the Battle of Ocaña, though highly disastrous, and, moreover, the loss of the Duque del Parque's army, might have decided much, if the French had forces to follow up their success, but as it is I think the *dons* will have time to recover themselves, and have (at least we hope so) gained in experience. The causes of their defeats are very apparent. Their cavalry are always placed in a situation where, even if they were brave, which we have no reason to suppose, they are exposed to certain destruction. Their officers are even worse than those of the infantry, which is decidedly brave and deserves much more our pity than contempt for their misfortunes.

In the battle at Ocaña, the genl. in chief left the field before his army, and left them to fight it out in their own way, and set off in a different direction, to avoid even the confusion of his own routed army. All the fine squibs in the papers about him are not true. The Duque del Parque's army, after having fought most gallantly and effected its retreat, dispersed in a panic occasioned by some Dragoons galloping in, and calling out *vienen, vienen*, (they come, they come) when there was not an enemy within several leagues. So much for their disposition and Officers, who could never rally them at all. The loss I most regret on these occasions are the arms, which the fools throw away in their flight, and more irreparable than men of which they ought to have no want.

The French will have a difficult job to drive us out, both from the nature of the country, want of provisions and means of transport, and the very improved state of the Portuguese Army, which in itself speaks sufficiently for Beresford's exertions, and the propriety of the severe, or rather firm, conduct he went upon from the first. In many respects he has been infamously used by both governments, but I suppose he has the good of his country and common sense too much at heart to complain or remonstrate. I think he could not feel annoyed at the appointment of Ld. Wellington to be Marshal-General and Comr.-in-Chief of the troops while in the field only, which he is, but the manner in which it was done has much disgusted us all. His own feelings I know not, and indeed I am not fond of writing or speaking on these subjects, and merely mention it to you as my own ideas.

The Portuguese Army, notwithstanding the numberless difficulties to which he is constantly exposed, from imbecility and mean contemptible jealousy and intrigue, will be a sufficient testimony, I have no doubt, both in its apparent discipline and conduct before the enemy, whenever it shall be our fortune to meet him. I confess myself rather anxious for the trial. It will shew us what officers are subject to *dores de bariga* and enable us to get rid of them, and make examples of this worst part of their army, though now there are really many very promising young officers, and the old ones have in great measure been got rid of. Lord W. as well as every British officer have been very much, though agreeably, surprised at the state of our troops. I am inclined to think that had they justice done unto them in the common comforts, I may say necessaries of life, clothing and food, they would make as good soldiers as any in the world. None are certainly more intelligent or willing, or bear hardships and privation more humbly.

As to Custine, (see Memoir) I see not the least occasion for your advancing him a farthing more. My obligations to him I think quite sufficiently repaid, and has behaved dishonourably about the bill. Therefore, in future I cannot think you have any occasion to answer his letters.

I am much obliged to you for your kindness to young Lacerda, but I certainly had no idea of your asking his family to stay in the house. The Louriçals are the only people I would think of asking so great an inconvenience for, and for them only for the great friendship they have shown me, and the very bad health of the *marchioness*, and this only had you been at Hendon. In town I know it is quite out of the question, and even at Hendon it would not much signify, as we could assist them in getting a lodging or house. But at all events I hope, whether I am in England or not, should they be forced out of the country, you will be very civil to them.

Pray give my kindest love to them and to all, the dear uncle of Hendon Place, when you meet again, and believe me ever, my dear father, your very affectionate son,

Wm. Warre.

I shall join Marshal B. at Oporto from Arouca, and when they make the tour of the Northern Province, which would have been very pleasant in summer. The marshal desired me to remember him most kindly to you and my mother, whom pray thank for her kind letter to me, which I will answer very soon.

NOTE ON BACK.

20,000 gr. coats	10,000 caps
20,000 blankets	40,000 half-stockings will be sent

84

10,000 jackets   40,000 shirts
10,000 pantaloons   40,000 knapsacks
4500 saddles   20,000 jackets
4500 bridles   20,000 pantaloons
4500 saddle bags

CHAPTER 4

1810

The beginning of the year 1810 saw the army of Lord Wellington withdrawn from Spain, and awaiting in Portugal the attack of the French, which seemed the inevitable. It was destined to wait many months before the blow fell. King Joseph and his advisers committed the error of invading Andalusia, the subjugation of which, and the siege of Cadiz, involved the employment of the larger portion of the forces at their disposal. Before they could invade Portugal, it was necessary for them to give time for reinforcements to arrive from France. The Emperor, having concluded peace with Austria, was now able to spare some of his legions for the complete conquest of the Peninsula. But the time of waiting was long. Astorga in the north did not fall till 22nd April; Ciudad Rodrigo was not taken till 9th July.

In July the opposing forces were brought into contact on the 24th in the Combat of the Coa, in which, owing to the obstinacy of General Craufurd, the Light Division was severely handled by very superior numbers and nearly cut off. Followed the advance of the French Army and the siege of Almeida, which was taken on 27th August.

Meanwhile, during these weary months of waiting, the Portuguese Army was growing in numbers and steadily improving in efficiency and discipline. The language used concerning it in the letters is full of confidence, and offers a contrast to the rather despondent tone of the references to it at the beginning of the previous year.

Major Warre, after a very busy time in August, seems to have been attacked by his old malady and to have been sent to Lisbon. He thus, much to his chagrin, missed Bussaco and the retreat to the lines of Torres Vedras. Early in October he had recovered sufficiently to rejoin the marshal at his headquarters within the lines. But the hard life and exposure resulted in a very serious relapse, which brought him to death's door, and the Medical Board determined that he must be sent home. He arrived at Falmouth, after a bad voyage of ten days, early in November, and the last two letters of this year's series, from Falmouth and Honiton respectively, indicate a very tedious journey and a precarious state of health.

LETTERS

Lisbon, Feb. 6, 1810.

My Dear Kind Mother,

I was made quite happy, on my arrival three days since at this place, by receiving your affectionate letter of 29th Decr, and 1st Jany. (I have also received yours of Dec. 12th). . . .

I own I think you very much more gloomy than necessary as to public affairs, and do not agree with you as to ministers, as I approve much of many of their measures. Our misfortunes in Spain they neither could foresee or prevent. Who could imagine the Spaniards would betray those who went to their assistance? Cowards they are not—that is the soldier. He is capable of being equal to any in the world. But without officers, or of course confidence, without discipline and betrayed by their government, what could they do?

Our last accounts, and their enemy being before Cadiz, was as unexpected as an earthquake, and quite as unaccountable, as that Spain has no army. They (the French) will find it very difficult to conquer this country, and though things in Spain are certainly very dispiriting, the game is not lost. Nothing, however, but a revolution (horrid as the idea is to humanity) can save it, and that is already begun, I suspect, and I hope the traitors will fall. I am quite of the opinion that public safety is the supreme law, and the cant of humanity, when the country is to be saved, I consider as weak and unmanly. They have paid dearly for a bigoted adherence to old absurd forms and prejudices. I do not mean that a revolution and popular government will now save them. But I am sure that it is the only thing that can. They are very enthusiastical and violent, and they abhor the French, against whom their fury will be directed as well as against their government and traitors; and in this tumult some great characters may start up.

As to Flushing, our expedition there was disastrous, but well meant. Who could foresee that Austria would so soon make

87

peace? And the diversion, had it continued the war, would have been of great consequence. Besides, as a soldier, I think we make too much fuss about the loss of men where a great object is to be obtained. Victorious or beaten we must lose men, but while we regret their loss individually, we should not as a public one, in so glorious and just a cause, that of our political existence as a nation.

I write to Tom some account of our tour, which was very pleasant, though rapid. We travelled near 200 leagues in less than two months. Nothing can exceed the beauty of part of the country we went through, and we had only one day rain, and our inspection of the progress of the discipline of the Portuguese troops was as pleasant as our most sanguine wishes could expect.

I am very sorry you had not received the letters I wrote from this in answer to that you wrote in company from Hendon, which I answered, each individually. I wrote also to my father and Emily in December, which letters I hope you have since received, and I only did not write from Porto, as I intended, from really not having time hardly to sleep or eat, what between duty and grand ceremonies and rejoicings. Nothing can have been more honourable or flattering to the marshal than his reception in that city, and indeed in every place we have been in throughout the country, and he deserves it for his unremitted exertions, and Herculean labour. There exists not a more honourable firm man or a more zealous patriot. His failings are mere foibles of a temper naturally warm and hasty, and great zeal to have everything right, without much patience. Those who accuse him of severity are either those who have felt it because they deserved it, their friends, or people wilfully ignorant of the state in which he found the army.

And of how much he has forborne, as to myself, I declare I do not know one instance of severity, and do know numberless ones of his mercy, and goodness of heart, where others would have been less lenient. You see I insensibly fall into politics, or the shop, so called, but one naturally writes about what one's mind is constantly occupied with, and as the subject is not uninteresting, I hope you will not be angry at my writing to a lady on such grave matters as politics and tactics, or rather more properly speaking, on public concerns.

I was three days at Arouca with dear Clara, who is a most amiable sensible woman. Her manners and sense are really quite astonishing for one so constantly secluded from the world. She was quite well. We put the convent in a terrible fuss by the marshal's arrival to breakfast there, on his way to Vizeu. It was very kind of him to go to pay her a visit, and he was very much pleased with her.

I have got an order from the Nuncio to remove her where I please, in case of danger, but it is not quite what I wanted, and I shall try to get a more general one, and bring her to Lisbon, when necessary, where my friends the Louriçals will be glad to receive her. The *marchioness* has just lost her sister the Duchess of Laffoes, and has the care and guardianship of the young duchess and her sister, nieces to the prince, a dismal prospect for her, poor thing, in the present state of public affairs, but notwithstanding she will not allow me to place Clara anywhere else, and she cannot be with more amiable charming people. *Adieu*, as I write to Tom and know that he will see this letter, and you his, shall say no more, but beg you will give kindest love to my dear father, with thanks for his letter, from your sincerely affectionate son,

Wm. Warre.

Lisbon, Feb. 17, 18 10.

My Dear Father,

I avail myself of Frank van Zeller's going to England to thank you for your very kind attention in sending me the books by John Croft, and it was odd that I had, not half an hour before, finished the translation into Portuguese of that on light infantry, when yours arrived. It is, however, not less welcome, as coming from you, and shall supply the place of the old one in our marches.

The great coat having brought a letter enclosed in it addressed to the marshal, it is a doubt whether it is for him or for me. It came directed to me, and the letter enclosed is very equivocal. At all events it does not fit me and does him, and therefore he shall keep it, and if it is intended for me, he can send for one in its place that will fit me. This sort of great coat, however, is of little use on horseback, as it does not cover the knees. And as we can carry but little weight on our horses and but very little baggage, a cloak lined with any warm *but light* stuff is much better, as we oftener want a cloak to sleep in than to keep out the rain, and I have latterly practised riding with an oil skin cape over my great coat, and not minding the rain, so long as I have anything dry to wrap myself up in, or sleep in, when we arrive. Indeed, my cloth coat gets so soon wet, is so heavy when filled with water, and takes so many days drying, that I never carry it with me, in order to save both myself and horse, and I find that we get as used to being wet, and mind it as little, as we do many other very disagreeable things.

Croft tells me you said something to him about a bear skin, which you would send me, but I feel equally obliged by your affectionate intention, and do not wish you to put yourself to the unnecessary expense, as I have already a very good one, a former present from Tom, and which I recovered after poor King's death at Talavera.

I wrote so lately to Tom that I have very little more news to communicate. Cadiz since the Duque d'Albuquerque got in with 6000 men, and the sailing of English and Portuguese Succours is, I think, out of immediate danger, and indeed if the accounts we have from Spain, and the non-arrival of reinforcements is true, as we suppose, I cannot imagine that the French Army can maintain itself in Andalusia, and the movement appears to have been a very rash one (though they succeeded in preventing the Cortes, a great object) and one which they may bitterly repent. It is, however, impossible to say. They are very clever fellows, and have too much experience to make any very great faults, and it is impossible for us to know the secret causes or encouragement which induced them to take such a step.

Even the people who are about a general officer commanding know very little of the motives which weigh in his mind and make him act, and but very few indeed are capable, at the moment, of judging of its expediency or propriety, even long after, when results are known, and time has developed many of the circumstances, and the real situation in which they were placed. We cannot be too cautious in blaming or approving the conduct of one entrusted with such a command. For we can never fully know what passes in his mind (unless greatly in his confidence), or the numberless combinations he must regard. We can only form to ourselves an opinion of how far, and with what propriety apparent, he has deviated from, or adhered to, the certain fixed principles of war, which are subject to as much modification as the variety of the ground to which they must be adapted.

They have also advanced a corps of 6000 to 8000 men upon Badajos, in which Romana is with 6000 men, and a lesser towards, Olivença, another upon Ciudad Rodrigo, which, I hear, is not strong, but am ignorant of their numbers, or of what garrison is in the place.

These corps threaten us direct, but I am of the opinion that it is merely a demonstration in order to deceive and restrain the British and Portuguese Army, by making them jealous of their approach, and collecting the forces for fear of an immediate attack, as I have a letter from a friend of mine in Spain who denies that any reinforcements have arrived, and says he had just spoken with a Spanish courier, who passed Bayonne on the 19th *ulmo.*, and reports that no reinforcements had arrived there at that period, or were any immediately expected, and that the state of the public mind in France was far from favourable to Buonaparte. Of this you may believe as much as you please, combining it with what reports you have in England. Spaniards more frequently report what they wish than what is true, as we all well know to our cost.

General Hill's corps, British and Portuguese, have been marched towards Elvas to cover our sick and wounded at that place. The Portuguese troops are in very high spirits and seem anxious to meet the enemy. They are in a very improved state of discipline, and promise well. It would be unfair to doubt them with these qualities. Poor fellows, they fight for everything that is dear to them. I never saw a regt. embark in better style or higher spirits than 20th Portuguese Regt. did for Cadiz a few days ago. They embarked 1400 strong, and lost only 6 deserted, which does them and their country great honour.

Several men came and enlisted at the moment the regt. was embarking, and one fine fellow I enlisted myself as the regt. marched off. The son of the Viscondessa de Misquetella also enlisted at that moment. Everything proclaims an active spring, and I am very glad of it. The French will, I dare hope, find themselves mistaken in the Portuguese troops, and though I am not sanguine as to the final result, unless Spain does more than she has done yet, I am sure the conquest will cost them very dear.

Pray thank —— for their affecte. letters by John Croft, whom I was much astonished to see in Lisbon, and also for the bonnets for Lumiaces which are much approved. I have also received your letters by Mr Knox and Stanhope and that from my Uncle Wm., and will, of course, shew them every kindness in my power, though I regret the state of the public mind, which is a bar to much society, and my mixing very little in any society whatever, will prevent my shewing them as much of it as I could wish. I have offered them my horses, and will endeavour to ask them here as often as I can.

Our stay is very doubtful, and of course very much depends upon the movements of the enemy, nor have I yet an idea as to where our hdqrs. are to be. Your most truly affectionate,

Wm. Warre.

Lisbon, March 10, 1810.

My Dearest Mother,

We have been unexpectedly delayed in Lisbon some days owing to the dreadful storms we have experienced for the last 8 days, during which it has rained in torrents, and blown almost a hurricane. Great damage has been done in the river, and for several days and nights we have heard nothing but signals and guns of distress in the river even above Lisbon, though I have not yet heard of many lives being lost. I comforted myself with the idea that it will fill our rivers for us, and render all the fords impassable. We are likely to remain a day or two longer in Lisbon and then go to Coimbra, which for the present will be the marshal's hdqrs. The enemy has latterly been very quiet, and we have had very quiet winter quarters, a luxury very rare in the present system of warfare. This, however, cannot now last long, and I hope ere long some movement will be made on one side or the other.

The supineness of the Spaniards is truly distressing. Poor devils, they have been most shamefully betrayed by their government, and public confidence appears in that country quite lost. It is really mortifying, for they are an enthusiastic and spirited people, and have shown on some occasions that they are not deficient in individual courage. I wish they were in half the state of discipline and organisation of the Portuguese, and the French would not then find it an easy task to maintain themselves in that country with their present force; and nothing but the French being perfectly well informed of the real state of that unfortunate nation could have induced them to make the rash movements which they have, for, in any other point of view, they appear much allied to absolute folly.

With regard to this country much is to be said, but my motto is *Nil Desperandum*. Our commanders are very clever, and of course know better than anybody how they can defend the country, and every officer who feels like a soldier should not form, or at least communicate, theories of his own, but make up his mind to share their fate, be it what it may.

To put my mind at rest I have obtained an order to remove dear Clara to the Convent of the Esperança at this place. This from the Nuncio who has also written a very kind letter to the Bishop of Lamego to facilitate the business. These I gave to the patriarch a fortnight ago, and he told me to set my mind at rest, and that he would arrange the whole business for me in the best manner. She will be within reach of the marshal's protection in case I should be at a distance in time of need, should it come to that extremity, and my friend the Marchioness of Louriçal has promised to treat her as if she belonged to her family, and it is to her exertions and friendly interference that I am indebted for having her admitted into this convent, which is the best, and the lady abbess a friend of hers.

Should they be forced to embark, of which I see however no present probability, she will take her with her, and even should that not be easy, I feel confident I can depend upon the marshal's friendship and protection, therefore pray tell my dear father, that he may set his mind quite at rest, and she is truly deserving of all our love and affection.

My stay in Lisbon this time has been anything but amusing. There has been very little gaiety, and my time fully employed with my friend John Campbell in compiling a set of regulations for the cavalry, the last I hope I shall be bothered with, for I know from experience that we may write out our finger ends, and nobody thank one, even if we were to put the regulations into hexameter and pentameter verse!

Pray give my kindest love to my dear Father, etc., and remember me most kindly to all my friends. Ever, my dearest kind mother, your truly affectionate son,

Wm. Warre.

I have not heard from any of you for some time.

Coimbra, March 21st, 1810.

My Dear Father,

We arrived here yesterday from Lisbon after a rather tedious and rainy journey, and have for the present established our hdqrs. here, but for how long it is impossible to say, or where we shall go when we do move. Both must depend entirely upon the enemy, who have given us a much longer period of tranquillity than I expected. The bubble, however, must soon burst, and I expect to hear daily of their making some movement, for we have very good reason to suppose they are much distressed by the want of provisions, a want they are not likely to mend by entering this country, in itself considerably exhausted, and where every means will be taken to place what is remaining out of their reach, or destroy it, in case we should be forced to retreat.

I am anxious that the campaign should begin; and to be able to judge of what our Portuguese will in reality do. I confess I have very great hopes of them. Their discipline is most wonderfully improved, perhaps fully as good as necessary for active service, and only wants confirming. I fear their relaxing, when they get out of the immediate control of British officers, before the enemy, and the class of their own officers, though very much improved and mostly young men, have scarce experience and firmness enough to control them as we could wish. Their pay, which has in some cases been more than doubled, gives them the means now of living like gentlemen and with respectability. In some cases, it is better than ours in proportion, and since the service becomes an object, they will, we must hope, exert themselves, that they may not be deprived of it, which they certainly will without remorse, if they misbehave at all.

Our cavalry is also getting into a very respectable state, and now very tolerably mounted. I saw the 4th commanded by Lt.-Col. Campbell, Augustus' brother, manoeuvre at Lisbon at a gallop extremely well, certainly beyond anything Portuguese officers had any idea of, and they are certainly equalled by the 1st brigade, and Madden's the 2nd, which is mounted on mares, and I doubt will be able to bear the work equal to the other. It is an experiment, and my private opinion is that it will not succeed. Two brigades of very fine infantry, the 1st cavalry, and 3rd brigade of artillery, are with Genl. Hill on the frontier of Alemtejo, and I believe several other brigades will be attached to the British Army in the Beira, and I think it most probable that some English regts., as a reserve, will be attached to Marshal Beresford's *corps d'armée*. But where we are to go, or what to do, I am perfectly ignorant.

I shall be much obliged to you to send me out a map of Spain and Portugal, published by Fadan, and compiled by Nantiat. It appears to be the best extant, and I am in want of a good one, so much so that you will much oblige me by sending it out by the very first opportunity, and Col. D'Urban, our quartermaster general, begs me to procure him one also. They must be pasted on canvas and in strong cases. I have just been calling on General Payne, who asked very kindly after you.

The Spaniards have attacked the French at Caceres and at Valverde and beat them, killing at each a general, one of division. Though these affairs are of no great consequence in themselves, they may revive the dormant enthusiasm and patriotism of the Spaniards, but I confess I have very slender expectation of it. At Valverde it was done in a very slovenly manner, for they completely surprised the French, and the French general was in bed, but they amused themselves murdering a few unfortunate devils whom they first met, and let him get away with some dragoons. At Caceres had their cavalry behaved as well as their infantry they would have taken or destroyed all the French, who prepared to receive them, but were completely beaten and followed for about a league.

Believe me ever most truly your affectionate son,

Wm. Warre.

There has been a little trifling outpost work beyond Almeida on the Agueda. We had one hussar killed. But this is of no consequence and leads to nothing.

March 23, 1810,   W.W.

Coimbra, March 30, 1810.

My Dearest Brother,

The last two days have been fertile in happiness, as in them I have received all the letters from my dear family. Yours of the 5th is this instant arrived. The breeches, etc., by Col. Brown I have received and not before they were wanted. I am much amused by the cause, though sorry for the fright you are all in. We cannot ourselves see any reason for this dread, and are spending our time pleasantly enough in peace and quietness, so much so that we are all sighing for a more active scene.

Now I confess I do not think this far distant, but that the result is to be so disastrous to us I do not believe. I cannot think where the people in England get their information, certainly not from Portugal. It must be from "Bony," or it would not be given such disastrous colours, alarming our beloved families without any reason. You know my opinion of the ultimate result of the contest, unless something unexpected turns up in the north, or in Spain. But we are only at the beginning, and there is a great deal to be done before we are forced to embark yet, if it should ever come to that.

What most annoys me is our British House of Commons, particularly the late debates. Bonaparte can never want spies or intelligence, while that House tells our exact force and dispositions. I love the liberty which distinguishes their discussions, but abhor the folly which makes each side sacrifice the interests of their country to their villainous party interest. They will tell the force, station, expense, of your armies; they will foment discontent and distrust, treat your allies with disrespect, and (with regard to what they said of Portugal) with falsehood, to vex ministers and get themselves in, and *vice versâ*, for I think one as bad as the other.

I am much delighted with your account of my mother, whom pray tell that she need not be in the least alarmed about her tall son, who will take great care of himself for her sake, and that at present he cannot see any danger except of growing too fat, from having little to do and good living, and I will write to her by the next packet.

I cannot tell you what will be done with the Portuguese troops, who are really in very high state of drill and appearance, and, I have no doubt myself, will do their duty. For I do not know very well myself; at all events, my private opinion is that it would be folly to leave them for the French, but these are after considerations, and no doubt when it comes to that push, proper measures will be taken.

Hdqrs., Mango Alde, May 3rd, 1810.

My Dearest Father,

It is indeed difficult to express to you the pleasure with which I read your very affectionate kind letter of the 8th of April. The approbation you express of my conduct (founded on the flattering accounts of my friends always willing to gratify a parent's feelings) is the greatest reward I can ever wish for.

I avail myself of a courier, which the marshal is sending to Lisbon, to write these few lines and to inform you that soon after my return from Porto to Coimbra, the marshal went over to Vizeu, but I remained behind to rest my horses. But on the 26th, owing to some movement of the *mounseers* upon Ciudad Rodrigo, our army received orders to march immediately, which they did on the 27th, on which day I arrived at Vizeu, and found, to my great satisfaction, that the marshal, who, I heard, was ill, was nearly recovered, and only suffered from a very severe cold.

We remained there till the 1st, giving time to our troops to arrive, and then moved the hdquarters to this place, and today, the 3rd May, we move on the Fornos d'Algodres, where we expect to remain a few days. This, however, must depend on the movements of the enemy, or Lord Wellington's plans, and I am as ignorant of the intentions of the one as of the other. I conjecture that if they persist in the siege of Ciudad Rodrigo, an action is inevitable. Our army is in the highest spirits—and we all wish it. Notwithstanding the very unfavourable weather we have had, as it has rained incessantly during the whole of their march, the Portuguese troops are in the highest spirits, and seem anxious to prove the good effects of their discipline and reorganisation.

English Hdqrs. are at Celorico and the army in that neighbourhood advanced as far as Gallegos. The French are about Tamames, St Espiritu, and advances before Cd. Rodrigo. Ballesteros, in the Sierra Morena, has been beaten, but not routed, "*que milagre,*" (what wonder!) Genl. Hill made a forward movement at the end of last month in order to disengage O'Donnel the Spanish general, who was at Albuquerque. But on the French retreating he returned to Portalegre. Their Germans and Italians desert in great numbers. I have seen several parties of them who are remarkably fine men, and very well clothed, but they complain of never being paid, and that the French treat them like *canaille*. Nor have they enough to eat. Many more would desert, but they are afraid of the Spanish and Portuguese peasantry, who murder everything that wears a French uniform. Yesterday 23 went through from Braganza. They were Prussians taken at Jena and forced to serve. They told me they had rather serve us than the enemies of their country. I never saw finer men.

I now come, my dear father, to a part that interests us more nearly, and I am very sorry to tell you that dear Clara has (notwithstanding the trouble I was at in preparing everything for her removal) refused to quit the convent. I have written to her in the strongest manner, and urged the propriety of this temporary inconvenience in the most forcible language, telling her how impossible it will be for me, should real danger occur, to break my trust by warning her even distantly, my principal reason for wishing to remove her, but all in vain. The nuns do all they can to prevent her, and every intrigue is used. It is their interest *they fancy* that she should remain, and you know the power those silly women have over her mind. She is, I fear, unwell with the agitation, and when Frè Bernardo went to bring her away, she pleaded illness not to see him, and he came away as he went. I am much vexed and annoyed at her *resistance*, but can do no more. It places me in a most unpleasant situation. I, however, enclose hers and the abbess' answers to my letters, and from them you will be able to judge of what I have had to fight against. I really believe, poor thing, that she is ill, and dare not press her farther, and trust only that neither herself or any of her friends may have reason to repent her folly.

I am very much obliged to you for the maps of the Tagus, Spain, and Portugal. The latter I much wanted.

I am not surprised at Wilson's not mentioning the marshal, who has no reason to be pleased with him. Nobody will deny him courage and talents as a partisan, but to those who know facts, the attempt at thanks in the House are more adapted to make him appear ridiculous, than to do him honour. He can never want a trumpeter while he lives, and no man better knows the *art de se faire valoir*. He must really be a clever fellow, to have, with 700 undisciplined Portuguese, checked 30,000 French, terrified them much, and at the same time covered upper and lower Beira, Almeida, Ciudad Rodrigo, and ensured the retreat of English detachments, which the enemy never attempted to impede. Many other of his deeds, mentioned by the Hon. member, we never heard of. He is a very good fellow as a companion, and a very able light troop officer, and if he would not attempt to be more than he really is, would be more respected. His conduct to the marshal I can never approve, and he himself must feel lowered in his own estimation by it.

I have been obliged to leave a horse I gave 80 guineas for lame at Coimbra, and am reduced to two. On my return to Lisbon, however, whenever that period arrives, I shall be able to buy another without drawing on England at all.

Pray give my kindest love to dear mother, etc.

Adieu my dearest father. Ever your most obliged and most sincerely affectionate son,

Wm. Warre.

The marshal desires to be most kindly remembered. H. Brown, who, poor fellow, has been very unwell at Lisbon, desires me in all his letters to say as much.

P. S.—Ciudad Rodrigo is a wretched place, considered as a fortified town, perhaps à *l'abri* of a *coup de main*, but I think would not stand a regular siege for a week. Our neighbourhood may encourage the inhabitants however, while it checks the assailants, and they may do wonders as many other Spanish towns have. I fear Astorga has fallen, though I do not know it for certain. We have lost a few men at Cadiz and Col. le Febre our chief engineer, while evacuating an advanced work, which the enemy had nearly demolished with their artillery.

EXTRACT FROM LETTER TO SISTER.

Fornos d'Algodres, May 9, 1810.

We have had our hdqrs. at this place for some days, nor do I for the present see much chance of our moving. It is a miserable little place, and in the whole of this house there are but half a dozen panes of glass in one window, and we are three in a small room, through the ceiling of which we receive light enough to save us the trouble of opening the window. It is, however, better than many we have had, and shall have, and therefore we are quite contented. Besides the house is full of *senhoras*, pretty enough, if they would wash their faces and comb their hair, but you know *fidalgas* and *fidalgos* d'Albea have a right *ab origine* to be as filthy as they please, so long as they have finery and tinsel. I am much amused with the airs and affectation of these *grands du village*, who however, we must confess, are very kind and civil, and, to their no small and *our* very *great annoyance*, dine and breakfast with us à *l'Anglaise*.

We went last week over to Celorico the English Hdquarters, and staid two days, on one of which we went over to Guarda and reviewed two Portuguese regts. under torrents of rain, such as I never before recollect. Indeed, for the last three months this weather has been constant, as in that time we have not had three fine days. It looks better today, and for the sake of the troops I sincerely hope it will settle. I was much flattered by Lord Wellington's reception and kindness to me, and respect him too much to be indifferent to his good opinion. He appears confident and in spirits, and all his army are in the finest order, as are indeed comparatively our Portuguese, who have all shown great spirit in this hasty advance, and the greatest wish to meet the enemy.

I forgot to mention to you our family consists of six or seven grown up young ladies, all of whom firmly believe that your letter was from a love, as I walked into my room to read it, and seemed much pleased at the receipt of it. They rally me very much about a *Minha Carida*, and I do not deny I love you very much! I have a *valet de chambre*, a Portuguese, one of the finest gentlemen I know, but not a bad servant, if he was less affected, and less fond of his ease. He is a much greater man than I am. I have also a man from the 23rd, a very decent quiet groom and very fond of his horses.

With kindest love, believe me, etc. etc. etc.,

Wm. Warre.

Hdquarters, Fornos D'Algodres,
15 May 1810.

My Dear Father,

I wrote to you a few posts ago from Mangoalde, informing you of the very bad success I had in my attempt to remove dear Clara to Lisbon. After having everything arranged, I am sorry to say that the agitation and distress it occasioned her was the cause of a slight fever. Poor thing! such is the effect of superstition and popish influence, and I have been much alarmed about her. However, she is much better, indeed, I hope, by this time quite recovered. My situation with regard to her is very unpleasant. I dread urging the business or committing myself by writing very strongly to her; and still, in prudence, I cannot be happy while she remains there. There is certainly no immediate cause of dread of the enemy, but a battle may decide much, and I know too much of war ever to wish any person that is dear to me to be even distantly exposed to its chances.

I am therefore anxiously waiting to know your wishes about how I am to proceed. I much fear her health would suffer materially by insisting on her removal, and on the other hand, when there shall be any immediate cause of alarm, how can I risk alarming a whole province by informing her of it. How difficult it is sometimes to reconcile private feelings to public duty! The latter, however, is imperious.

I have been much flattered lately by Ld. Wellington's reception of me, and lately remained two days at his hdqrs. at Celorico 2 leagues from here. He has applied to me to procure him one hghd. of very fine old port. He does not care about the price, and wishes me to get you to take care of it for him in London. At Oporto it is impossible to get any old wine, and I therefore told him I would write to you, and beg your assistance. It is, I suppose, for some very particular purpose, and I shall therefore be glad to know how far you can assist me. It may be *bem empregado* (well employed) and may lead to an acquaintance on our return to England between you and a man of first-rate abilities. He says he thinks you ought to get one for him in return for his having taken away my snuff-box, though I am sorry to confess he has not made me leave off that vile custom, though he made me promise not to carry a box, to the no small annoyance of my friends on whom I must trust for my supply.

I have received the price of the pipe of wine shipped by you for Sir David Dundas, and delay sending it, in the first place, till I can get a bill, and in the next, that having received it in six Milfour pieces, I can scarce bring myself to part with them, as they are very scarce, and dollars most inconvenient to carry about. I will write to Mr John Bell, who pays us, to buy a bill for the number of dollars, and remit it to you, or will buy one myself, if I can, before next packet.

Our accounts from the French Army are that they are very sickly; in Salamanca are about 2000 sick, who die 30 or 40 of a day. Their troops are also much dissatisfied, particularly the Germans and Italians, who compose the chief part, and those desert very fast, and would much more, if they were not exposed to be murdered by the Peasantry, whether deserters or prisoners. It is really horrible, and defeats the exertions which are making to entice them to fly from their oppressors, and they are willing enough but for these difficulties. Some have come over horses and all. I never saw handsomer or finer looking men. They all agree in complaining that they are never paid, and but indifferently fed, and that they are constantly harassed and marched about.

From the accounts we have, the French force immediately before us may be of 30,000 men, more or less, and certainly sickly. The constant rains which have continued for the last 3 months have been much against them. It is pretty sure now that they intend to attack Ciudad Rodrigo, which is a place of no strength, and their heavy artillery is on its march to that place, which has been summoned in a very imperative manner. Masséna is reported to have arrived to take the command of the whole of this army. I am most anxious to know what steps Lord Wellington will take to prevent the reduction of Ciudad Rodrigo. It is of, I consider, the greatest consequence that it should be protected, if possible. It is a sort of outer door to our house, and, in the possession of the enemy, would enable him to establish his magazines, hospitals, etc., nearer to our frontier than we could wish. Ld. Wellington and Marshal Beresford know best however, and I shall feel confident of the propriety of whatever they do. I shall rejoice very much at quitting this miserable village, where we are very badly off.

Our troops as well as the English are well, and in high spirits, though in my opinion these cantonments in small detached villages are greatly detrimental to their discipline, of which, however forward and astonishing, they cannot have acquired yet that habit which will admit of any relaxation. I am, however, confident that where they are commanded by British officers they will behave well, and that, at the end of the campaign, they will have acquired a character as troops. It will indeed be heart-breaking to poor Marshal Beresford if they do not.

His exertions have been Herculean and indefatigable, and their good effects felt in every branch of the legislature, and has even now done enough to establish his character as a very superior, strong-minded, clever officer, and should his labours be crowned with the success they deserve, he will become one of the most eminent men in England, and have deserved more of this country than they can ever repay.

I cannot sufficiently admire the firmness and understanding with which he has overcome difficulties, which would have disheartened and overturned the plans of most, even very superior men. He is just the man for this particular service. Waters passed through this place yesterday with General Stewart. He is quite well, and gave me great pleasure by the accounts he gave me of all the dear family. By him I received the chart of the Tagus, for which I am very much obliged to you, as also for the drawers, which I fear are somewhat too small for me, but must do.

I feel considerably distressed at the accounts from England. I always felt that we had nothing to fear against our foreign enemies whilst united amongst ourselves, and have long observed the struggles of a particular and very infamous set of men, to sap the public confidence in their government and constitution, for it is at that they now strike direct, and neither the respectability of the king, nor the critical situation of the country, can prevent these fellows from endeavouring to create confusion and a revolution, in which the mob are to have the lead, for by that alone can such designing unprincipled miscreants be countenanced or exalted to any power.

I consider the question as no longer one of opposition against ministers; that I should not mind. It is in the very nature of our constitution. But the question is now whether the country is in such a distressed situation from unhappy political circumstances—whether the want of unanimity of ministers, and the state of mind of the dregs of society, are in such a state, that Sir F. B. (Francis Burdett) and his gang can expect to be able to overturn the constitution, and raise themselves upon the wreck of their country. I have no patience that such fellows have so long gone on without punishment, and the seeds of civil discord once sown, there is no knowing where it may end. There are never wanting factious, needy men to foment it, who, having nothing to lose but their lives, would sacrifice their country to gain something in the appearance of power. Respectability is out of the question.

Adieu. Pray now and then send me the general opinions of the day. To us at this distance they are highly interesting. Pray give my most affecte. love to my dear mother, etc., etc., etc., and believe me, Ever my dear father your most affectionate son,

W. W.

P.S.—   Fornos D'Algodres,
                                              May 23rd, 1810.

Masséna is just arrived to take the command of the army of Portugal now between Ciudad Rodrigo and Salamanca, which consists of Ney, Soult, and Mortier's divisions. He is one of B.'s best generals. I dare say he will shortly attempt something, but we are too well prepared to fear much his first attack, but how far we shall ultimately be able to resist numbers upon numbers, unless Spain assists us, is another question.

Hdquarters, Fornos D'Algodres,
May 23, 1810.

My Dear Ellen,

As you desire to hear from me immediately, I will not lose a moment in thanking you for your dear letter of the 15th and 24th April, and for your affectionate kind wishes on my birthday. . . .

We have been in this quarter near a month and most heartily tired of it. It is a miserable little village on the side of a very high mountain, opposite to the famous mountains of the Estrella, and about a mile from the River Mondego, and 8 from Celorico the hdqrs. of Lord Wellington.

I have lately changed my abode, as in the last the rain ran in upon my bed, and we were three in a very small room with one window without a pane of glass. Indeed, in the whole of the marshal's quarters there are but 6 in one window. We only had one bason and one jug, and you may imagine the squabbling as to who was to wash first. I have deposed some silkworms from my present room, and have at least the luxury of being alone, and having a broken pewter bason, none of the cleanest, to myself. There's luxury for you! The rain however, which has been incessant for the last 3 months or more, has found its way in, and runs in tolerable streams in four parts of my dismal abode.

My bed escapes, and my bason and some broken jars catch water. Therefore, I am rather well off.

At the general's, my last quarter, we had 7 or 8 grown up young ladies, *des grands du village,* the most affected stupid misses I ever met with in *any barbarous country.* They never were three miles from home, and ape notwithstanding from hearsay what they fancy great people should do. They think me I believe very proud, and the young ladies are mighty shy. I am not, however, quite safe from the attacks of a maiden aunt of 30 to 40 with little cat's eyes and bad teeth. I think she will find I am bombproof to her kind looks and sighs. She has already begun to try what disdain will do, to my great joy and amusement.

You would be much entertained to see us assemble at breakfast and dinner, near 20 people. We have succeeded at last in making them wash their hands and faces, and if we remain long enough no doubt will also attain the desideratum of combing their hair, even for breakfast, or rather before breakfast, and once or twice a week, oftener than on Sunday morning.

Public news I have none to tell you, except the arrival of Masséna to command the army of Portugal, which is between Ciudad Rodrigo and Salamanca. He is a very clever enterprising officer, and will soon give us something to do, I have no doubt, but we are not at all afraid of him, as our troops both English and Portuguese are in the highest spirits, and the latter so much improved that they hardly know themselves again. I have no doubt they will do their duty, but should wish to break them in by degrees.

Ever yr. most affectionate brother,

Wm. W.

EXTRACT FROM A LETTER OF THOMAS WARRE

London, June 20, 1810.

My Dear Father,

I write these few lines to inform you I this morning received a long letter from William, from Fornos d'Algodres, *June 6th,* the same place they were in before. He is very well and writes in very good spirits. They have had dreadful bad weather by continual rains.

The French have invested Ciudad Rodrigo closer, but William thinks before they attack that place, they will drive in our advance corps, General Craufurd's division, which overlooks their operations, and should they succeed in driving them in, Beresford's forces must retire to concentrate. But William does not expect they will succeed, not being in sufficient force. He still speaks favourably of the native troops, who are kept a good deal on the alert. They have lately had great feasting. Ld. Wellington on the 4th inst. gave a dinner to Beresford, which was returned by him, and all went off remarkably well.

William has again written to poor Clara, but fears nothing he can urge will induce her to move at present. I lament it exceedingly. . .

On getting to Throgmorton St. I found a few lines from Capt. Hardy. The date is 28th of May off Fernesen in the Gt. Belt. He merely says that he is quite well, and that they are proceeding on to the Baltic, that is the *St George, Formidable, Stately* and *Resolution*, and that nothing had occurred worth noticing.

Extract from a letter of Thomas Warre

Hendon Place, July 8, 1810.

I deferred writing to you as I expected to find letters in town from Wm., which we did of *13th June.*

He wrote as usual in great spirits, but the crisis of their fate approaches. The French had completed their bridges across the Agueda, so C. Rodrigo was invested, but their heavy artillery had stuck in the mud near Tamames, somewhere between Salamanca and C. Rodrigo. They have three *corps d'armée, viz.*: Junot, Ney, and Regnier's, which is opposed to Genl. Hill to the Southward. Their force he supposes to be 60,000 to 70,000, very sick and discontented. Much will depend on their first sweep, but if the Portuguese troops fulfil the promise they give at present, he has no doubt they shall give them a good licking. Ld. Wellington's Hdqrs. were at Celorico. The front of the allied army extended from Pinhel to Guarda. Adv. gd. at Gallegos, 2 leagues from C. Rodrigo and the advanced picket at Marialva, close to the French outposts.

I saw Col. Ross yesterday. He has exchanged into the 48th; both batts. of which are in Portugal in Genl. Hill's division. He had seen a letter from Ld. Wellington to one of Mrs Ross's brothers. He writes in great spirits. My father likewise saw a letter yesterday from general off. of high rank, who said that their position was an excellent one, and that the c. in. c. has made the most judicious arrangements. All this is very good as far as it goes, but I shall look for the next arrivals with much anxious impatience.

Hdqrs., Fornos D'Algodres,
June 20, 1810.

My Dear Father,

I am sorry to tell you that the marshal has not yet received any answer from the government respecting the admission of rice and grain free of duty; and I begin to fear that their usual narrow and absurd policy opposes more obstacles to this very desirable object than was at first expected. Indeed, if so, nothing can be more absurd, as although the harvest promises very well, particularly rice and barley, owing to the uncommon lateness of the season, the Indian corn is in most places but just sown, and in many not yet. Much must therefore depend upon the dryness of the latter end of the autumn, and before that I think the scarcity will be so great, that they will be forced, though late, to open their ports, and give every encouragement to importation, or starve.

The men and oxen have been kept away from their agricultural pursuits, to attend the armies with their carts, and this has delayed and impeded very much the ploughing, and hoeing, and reaping, as has also in some degree the very great consumption of cattle. The moment the marshal gets an answer I will write to you, and to Porto to Pedro Alvez, which I have not done hitherto, because in the first place I could tell him nothing decisive, and in the next, it appeared to me prudent that it should be kept quite a secret that such an allowance in point of duties was in agitation.

The weather has at last set in very hot, which I hope will increase the great sickness of the French, who have been mostly exposed to the continued rains we have had till now. Our people, both English and Portuguese, are getting into the most satisfactory state of health, having been under cover and quiet.

The enemy continues almost in *statu quo*. They have completed their bridges over the Agueda at Val d'Espino, and covered them by a small *tête de pont*. By their means the investment of Ciudad Rodrigo is completed. Their heavy artillery and mortars are, I believe, still fast in the mud halfway to Salamanca, but this hot weather will now soon enable them to bring them up. After which I have no idea that Ciudad Rodrigo can hold out a fortnight, from its construction, which is completely irregular and very defective, besides being in some degree commanded at about 800 yards. This will probably be the prelude to our play, and then we shall all become actors.

They seem very shy of us, and I do not believe have as yet completed their preparations, or collected a sufficient force to attack us. Their foreigners continue to desert in considerable numbers, and more would, I am sure, come over, but for the steps the French have taken to prevent them. Our advanced picquets have frequent skirmishes with them, which lead to nothing but wounding a few men and horses on each side.

We went over two days ago to Francozo to inspect a Portuguese brigade with Lord Wellington, and afterwards to Minucal (?) to see the 16th Lt. Dgns., who are in very fine order, and made a most excellent review. At Francozo we visited the nuns. The *porteress* gave Lord Wellington, etc., etc., leave to enter, and some of us rambled all over the convent. I never saw more poverty, misery, and dirt, except indeed some of the cells which were tolerably neat. Most of the nuns were in the Choro at prayers, and not a little astonished at seeing a large party of men appear at the door from the inside. There were some pretty girls enough, but they were so long at prayers, that we could not stop to speak with them, and had the full and free range of their abode. This visit of the great people will furnish conversation, I dare say, for years!

The price of Indian corn at Montemor Velho, which regulates for Coimbra and all that neighbourhood, was last week at 11 *testoons* the *alqueire*. (*Testoon*= about 5d. Alqueire = about 3 Imp. gallons.) It had been at 12 *t*. the fortnight before.

Believe me ever, my dear father, Your most sincerely affectionate son,

Wm. Warre.

To His Brother

Hdqrs., P.A. Francoso, Nr. Pinhel,
June 27, 1810.

My Dear Tom,
We removed our hdqrs. here two days ago and the English

Hdqrs. to Almeida, on account of the very interesting situation of Ciudad Rodrigo, and to be within reach of immediate information respecting any movements of the French Army, which becomes every day more interesting. Their heavy artillery being arrived, they on the evening of the 24th commenced a brisk fire on the place, which was returned with great vivacity by the besieged, and continued until 10 o'clock on. the 25th in the morning, when a most tremendous explosion took place in the French lines from their powder magazine blowing up, (N.B. has since been ascertained to have been in the town), and immediately after two lesser explosions (which were in the French lines).

The quantity of powder must have been very great, as it was seen at this place by several of our officers, nearly 40 miles off, and at Almeida, half-way between this and the Ciudad Rodrigo, the shock was very strongly felt, and Governor Cox writes that it shook the whole place. Certain it is that the French batteries ceased firing and the Spaniards continued for two hours after.

If their loss is what we suppose from these circumstances, it will be a most serious loss to them, as I know not how soon they can replace it in Spain, and will probably delay their attack upon us for 6 weeks or 2 months, a great point gained for us, whose object is by gaining time to complete the discipline of our army, etc., and who are getting very healthy. These, however, are the effects we wish for, and, like other people, we are very apt to fancy the probability of what we wish for, though at the same time you must not imagine that we are the least afraid of them even now. We know that their army is very sickly. They average deaths 46 to 50 a day, are in want of everything, and their intercepted letters show that they are very much disgusted. The Spaniards carry on a desultory and most destructive warfare. They scarcely dare move out of their quarters without risking to be assassinated, and their losses in this way and by desertion are very great in every part of Spain.

They drive in our picquets now and then. They have a great superiority of cavalry, but nothing of any consequence has taken place. But if the greatest part of their powder is not destroyed, we may expect something every day. I cannot think they will let Craufurd with the advance guard remain so near them. Their and our vedettes are 400 to 500 paces from each other and we overlook their camp, which is very extensive, I suspect more so than they have any occasion for, considering the number of men they have. They are quite up to all this sort of humbug. If our Portuguese do as we expect, we are not uneasy as to the result, and if we lick them what a glorious day for Old England! I like this place better than Fornos, though we are not very well off either, and have a large brigade of infantry with us in the town. I am very well, the only annoyance is my face, which as well as my lips always peel and are very sore. By the end of the campaign I daresay we may pass ourselves off for Portuguese Indians, or any other tawny gentry you please. *Adieu*, etc.

Francoso, July 9, 1810.

July 2.—Hardinge and myself left Francoso about 6 in the evening to visit the advanced guard and outposts of the army under Br. Genl. Craufurd stationed in front of Gallegos, in New Castile, with his hdqrs. at Almeida, about 4 miles in the rear. We arrived late in the evening at Pinhel, where we remained the night. Next morning set out after breakfasting with our friend Major Murphy of the 88th, (the Bishop of Pinhel being absent from Pinhel,) having dined at Francoso the day we left it for Almeida, the direct road to which we missed, and proceeded by an almost impassable path down to the Coa, which here on either side presents a most formidable position, totally impracticable for cavalry and artillery except over the bridge and high road leading to Almeida from Freixedas, Guarda, Pinhel, etc.

According to the reports of its whole course from its confluence into the Douro to near Alfaiates, with the exception of two leagues beyond Almeida towards its source, it presents, from the very great steepness and rocky soil of its banks, a most formidable barrier to any army attempting to advance towards Vizeu, Celorico, Guarda, or Francozo, from the neighbourhood of Ciudad Rodrigo. It is, however, liable to be turned by Sabugal, or Castello Branco, and opposed to a superior army its great extent is a very serious inconvenience, as any part of the line being forced must oblige the rest to retire.

While Almeida, which is about a mile and a half from the river on the Spanish side, holds out, I consider any attack by that road as not to be feared. Though the greatest part of the descent to the bridge is out of sight of the town, the enemy's movements would be very much impeded in attempting to advance. Considering all circumstances, the great superiority of the enemy and nature of a great part of our troops, I have much doubt in my own mind of any position being attempted to be defended on the Coa, as a general one for the army, but this a few days must show, and I am no way in the secret.

We crossed the Coa at a very bad ford called Veia, about a mile below the bridge, and arrived at Almeida, waited on Governor Cox; and, after walking round the works (which from their nature I do not at all envy him the defence of, considering the troops he has, mostly militia,) continued our march to Fort Conception to see our friend Lt. Col. Sutton, who had been appointed governor, when there was an intention to defend it. But since the great superiority of the enemy rendered it impossible to attempt to relieve the brave Spaniards in Ciudad Rodrigo, it has been resolved to blow it up, and it has for that purpose been mined all round. When the enemy seriously advance this beautiful fort will be entirely destroyed.

It is a thousand pities. I never saw a more complete or perfect fortification with every part bomb-proof, even stabling for 200 horses. Its outworks are admirably adapted to defend the approaches, which are all round a perfect natural glacis to several hundred yards. Of the necessity of the measure I am no judge, but fear it will much vex the Spaniards.

We arrived about 3 o'clock at Almeida, and dined with Genl. Craufurd, with whom after dinner we rode out to look at the French posts beyond the little River Azara, over which there is a bridge of stone leading to the village of Marialva, and about a mile beyond Gallegos. Along this line were about 3 squadrons of the German 1st Hussars doing the outpost duty, their reserves in Gallegos. I went down to the bridge and endeavoured to persuade two French officers to come down and speak to me. They were, however, very shy, and only came near enough for me to tell them. that some friends of theirs, who were taken prisoners near Chaves a year and a half ago, were well.

I observed they were constructing a wooden bridge a short distance to the left of the former, and from the exhausted appearance of the forage on the other side, their having removed the cars from blocking up the stone bridge, and certain reports of deserters, it appeared very probable they would drive in our posts next morning, the 4th July. They had there and near Carpio about 5 or 6 regts. of cavalry and some infantry, 4000 to 5000 men I should guess in all. Our infantry, consisting of the 43rd, 52nd, Rifle Corps, and two Portuguese *Caçadores* battns., one very good and the other very bad, were stationed in the woods in front of Alumeda, about 3 or 4 miles in our rear.

At daybreak they crossed the little River Azara over their two bridges, and drove in our picquets. They had 12 squadrons and 2 brigades of infantry, but our three squadrons were supported by a troop of horse artillery, which kept them in check and enabled our little body to retreat in safety on the infantry though close pressed and skirmishing very sharply the whole way. It was the prettiest thing, *en fait de guerre*, I ever saw. The retreat was very well conducted. Their artillery could not come up till near the end of the affair, and ours killed a great many of their men and horses, while our cavalry were in comparative safety. Their numbers enabled them constantly to turn our flanks, and the superiority of our horses as often to get out of the scrape.

A party of the German hussars under Capt. Kranckenberg behaved particularly well, charging at the passage of a small bridge a very superior number of the enemy, though supported by four squadrons within pistol shot on the other side. It was very well done. Two French officers were severely wounded and some men, and one prisoner was taken, though, poor devil, he was covered with wounds, 6 in the head, and his arm nearly cut off, also run through the body, and wonderful to say, he is expected to recover. The French seemed much irritated at this check, and kept up a very brisk fire up the road we retreated by, within about 50 yards from us.

Nor were they sparing in abuse, and confident of still cutting us off, when we arrived at our Infantry which checked them, and a squadron of their 3rd Hussars coming unexpectedly on the 3rd P. Caçadores (an excellent corps commanded by Lt.-Col. Elder) received a very warm salutation which dispersed them. The battalion behaved very steadily and well, and give us hopes of the Portuguese troops, on whose conduct the issue of this campaign must in a great measure depend.

The division commenced its retreat towards Fort Conception covered by the cavalry, whom I here quitted, having offered myself to act as *aide-de-camp* to Genl. Craufurd. The infantry returned in very good order through Alumeda towards Fort Conception, and General Carrera with his Spaniards, who were in our rear, by the fords of Algardon to a very strong position covering the roads that way. These Spaniards are remarkably fine men, about 3000 well clothed, though not uniformly, and armed. I did not, however, think much of their discipline or regularity. Hardinge placed them, and seemed to be much pleased with General Carrera's appearance and manner.

The French gave up the pursuit about half a league from Fort Conception, and retired again to Gallegos, on this side of which place they established their vedettes, having attained, what I suppose was their intention, a new ground to forage on, and having reconnoitred our force, to ascertain whether or not Lord Wellington had come up with the army. Our loss was about 4 or 5 men wounded and as many horses. That of the French, so far as we could see, and have since heard from deserters, several officers and about 30 or 40 men killed and wounded. After halting about two hours near the fort, our advanced guard took up a position at Val de la Mula, on the Portuguese frontier, with the cavalry about a league in front, leaving a space of about a league between their vedettes and ours.

And this ended this little affair which Hardinge and myself had so much wished to see, and which was certainly very instructive. *Au reste* a great deal of firing to very little purpose. A strong proof of how ineffectual the skirmishing of cavalry is, except to cover the retreat of larger bodies, and prevent the columns being fired into. Our people and theirs were constantly within 30 yards of one another firing with no effect, though neither party had any idea of fear. When it can possibly be avoided the less powder wasted this way the better. The best arm for cavalry is the sword or sabre, a well broken horse and firm presence of mind, reserving the pistol or carbine merely for the purpose of vedettes, or covering some movement.

At Val de la Mula Col. Pakenham asked us to breakfast and afterwards to dinner, and during the whole of our stay we are much indebted to his civility, as also to Capt. Rowan and Wm. Campbell, brother to Augustus, who prevented our ever wanting a meal or forage for our horses during our stay. General Craufurd was also very civil to us. While retreating he sent me with some letters to Governor Cox at Almeida, whom, however, I was fortunate enough to meet at Val de la Mula, which saved me a very tiresome ride, and enabled me to return immediately, but everything was over, and I was so tired that I was very glad to lay down in the guard-room of the Fort, which was evacuated, to take a nap, which was not of long duration, as I had taken possession of the mattress of a Spanish shepherdess of no very gentle nature, who was so clamorous and violent in claiming her property, that I was forced to yield it up for fear I might not escape so well from her gentle paws, as I had from the French.

Besides, poor things, I could not but pity them. It was most distressing to see them abandoning their habitations, and flying away from the miscreants, loaded with what little property they could carry away, crying and lamenting, followed by their helpless children, while the men drove away their cattle, and all uncertain where they might find a place of safety. In Portugal the natural animosity which exists so violently on the frontiers, and which even the similarity of their misfortunes and distress cannot do away, they had but a dismal prospect of meeting with a friendly reception. I pitied them from my heart, to relieve was not in my power. How little does the independent happy English peasant know how to value the peace and security in which he lives!

And how would those miscreants who preach discontent and faction through the country, giving them ideas of wants and liberties which are incompatible with society and government, how would they blush if they were to witness the sufferings and oppression which these poor people undergo! They would see that in England alone the peasantry are now happy and free, and would see their own infamy in sowing the seeds of discord and civil dissension among that happy people, when every mind should be united and heart joined to resist the oppressor of mankind!

If reform is necessary let us wait for moments of peace with foreign enemies, when we do not risk, by dividing amongst ourselves, the entire ruin of the most perfect fabric of government that ever existed, even with all its faults, and give every advantage to our enemies by exposing as some of our senators do, by way of opposition to ministers, or to get themselves in, our forces, intentions, weakness, faults, etc., etc., in fact, for the sake of a popular speech in the House, tell the enemy everything they ought most to conceal, even the stations and exact numbers of the troops, of ourselves, or of our allies. This conduct leads us half way to our ruin, and we shall repent it when it is too late.

On the 5th, early in the morning, Hardinge and myself rode out beyond Alumeda, towards Gallegos, till near the enemies' posts, to see what damage we had done them the day before and what they were about. We found in the road two of their dead and some horses, evidently from the effects of our artillery, as they were much mangled, and we also saw some more to the right and left of the road at a distance. A very large flight of vultures of very large size were flying about them, and on the ground, which added much to the disgust of the scene, and after ascertaining the positions of their vedettes, we hastened to return. Being but indifferently mounted, and at a great distance from our outposts, we were very much afraid of being cut off by some of their patrols, and, returning through Alumeda, I was just observing to Hardinge that we should look very foolish if we were to be taken, when I turned my head and saw a French hussar close to us.

Hardinge had not even his sabre, having broken it the day before, and I saw nothing was to be done but to charge him, for which purpose I drew my pistol and galloped at him, when he surrendered, a no very glorious prize, as his horse was so tired that he could not move out of a very slow pace, and it was with difficulty and anxiety we got him into one of our picquets. He was a French lad, and told me he had deserted that morning, owing to the ill-treatment of his chief, and the want of everything they experienced in their camp, and said he intended to go to England and work at his trade, a cabinet maker, as he had a cousin there, whom he intended to enquire for at the *commune* (police office), though he had not heard of him for 4 years. I have great doubts of his being a deserter at all, and rather think he was as much surprised to see us, as we were to see him. He is quite a Frenchman, and contradicted himself twenty times!

We arrived at our quarters at 8 o'clock, and breakfasted with Col. Pakenham. After which we set out, 5 in number, well-armed and mounted, to reconnoitre the enemy on our left, and proceeded without meeting any as far as Villa de Porco and Barcilha, from the heights above which we distinctly saw with our glasses Ciudad Rodrigo, which was keeping up a very heavy fire, and defending itself as if it were manned by heroes. Let them now surrender when they may. They have done their duty, and it is heart-breaking to think we can in no way assist them.

At Barcilha our party divided. Hardinge, Col. Pakenham, and Capt. Cotton went by the right, and Capt. Shaw, A.D.C. to Genl. Craufurd, and myself agreed to go and visit Villar de Ciervo, and all that line, and ascertain whether the French had occupied all those places, or Villar de la Egoa, where there are some excellent fords over the Agueda, and which, being in rear considerably of our left on the 4th, gave Genl. Craufurd no small anxiety. We met nothing, and returned about 4 to dinner, having suffered only from the extreme heat, which fagged me a good deal, being rather bilious, and prevented my accompanying them in the evening, instead of which I paid a visit to my friends in the 52nd, whom I was very glad to see looking as well as ever I saw them at Shorncliff, though perhaps with less pipeclay.

Next day was spent nearly in the same way. In the morning we rode out reconnoitring to Alumeda, dined afterwards with General Craufurd, and set off on our return to Pinhel, 4 leagues, where we arrived late at night and slept, and next day came home, after a most delightful trip, and having just seen what we wished and expected. The retreat of the advanced guard had for some days appeared inevitable, and it was to see how it would be conducted that we went over.

The desertion continues from the French in great numbers, 8 to 12 of a day while we remained with the advance guard, and they all agree in stating that their army is badly off for provisions, and the foreigners much disgusted, and would desert in greater numbers but for the vigilant means that are taken to prevent. Junot and Ney with their corps are before C. Rodrigo, and I believe also Masséna, as are also the traitors Alorna, Pampeluna, Sancos Mezeude, against whom no measures are taken by this Government, and we know they are supplied with money, etc., from their estates in this country, which are not sequestered or disturbed. So much for weakness and infatuation! The Count Doidga (?) has been declared infamous and his offspring for three generations, and his property sequestered. He is a poor wretch and can do no harm, though not less a traitor, while these scoundrels, with arms in their hands, known traitors before the prince embarked, and treated by him with great lenity, are suffered to attack their native country with impunity. It is most disgusting.

I do not think the French will attempt anything till C. Rodrigo falls, which, notwithstanding their heroic conduct, cannot be long delayed. It will enable the French to establish their magazines and hospital. What the plans for the campaign are I know not. Everything promises a very warm one, and I confess I look with some anxiety to the conduct of the Portuguese troops, on whom much, nay everything, must depend. They promise well, it is true, in every respect, but still they are very young troops and never tried. The force against us is very superior. But on the other hand, the greater must be the difficulty of supplying them and means of transport. We retire on our supplies while they advance from them. And everybody has great confidence both in Lord Wellington and Marshal Beresford, and if the native troops fight like men, I have not a doubt we shall succeed, though the loss must be inevitably great on both sides.

My own idea of their attack is that they will keep their principal corps in our front, leave Regnier with his corps, and keep Hill in check in the Alemtejo, while with a strong column they endeavour to force the passes near Castello Branco, or by Sabugal, endeavouring to unite near Thomar. By this means if Hill retires and crosses the Tagus, either at Villa Velha or Abrantes, the Alemtejo is left open, and we cannot but feel some anxiety for the capital, or rather for the opposite side of the river, which would occasion great confusion. Hill must then defend the passage of the Tagus, which abounds in fords as low as Salvaterra, and also endeavour to check the enemy's advance by the passes of Salhadas, etc., from Castello Branco or Abrantes, and if either of these movements of the enemy succeed, I should imagine the whole army must fall back from the Upper Beira upon our works round Lisbon, that is Torres Vedras, Bucellas, etc., etc., for fear of its communications with Lisbon and our stores.

Or if they do not attempt Alemtejo, I think they will attempt advancing in three columns by Castello Branco from Coria and Placencia, and from Guinaldo, etc., by Sabugal, and in our front by Celorico or Guarda, endeavouring to unite beyond the Sierra de Estrella. In this case we shall come into play immediately. Almeida, I think, they will merely mask by a strong corps, and leave in their rear. If they succeed, the place must fall of course. If not, there is not force enough in it to annoy them. These are my own private opinions, and, from the very little means I have of information, must be considered as mere speculations, and as such, if erroneous, I may be excused, as I really know not how far they may agree with any others.

Hdqrs., Francoso, July 10, 1810.

My Dear Father,

I received your letters of 13th, 15th June, on the 1st of this month, and my having been absent at the outposts alone prevented me writing by last packet to thank you for the very interesting information you give me about Ferguson in particular, and the other occurrences of the day, as also for the affectionate friendship and solicitude on my account, which would be a sufficient reward in themselves for anything I can ever do.

I send you, annexed, a sort of journal of my proceedings during my little excursion to the outposts, which was very interesting. It was written in considerable hurry and just as the things occurred to me. The opinions also merely speculative, as I have but little means of positive information. I should therefore wish you to consider it as merely for your amusement and confidential, and for those few who can feel any interest in such trifles because they concern me.

Our situation becomes every day more interesting. The heroic defence of Ciudad Rodrigo has delayed the operations against this country, but I consider that it is impossible the place can hold out much longer.

What the issue of this contest may be, it is very difficult to guess. The enemy have certainly from 70,000 to 80,000 men, and we as certainly Troops of the Line not so many, though we have other advantages which they cannot have, particularly the people and the country in our favour. Lord Wellington and the marshal appear very confident and in high spirits, and so does the whole army, who are in excellent order. Our chiefs know best the real situation in which they stand, and the confidence everyone feels in them will make the army do wonders. Much must depend upon the Portuguese troops.

At all events I think prudence would dictate the removal of all property from this country, and leaving as little to chance of war in point of business as possible, and although I by no means wish to croak, when I consider the great superiority of the enemy in numbers, and the nature of our troops, with many other circumstances, I confess I do not feel quite so confident of our ultimate success. But I shall not form any decided opinion till I see our people tried.

Pray thank my dear mother for her kind letter of the 30th May from Hendon, and Tom for his of the 19th June, and for Greenwood and Cox's abstract of my account. I am a good deal surprised they have not received my claim for losses. By the account I see they have received no part of them and suspect they do not much exert themselves, as I know other officers have received theirs. By Tom's letter I observe a warrant has been issued for £36, 15s., I suppose for my horse shot at Vimiero.

I hope you have had a pleasant trip to Woburn and Holkham. I am always happy when I hear of your amusing yourself in a way I know to be so much to your satisfaction.

I have got at Lisbon two Merino rams and 3 ewes. They tell me they are very fine, and my difficulty now is how to send them to you. I write by today's post to Messrs Bulkeley to beg them to take charge of them for you, and send them by the first ship to London, and shall inform you of their answer. If you had no place to keep them yourself, and nobody else you wish to give them to, pray present them to my Uncle Greg with my kind love. I am, however, a good deal bothered about getting them home, being myself at such a distance from Lisbon.

Adieu; pray give my kindest love to my dearest mother, and believe me ever your most truly affectionate and dutiful son,

Wm. Warre.

I will tell Ld. W. about the pipe of wine when I see him, and am much obliged by your attention about it.

July 11th.—A very heavy firing and cannonade was heard yesterday morning at Ciudad Rodrigo, which is a proof that the place still holds out. Poor fellows, I fear they will pay dear for their heroic gallantry, since we cannot assist them.

I have been able to hear nothing further about the free importation of rice and grain, and I fear it will not be allowed from the delay.

Hdqrs., Francozo,

My Dear Father,

I have but just time to write you a few lines that neither you nor my mother may be anxious about me, when you hear of the unfortunate affair of our advanced guard yesterday, at which, however, I was not even present. The French attacked Br. Genl. Crawford's Division, consisting of 43, 52, 95, and 1st and 3rd Portuguese Caçadores, about 3000 men, and some squadrons of cavalry, with 23 squadrons and about 10,000 to 12,000 infantry. I fear there was some delay in retiring across the Coa, and, being very close pressed in their retreat, our brave fellows suffered very considerable loss, about 300 killed and wounded and 30 officers.

The 43rd I hear have suffered most, and have 14 officers killed and wounded, as also the 95th, of whose loss I am ignorant, except of the death of poor Capt. Creagh. Col. Nutt of 43rd is killed and Capt. Hull wounded. They had arrived from England the evening before. The 52nd also lost some men and Officers, but I have not been able to hear any names, except that of Lt.-Col. Barclay being slightly wounded in the head. The 3rd Caçadores under Col. Elder behaved very well, and suffered some loss.

I am sorry I cannot add as much for the 1st, who did not behave so, and ran off at the very beginning, though their Col. d'Arilez, a very fine young man, behaved very well, as also some of the officers. So much for want of discipline and confidence. I had before expressed my fears about them. I am just about setting off to enquire into the business, and I hope a most severe example may be made to prevent the recurrence of such a horrid disgraceful business. If they will not fight from feelings of patriotism or honour, they must be made to do so from fear of a more infamous death, and a more certain one, if they deserve it. It is a measure of peremptory necessity; though I have much pleasure in being able to add that in an attack which Regnier made on Salvaterra away to our right, the 1st Portuguese Cavalry commanded by Col. Pays of Mangoalde behaved most nobly, charged three times, and as often repulsed the enemy, and at last completely drove them back, and I believe the French had the superiority in numbers.

Our advance guard having effected its retreat at all before so very great a superiority is most fortunate, that is across the Coa, whose banks are tremendously steep, and the road narrow. The French three times attempted to force the bridge after them but were repulsed, and lost a good many men on it. The tremendously heavy rains and storm we have had these last two days had fortunately spoiled the fords of the river entirely. Otherwise I much fear our little corps would have been entirely cut off and taken.

The English kept possession of the bank till early this morning, when the whole line was abandoned and our advance established at Carvalhos or Carvalhal. The French vedettes are on this side the river, and Almeida is consequently in some degree invested. I scarce believe they will besiege it, but rather content themselves with blockading and starving it, which will not be easy, as they have 4 months' provisions complete. Pray send Augustus Campbell word that I hear both John and William are well, the former I am not sure was engaged. Wm. was of course with Craufurd. I fear you will be scarce able to read this very hasty scrawl, but I have at this moment so many things to do in order to get away before late in the evening to reach Freixedas tonight, that they must serve as my excuse. You shall hear from me every opportunity. *Adieu*. Pray give my kindest love, etc, yr. ever dutiful and affectionate son,

Wm. Warre.

Lagiosa, August 8, 1810.

My Dearest Father,

Many many thanks for your very kind letter from Eastley End of the 16th July, and for the excellent account you give me of all my friends.

We continue here very quietly, and except the taking of a few prisoners at the outposts in front, and the peasantry having risen and killed a good many of the enemy, who straggle into the villages to plunder or seek for food, nothing of any consequence has occurred since my last.

The French appear to be preparing for the siege of Almeida, but have not yet established any batteries. From the accounts of all deserters and prisoners they are much distressed for provisions, particularly bread, which as the peasantry all fly from their ill-treatment, they are forced to thrash out, carry to the mills, and grind and bake themselves. In some places the officers alone have bread, in others they sometimes receive 3 lb. between 8 men. They are also much in want of shoes. A very intelligent Italian sergeant, who was brought in yesterday, assured me that their 66th Regt. lost on the 24th *ultmo*., in the attack near Almeida, 500 killed and wounded, and the other two Regiments also a very large proportion. They therefore must have lost upwards of 1000 men in all, which is more than we supposed. They continue to desert in great numbers whenever they have the opportunity.

Our Portuguese troops are behaving very well. The 1st Regt. of Dns. at Atalaya towards Castello Branco attacked 80 French who were in the town, killed 25, and took 20 men and horses. Yesterday evening an account arrived from Bragança that a squadron of the 12th Dns. had been attacked by a French squadron, which they defeated, took 40 men and horses prisoners, and killed all the rest, except 2 officers and a soldier who escaped. Many of these prisoners are badly wounded. The Portuguese squadron must have behaved very well to have done the business so effectually, and although these small affairs are of no great consequence (in themselves), yet they give us very pleasant hopes of what the Portuguese troops will do when more seriously engaged.

I have this instant been to see three French cavalry, who deserted yesterday evening. They say they did so because they are starved, and that 25 of the 3rd Hussars and 8 more of their men had deserted the day before. These men, who are native French, come over mounted and completely armed. They say that nothing but desperation could make the infantry go leagues from the army to get food at the risk they run from the peasantry, and that their regt. of the 15th Chasseurs à Cheval have in 4 months been reduced from 900 to 400 men by sickness (which is very great in their army) and loss of horses. These men belong to the 6th Corps, Ney's, and could tell us nothing about Almeida. *Adieu*; Believe me ever yr. most truly affectionate son,

Wm. Warre.

I hope my father will receive the Merinos safe which I sent him, and that they will turn out well. I wish him to keep them or dispose of them just as he pleases.

I send a letter from Clara, which pray deliver to him.

My Dear Father,

I intended to have written (you will be amused at this beginning and the length of the letter, which I write at a gallop, expecting every moment that the marshal will mount) you *a long
letter* today, but, being on the move, I have only time to tell you
that our army has again made a forward movement, and we this
day change our hdquarters to Avelans da Ribeira, to the right of
Alberca, which becomes for the present Lord Wellns.' hdquarters. The army is all on the move, but I am ignorant of what the
intention of our generals is, whether to cross the Coa and raise
the siege of Almeida, on which place they have not yet that we
know of opened their batteries, or whether by a diversion on
this side favour the disturbances which have been reported to
have arisen in Spain. Whatever it is, it is a forward movement.
Everybody is in high spirits.

The distance to which Junot has removed with his *corps d'armèe*,
and Regnier being occupied by General Hill, it leaves only the
6th corps, Ney's, to besiege Almeida, and, if the other corps
are really at such a distance as not to be able to support it, it
would be a shame for us to let them take that place before
our faces. As yet we know pretty correctly from deserters, who
continue to come over in considerable numbers, that they have
only completed the first parallel, and were at work at constructing the batteries in it. Their heavy guns had arrived but were
not mounted. The garrison keep up a very brisk fire, and the
enemy have lost some men. They press forward very boldly at
daybreak, their light troops close to the place, and fire into the
enclosures to annoy the gunners.

But Br. Genl. Cox, the governor, by telegraph informs us that
he does not much mind them, and that the garrison is in excellent spirits. Hitherto the Portuguese have had all the firing on
their side. When the batteries open from the enemy, we shall be
better able to judge how resolute they are. I daresay they will
do very well.

I can, however, assure you that the situation of the French in
Spain is most distressing. officers of rank from Madrid write
to France (intercepted correspondence) that they are reduced
to the greatest necessity. Joseph the usurper, with an army of
250,000 men in Spain, is only in possession of that part of his

kingdom which the troops occupy. The supplies from Cordova and Grenada to Madrid are no longer sure, indeed most precarious. In short, all orders write almost in utter despair, and conjure Buonaparte to alter his system with regard to that wretched country. The army have not been paid for ten months, and in many parts, particularly Almeida and its neighbourhood, are dreadfully distressed for bread, and all the foreigners ready to desert the first opportunity. Buonaparte says he can only give them yearly 24 millions of *francs* (1 million sterling), what folly! The tyrant recommends rigour, which is all in our favour, and his party from Spain write that if the emperor cannot be got to alter his plans with regard to the Spaniards, they cannot with all their force and advantage answer for the consequences.

Kellerman with all his divisions of cavalry cannot prevent the excursions of the peasantry to the very gates of Valladolid. We have also reports of great disturbances in Madrid, and the movements of the French Corps make me believe it.

We have had no affair of consequence since my last to Emily. The eagle which Silveira took with the Swiss battalion at Puebla de Senabria arrived here. It is an imitation of the Roman Eagles, and I think an ugly one. It has, however, its effect upon the volatile courage and vanity of the French. To them a cap of liberty, or emblem of slavery, is equal, so long as it flatters the self-sufficiency and vainglory of the grand nation. The battalion is gone to Coruña to embark for England. None will return to France. They will almost to a man enlist with us.

I must again request, my dearest father, to consider this information about Spain as confidential for the present. At all events not to mention my name, though I do not see any harm in your mentioning it, though not as coming from me.

This is the anniversary of the Battle of Vimiero, and at this time that day we were warmly engaged. I hope our next day may be as brilliant. Our army both English and Portuguese is in excellent health and spirits. I have great faith that our Portuguese will astonish the French most unpleasantly for them.

Adieu. Kindest and most affecte. love to my dearest mother, etc., etc. Yr. ever affectionate and dutiful son,

Wm. Warre.

I have written this letter in such a hurry that I fear you will have considerable difficulty in either reading or understanding, but pray excuse it, as I have been every moment expecting to be called away. *Adieu, Adieu.*

May every blessing and happiness attend you and all my dear, dear family.

P. S.—I had little idea I should have had time today to write when I wrote this yesterday.

By the enclosed, which I send open, you will see that we have halted two days. But as I am completely ignorant of what the intentions were of our chiefs, it would be folly to attempt to account for it.

W. W.

Avelans da Riveira, 22nd Aug.

Hdqrs. Lagiosa,
29th Aug. 1810.

Many many thanks, my dearest Father, for your letter of the 1st, and the expressions of your affectionate approbation which will ever make the greatest pride, as well as the greatest happiness of my life. You will see that we have again retired to this place, on the unexpected fall of Almeida, which *we suppose* surrendered on the 27th. The enemy's batteries opened from different sides and very briskly on the night of 25th to 26th. We could distinctly see and hear them firing. On the 27th I was dining at the outposts with General Slade, when a report arrived that, no firing being heard for several hours on either side, the place must have been taken. I hurried up to the telegraph in front of Freixedas and from what I could see through the glass I had not a doubt of the event, as I could see people coming in and out and the rampart crowded over the gate.

Many officers who were present saw the same. But the next night a heavy firing was heard, which has confused me a good deal, as I thought myself positive, and do, of what I saw through a glass, and this certainly appears a contradiction to it. Next morning Ld. Wellington and the marshal went up at daybreak, and I suppose thought there was no doubt of the place being taken, though still some doubt of when, and orders were given for the army to retire again, which was done yesterday and continues today, though we do not leave this place, nor, I suppose, shall till the enemy advance.

There was a little skirmishing at the outposts yesterday, and

I am sorry to say Capt. Ligon of the 26th is wounded in the neck, I do not know whether badly. Our advance vedettes remain where they were, in front of Freixedas, extending towards Pinhel, in which place the French are. How long things may remain in this state it is quite impossible to say. My opinion is that the enemy is not yet in force to advance. Nor will the state of affairs in Spain allow it for the present.

At all events they must have considerable garrisons and posts of communication, and by drawing them into the interior, destroying the means of subsistence, mills, and forcing the inhabitants to fly on their approach, which they are ready enough to do, I trust we shall be able to meet them on equal terms, and where we please, to give a good account of them. I hate grumbling and croaking, and think it most unsoldierlike in an army such as ours, even were we less strong. We must trust to the *fortune de la guerre*, and the abilities of our generals. I wish that every English officer thought the same and wrote less nonsense to their friends at home.

As to Almeida, it is quite an enigma, how it came to yield so soon. No breach can have been made, and from the opinion I have of General Cox, I much fear either he was killed, or the garrison forced him to this step. As, however, we know nothing but on conjecture it is as prudent and liberal to suspend our judgment. A week more or less must at all events have brought us to this, and it is a most ridiculous idea to despond at the event, as if it altered our situation.

On the 22nd there was a very gallant little affair at Ladoeiro between Castello Branco and Salvaterra. Capt. White of the 13th Lt. Dns. with a troop of that regt. and a troop of the 4th Portuguese Cavalry (our friend John Campbell's Reg.) attacked 60 French cavalry, and without the loss of a man or horse, took 50 men, 7 corporals, 3 sergts., and 2 officers. The capt. and some men endeavoured to escape on foot, but were afterwards killed by the peasantry. So that not one went back to tell the tale, and the French, thinking the whole had deserted, sent out another party in search of them. They had 7 or 8 men wounded, and Capt. White speaks very highly of the gallantry and good conduct of Cornet Raymundo Oliveira and the Portuguese Troop, who charged in very great style and tumbled the *mounseers* over in a minute.

I am quite delighted that you are pleased with my having got the Merinos, which I am sorry to say missed their passage to London owing to a mistake. They are in the care of Messrs Bulkely, who have promised to forward them by the first opportunity. Should I be able to procure any of a very good breed, I will, you may depend, never forget you. I am quite vexed I did not get 15 when I got these, which I hear are very fine, but I was then quite at a loss how I should get them home.

I received a very kind letter from Col. Ross from Sarzedas. He was quite well, and I am happy to hear is coming into the Portuguese service, where he will, I expect, command a brigade. I have said everything in my power to the marshal about him, and I have no doubt he will do everything for him. Mrs R. and the children, he tells me, are at Weymouth.

Pray thank Tom for his letter which I will answer on the first opportunity. Also pray tell my Uncle Wm. with my kindest love that I have received a letter from the Honble. A. C. Johnstone with his letter enclosed, requesting me to procure him a letter from the marshal to the Marquis de la Romana, which I have done, and in very strong terms, and I shall be happy to hear it has answered his purpose. Should he come into our neighbourhood, I will shew him every attention in my power, as he may depend upon, I will to any friend he may recommend to me. *Adieu*, my dearest father; pray give my kindest love to my beloved mother, Emily, etc. Yr. ever dutiful and most truly affectionate son,

Wm. Warre.

I am astonished at Greenwood not having received my Coruna losses. The Board of Claims is dissolved; I think it very hard.

I have this moment seen a letter from Guarda stating a French colonel to be arrived there a prisoner, and that a lieut.-col. was killed. They were, it is said, reconnoitring with Masséna at Naves d' Haver, and missed their way in the fog and rain, which was not improbable, as I never saw such tremendous thunderstorms as we had yesterday and the night before. The same letter also says Almeida is taken, and the governor reported to be killed.

6 in the evening,
August 29, 1810.

My Dear Father,

I have since writing this morning heard the official account of the surrender of Almeida, and the fact is this. On the morning of the 27th a shell fell near the principal magazine as they were in it and making cartridges, the door being open the whole blew up with an explosion that destroyed a considerable part of the town, and of course created the greatest confusion in the place. Cox, finding all his ammunition gone, except a few rounds, sent to propose surrendering in case the garrison might be allowed to join our army, which in consequence of the intervention of the Marquez D' Alorna, Pampeluna, and other Portuguese traitors, was refused by Masséna. Cox declared he would not surrender under other conditions, and recommenced the fire till next morning (the 28th) when every cartridge being used, he was forced to surrender as prisoners of war.

As the garrison marched out and were formed on the glacis, it was offered them to either march prisoners to France, or enter the service of Napoleon. To a man they refused the former (*sic*) (except one major of artillery who had been before tried as a traitor), a most noble act on the part of a garrison mostly militia, which strongly shews the spirit of the people. (There is some confusion here; to make good sense "the latter" should be read not "former". See *Oman*, vol. iii.) I also much rejoice in my friend Cox having got off with honour and credit to himself and the British Nation.

The French colonel and some men who were taken with him, passed through this since I wrote. He belongs to the *gendarmerie* and is a handsome looking fellow, though he has a very sneaking appearance. He as well as his companions were wounded. The lt.-col., his friend, was killed. We last night took 9 dns. prisoners at Freixedas which the French occupied, and have since again abandoned. *Adieu.* Yr. most affecte. son,

Wm. W.

I am writing as hard as I can, so pray excuse the difficulty you will have in reading this postscript.

The Major of Artillery Barretto, who proved a traitor, was sent by Cox as a flag of truce. The scoundrel told all he knew, and never even returned to the place. I suppose he found it too warm a berth, and was devilish glad to get out of it. A traitor is almost always a coward. He flies from a greater hoping to find a lesser danger with the enemy, or from the same reason that a man robs or murders, from natural vice or villainy. What miscreants are Alorna, etc., etc.

EXTRACT FROM LETTER, DATED HENDON PLACE, OCT. 2, 1810.

Hendon Place,
Oct. 2, 1810.

No arrivals, and of course no news from dear William. Lord W. had retreated towards Vizeu. We presume things were going on as usual on the 11th, as Paris papers to the 23rd are in town, and they hear at Paris in eleven days from the army.

EXTRACT FROM LETTER, HENDON PLACE, 16TH OCT. 1810.

Hendon Place, 16th Oct. 1810.

I give you joy of the glorious news. How delightful it is that the Portuguese have behaved so nobly. They have shown Bony's 'spoiled child of Fortune' what they can do when well organised and commanded. Some of the regts. were commanded by Portuguese. It will give dear William great satisfaction, though he will be sadly disappointed at not being there. He had been afflicted with his old complaint—was gone to the rear to recover.

I do pity him not sharing in the glory when he has partaken so much of the fatigue, and General Beresford's army having borne the whole brunt of the action makes it doubly mortifying as such an opportunity may not again offer. I long for letters from him, but fear we have no chance till the packet arrives. Capt. Burgh told papa he was quite recovered.

The French have concentrated their whole force, and were so determined to carry the day they only brought *Frenchmen* into the field. They would not trust their foreigners, who continue to desert in great numbers. Masséna applied to Lord Wellington for permission to bury his dead, which was refused, as Ld. W. wanted to ascertain their numbers.—Above 2000 were interred, and the general proportion is 3½ wounded to 1 killed. On this occasion it is supposed to be much greater, as the French had no artillery or cavalry, and we played away after them with grape and shot from our artillery down the hills.

Four of the Pintos are among the wounded or killed. A cousin of theirs is wounded.

EXTRACT FROM LETTER DATED HENDON, 25TH OCT. 1810,
REFERRING TO W. W.'s LETTER, OCT. 6.

Hendon, 25th Oct. 1810.

At last we have got letters from dear William. They are of a
very old date (6th Oct.) and must have been unaccountably
delayed in London, as the Packet of the 8th has been long arrived and one of the 16th arrived on Monday. Poor dear fellow,
he has had another dismal voyage of pain and suffering from
Figueira to Lisbon, but again met with kind friends, and is, God
be praised, restored to health—in one of the letters he says Jack
Croft joined him as soon as he heard of his being ill at Coimbra, and accompanied him in a crowded transport of sick and
wounded, sharing the floor and his bearskin, and administered
to him and his fellow sufferers every comfort in his power, and
on his arrival at Lisbon took the trouble off his hands of seeking
for a lodging for a poor little fellow under his protection, who
had lost a leg and been obliged to suffer two operations for it,
but is now likely to do well.

A son of Sir J. Frederick's, Major Stanhope, saw William on the
12th at Belem. He was then so much recovered that he talked
of joining the marshal (now Sir W. B.) in a day or two. I suppose
you will like to have an extract. The first part of his letter is all
about my mother's illness, as he had just received my letters ac-
quainting him of it. He then says he has recovered his strength
and looks so wonderfully fat, everyone is astonished at it.

"It will, however, require a fortnight or 3 weeks' quiet sea-
bathing to confirm the tone of my nerves, which have been
a good deal shook by resisting a very tedious and debilitating
illness in hopes of sharing in the glory of my companions: and
it has been a bitter disappointment to have been in the rear
during the late glorious actions, when the Portuguese troops
behaved so nobly. "

What a pleasure it must be to the marshal. And he deserves it,
for his exertions (for which success is the best payment) and for
his excellent honourable character. I believe everybody now
does him justice for the honour and rectitude of his intentions.
Of the movements of the army I know little, but believe they
are falling back on the positions at Mafra, etc., which are en-

trenched and prodigiously strong. If the French press forward, I think a decisive and good battle inevitable, but I do not think they will, and, if they do, I have not a doubt of the result, and Nap. will have got into a pretty scrape. If they beat us, we have equally strong positions at St Juliens, but this God forbid. For the sake of the poor natives I trust all will be well. They deserve it for their loyalty and willingness, but I really have great confidence that the infamous invader will get a complete defeat. The French left 3000 dead on the field at Busaco. How they could attempt to attack such a position I know not, nor can I conceive, except that they entirely despised the Portuguese infantry. Inganarao says they were mistaken! but we have yet to give them better proof of it.

Clara is safe and well at Porto, and her obstinacy in staying in the convent has caused me great anxiety—

A. E. W.

Major Elliot's treatise on the defence of Portugal is remarkably well worth reading, and gives a very just and true and impartial account of the people and country.

Hd. Qrs., P.A., Casal Eschin,
a mile to the Eastward of
Enxara dos Cavaleiros, 5 l. from Lisbon,
Oct. 20, 1810.

My Dearest Father,

You will see from the date that I am quite recovered, and have joined the army and my excellent friend the marshal, who, to my great joy I found on my return two or three days ago, quite well notwithstanding the fatigue he has undergone, I was in such a constant fidget in Lisbon, and so uncomfortable that I could not remain any longer, particularly as the weather did not admit of my sea bathing, which was my principal object in going to Belem.

I am much disappointed at not hearing from the family last packet. A packet is daily expected and I trust I shall be more fortunate.

On my return I found our army in a position as strong as anything can well be imagined, studded with redoubts and batteries, extending from the front of Torres Vedras to the Tagus at Alhandra, by Bucellas, on the chain of hills which runs behind

Sobral, nearly from the sea to the river. It is rather an extended one, but a part is so strong by nature, and by art, that the troops can with great safety in great part be spared to repel the enemy wherever he may attack, and I feel not a doubt of his being forced to abandon the enterprise and retreat, or that if he attack us, scarcely a more desperate measure than the other, he will be completely defeated and destroyed.

Masséna, as far as my very slender knowledge of these matters goes, is in a most desperate scrape, and I scarce see how it is possible to get out of it without the loss of a great part of his army. I cannot account for his incautious advance, for he has little reason to doubt the conduct of the Portuguese after the Busaco business, and could scarce be such a fool as to imagine that because we retired, we were hurrying to embark without fighting a battle, after having so completely beaten him at Busaco. I dare say he had no idea of the great strength of these lines. I had none myself, though I had seen parts of them. But now that he is close to us, I cannot see how he can avoid fighting us. Even should we be unfortunate, we have other strong lines to retire to, and we must fight him again.

As for embarking, I do not see how that is to be accomplished, if we are defeated, and did I feel less confident of victory, and less fearful that they will not attack us, I should think the game as desperate for us as for them. However, nothing can exceed the confidence and spirit of our army, who are very well provided, while we know for certain the French want entirely for bread, and must soon for meat. At present they have enough. Their officers tell them they are to be in Lisbon in a fortnight, but the reports of their deserters, and their number, sufficiently prove how little they are believed.

Trant and Genl. Miller and Colonel Wilson advanced suddenly with a large body upon Coimbra, and took about 5000 sick and wounded, 80 officers and a whole company of the marines of the Imperial guard, who have all except about 200 arrived at Porto, and are long e'er this embarked. It was a dashing movement which completely destroys the enemy's communications that way with Spain, and has spread the greatest terror and dismay in the French Army, as well as great disgust at their sick being abandoned, with so weak a garrison as 300 men. Many of these wretches must die and have died. Such are the horrors of war, but one cannot pity them, when we consider the enormities and cruelties they commit everywhere, where they pass, they are a horde of the most savage *banditti*, and, desperately miserable themselves, they spread terror and desolation wherever they approach.

We go every morning to a large work near Sobral, in which place they are, and from whence we see almost all our own position, and what they are about. Their posts are about ¼ mile from it, and close to ours. Junot's and Ney's *corps d'armée* in our front in the different villages, but most encamped near a large pine wood, and in it, about 3 miles in our front. And this is their principal force, about 30,000 to 35,000 men; and Regnier's corps is on our right near the Tagus in front of Hill. Ld. Wellington's dispositions are very much approved by everybody, and said to be masterly. As far as I can judge, I think so too. The greatest cordiality exists between the Portuguese and English troops, and they are so disposed as mutually to support and encourage each other, without much being risked by their misconduct should it be so, which nobody now fears, or could in justice the most captious, after the proofs they have given of their courage and good will.

J. Croft came yesterday and shared my bearskin with me on the softest straw I could procure, and this morning he rode at daybreak with me to the battery, where I showed him the lions. It was very interesting, as there were several movements on the part of the enemy, who appeared to be concentrating their force in the wood I before mentioned, and near it, fronting our centre. But my own private opinion is that if they attack us at all, they will attack the left.

Croft afterwards set off again for his son, and as I did not think I should be able to get back again in time to write, I begged him to mention that he had seen me and I was well. I have, however, fortunately returned in time to write this hasty scrawl with a wretched pen and greasy paper, which must excuse me with you for the difficulty you may have in reading it.

I have received the second part of the translation on the defence of Portugal, but have not had time to read a line yet, for we breakfast at ½-past 4 and dine at six, which, with a good deal of riding, makes us most ready to avail ourselves of all leisure moments to sleep.

Adieu. I hope my next may be to announce a most glorious victory, of which I have not a doubt, whenever they attack us, and which from circumstances I do not think they can long delay, and we are quite ready to receive them.

Believe me, my dear father, Ever most gratefully and most affectionately, yours,

Wm. Warre.

From some deserters from the enemy's cavalry who are come in we hear that they are practising or rather drilling their men to charge with the bayonet. It is rather ridiculous at this time of day, after pompous boasting of having carried everything at the points of their bayonets. They cannot drill their hearts and minds, and we shall always beat them at that work, as our fellows' minds and nerves require no drilling.

Falmouth, Nov. 14, 1810.

My Dear Father,

I am very much afraid you will receive this letter before that I wrote to go by last packet, and which, owing to a provoking mistake, was left behind and goes in this. By it you will see that after I rejoined the marshal my illness and pains returned with increased violence, and it was intended to prepare you for what I feared would be the consequence, my being forced to return home. But still I was most unwilling to quit my post, and give up at such an interesting crisis, the chance of an opportunity of making myself known. And this made me bear for upwards of a fortnight the torture of laying on the ground with but little comfort and less rest. It could not, however, last long, and my horse falling with me and on my bad leg and bruising it, forced me to go to Lisbon, and have a consultation on my case, when after some deliberation it was determined that I should go home, and I accordingly embarked on board the *Walsingham* Packet, and after a very rough and tiresome voyage of 10 days, we are at length arrived at this place, at which I shall be forced to delay a day or two before I can venture to travel.

When I came on board, I was almost a cripple, and suffered an agony of pain beyond anything I can describe. However, I have, thank God, for the last two or three nights been able to sleep a little, though I am very weak, and the cold pinches me much. By avoiding with great care catching cold, and by slow journeys, I trust when I arrive in London that I shall at least be free from pain. I hope to be able to get to town in about 8 days or less, if I find I can bear the journey well. Poor Ross is arrived with me and will remain a few days. He is better, I think, considerably than when he came on board, but still very weak and low. He goes to Bath, as soon as he can travel. My last will give you all the news, since which things remained *in statu quo* when we sailed. The general opinion was that Masséna was about to retreat. Loison's division had passed the Zezere. With most affecte. love, etc., etc., yr. affecte. son,

Wm. Warre.

Honiton, Nov. 18, 1810.

My Dear, Dear Father,

I arrived at this place this evening after being three days on the road since I left Falmouth, and most completely tired of Cornish moors and Cornish travelling at 4½ miles an hour. I only reached Bodmin instead of Launceston the first day, and Oakhampton on the next, and though I intended to have remained this day at Exeter and rested, I resolved, having lost a day, to push on, and, except I find myself unusually unwell, shall proceed by short stages to London without halting an entire day anywhere, and about the 22nd I hope to arrive. I am happy to say I have borne the journey better than I expected notwithstanding the weather, which has been much against me. I am, however, a good deal fatigued, and it is not unlikely I may be forced to remain a day on the road.

I did not send you the reports by the *Stag* merchant vessel from Oporto, as considering dates and circumstances they appear to me quite improbable, not to say quite impossible. That a battle took place so that accounts reached Porto on the 7th is impossible, (as we sailed on the 4th, and such a thing was not expected), except indeed we can do away all improbabilities, those of the French attacking us, .and then, *en militaire*, I do believe their defeat inevitable, and that Ld. Wn. attacked them I do not believe. Pray give my most affecte. love to my beloved mother, I am, etc., etc., yr. ever affectionate son,

Wm. Warre.

CHAPTER 5

1811

During the early part of the year William Warre was at home, an invalid, under the care of his family. He gradually recovered his strength, and by the end of April was pronounced convalescent, the medical authorities allowing him to start for Portugal as soon after 1st May as he could find conveyance.

Meanwhile great events had occurred in the Peninsula, absence from which fretted him much. In January 1811 Marshal Soult had invested Badajos, which was surrendered by Imaz on 11th March. After securing Badajos, Soult, whose presence was required in Andalusia, returned to the south.

Masséna had early in March retired from Santarem, but still held on tenaciously to Portuguese soil, from which he was not driven till after the combat of Sabugal on 3rd April. In the interval Beresford had recaptured Campo Mayor and Olivença. He had now 22,000 men under his command. With these he proceeded to lay siege to Badajos. Wellington, who on 20th April had come to Elvas, was soon summoned back to his army, which was investing Almeida, by the news of a forward movement on the part of Masséna. Reinforced by detachments from Bessières, he had now a force of full 40,000 men at his disposal, and was strong in cavalry, in which the allies were weak. Followed on 5th May the Battle of Fuentes d'Onoro, which was fought to cover the blockade of Almeida, and was almost not a victory for Wellington.

On the 8th the French retreated. On the 10th the French garrison of Almeida, under General Brennier, made their escape. Meantime Soult from the south again advanced to relieve Badajos, which Beresford was besieging with no adequate battering train. The latter took up a position at Albuera, a few miles to the south-east of Badajos, where, on the 16th of May, was fought the fiercest battle of the war, the memories of which have been enshrined in immortal prose by Napier. Towards the middle of May, Marmont succeeded Masséna in the command of the army of Portugal. Poor King Joseph about the same time attempted, but in vain, to divest his head of the crown, which caused it so much uneasiness, and to retire into private life. On 25th May Badajos was for a second time surrounded, but not for long. The siege was raised again early in June. At the end of May, Wellington was blockading Ciudad Rodrigo.

Hostilities after this dragged on without any events of great moment, until in September Marmont advanced to relieve Ciudad Rodrigo. After the action of El Bodon, the allied army, which was .in a critical position, in the face of superior numbers and a vastly superior force of cavalry, withdrew to the hilly ground of the upper valley of the Coa, and the French marshal, having missed the opportunity of striking a decisive blow, retired, with the result that Ciudad Rodrigo was again invested. The fact was that the country was exhausted, and the French Army, which had lived upon the country, could no longer find supplies.

Major Warre, who reached Beresford's headquarters towards the end of May, found the marshal rather failing in health after the stress of Badajos and two unsuccessful sieges, and the tremendous anxiety of Albuera. His first letter after his arrival is written on 20th June from St Olaia, about eight miles from Campo Mayor. With the exception of a reconnaissance in force by Soult, which had no important result, nothing of moment occurred, and during the hot months the armies on either side were comparatively quiescent. The marshal, whose health was much impaired, spent the rest of the year at Lisbon and Cintra. Meanwhile, the organisation and improvement of the Portuguese Army continued, notwithstanding the difficulties arising from the impecuniosity and incapacity of the Portuguese Government, of which frequent complaints recur in the letters.

LETTERS

Portsmouth, May 5th, 1811.

My Dearest Father,

Here we are still with very little progress in obtaining a passage, as both the *Port Mahon* and *Spitfire* are very much crowded. However, if the worst happens, I think Jack will be able to get a berth in the latter, and I will go in the *Westmorland* with my horses. But perhaps some new conveyance may start up, and while the wind continues in this quarter, (nor does it appear likely to change) we must wait patiently for what may occur, though it is really a trial of patience to be mewed up in this stupid place without exactly knowing what to do, or how we are to get away. Jack is a dear fellow, and a most agreeable companion, and I shall really feel very much annoyed if we are separated, though I certainly think it is best to go anyhow in the same convoy, and we can then unite again as soon as we arrive in Lisbon.

As to how I go I do not much care. I am very well in health, though a little heated, and I do not see that it signifies much whether I take Epsom salts in a transport, or crowded in a sloop of war's cabin, and God knows of late years I have been pretty well used to roughing it. We yesterday fed Capt. Digby, and Capt. Ellis of the *Spitfire*, who has been very civil to us both, but appears rather an odd one. He said he would try to get one or both of us (yesterday morning) with his Officers, but has not since mentioned the circumstance, which makes me think that either he has not communicated with his ship from the badness of the weather, or that it is impossible to accommodate us. Tomorrow we dine with Capt. Bouverie of the *Medusa*, if the wind does not come about, and now you have all our plans. . . .

Portsmouth, May 7th, 1811.

My Dearest Father,

Many thanks for your very kind letters and for the enquiries you have made about my passage. My last will have informed you that we had given up all hopes of either the *Spitfire* or the *Port Mahon*, and from yours I have but slender hopes of the *Romulus*, and have therefore this morning desired my servant to purchase some stock, and have made enquiries about a transport that I may apply for an order, which Capt. Patton will give me. However, as the wind is still set in to the S.W. we may be here some days, and something pleasanter may turn up. What I most regret in this arrangement is being separated from my friend Jack, whom I really cannot advise or approve of going in a transport at all.

Capt. Patton knows nothing of the *Braave*, nor is she yet come round. Should Mr Sydenham certainly go, I would, if I was sure of a passage with him, wait, for we should be before the convoy at all events. I shall, however, go in a transport should I hear nothing further. I have seen Capt. Knox of the *Fiorenzo*, who left Lisbon the 27th. He brings no news whatever, but says the natives were in the highest spirits. I have not been able as yet to obtain a passage for Jack's horse in the fleet, but as he has got the butcher's horse from Plymouth, I do not think it of any consequence whether he goes or not. . . . Walker and the horses are quite well. He has behaved very well, and I have therefore sent him some fresh stock on board, for which he is very grateful. My new groom also seems to be a good lad. Yrs., etc.,

Wm. W.

My promotion will be in course, and we can do nothing further. As to . . . . letter, it does not much signify what he wrote, *com todos nada*, (with all nothing) the best way is not to irritate the little worm, who will be vexed enough to find he has outwitted himself, and will no doubt try his ingenuity in plaguing me whenever he has an opportunity.

Portsmouth, May 9, 1811.

My Dear Father,

I am much obliged to you for your letter of the 7th and for ensuring my horses' lives, as well risk of capture, etc., which, everything considered, is as well, and I will direct great care to be taken of them, which I have done, at all events for my own sake, as money would be a very trifling compensation for what I could not replace. I have made every enquiry about the *Braave* charter, but can hear nothing of her. Capt. Patton from her description says he thinks she must be a navy store ship, and that they are out of his jurisdiction. I enquired about her at the dockyard, but they also know nothing of her.

I however ascertained that to go in her, if she is what I suppose, I must pay my passage, which would not be worthwhile, as I can have one for nothing in a regular transport. As, however, the wind continues still in the S.S.W. I shall take no further steps till the morning, in the hope of hearing something further from you about Mr Sydenham, as the *Port Mahon*, which is named and certainly waiting for a messenger, is so overcrowded already with Generals Hill and Campbell and their staffs, that I can see no possibility of their stowing any more on board of so small a brig. I have not been able to hear anything about my shirts and servant's livery, though I have enquired everywhere here about them. At the Crown, where my mother says they were sent, they know nothing of them. It would be provoking to lose them as well as the bearskin, which Mr W. Turner says he knows nothing of. I would therefore be much obliged to you to desire Dunn to enquire at the place from whence they were sent, and to let me know by what conveyance, and when forwarded, also how directed. I am at the Fountain Inn.

Jack is quite well and desires his kind love to all in George Street. We are, as you may suppose, not a little tired of Portsmouth, but as the weather is clearer now perhaps the wind may change, and then it will be most provoking to be separated, but my anxiety to get out increases, and I shall go anyhow.

Ever, my dear father, most affectionately yours,

Wm. Warre.

I have got Jack's horse on board in the *Westmorland* with my horses, and, as he will have thus two horses at Lisbon, think he is very right in taking out his groom with him. *Adieu.*

Hdqrs., St Olaia,
June 20, 1811.

My Dear Father, . . . I am very much obliged to Arbuthnot and to you for your trouble about my promotion, which, I suppose, is by this settled. I think your letter to Torrens a very proper one, and I myself wrote to him by last packet and to M'Mahon, which I thought right, and really felt a strong inclination to do, expressing my gratitude for all his and Mrs M'Mahon's kindness, which has been uniform and most obliging, but we must not press any business there for the present, though after all, what I have got, I must have had without any interest, except Beresford's.

The marshal is, I am happy to observe, somewhat better, though he will require some time of quiet of body and mind to put him quite right again, and I really hope, if Marshal Soult leaves us alone for the present, as I think most likely, that the marshal will go to Lisbon for a month or six weeks, and try sea-bathing and a change of air. But till the intentions of the enemy can be positively ascertained, I know he will not be persuaded to move to the rear.

This movement of the army to the rear will, I hope, satisfy our newsmongers as to the propriety of raising the siege of Badajos. It was about just in time, or we should have had to fight a battle, perhaps against a very superior force, and under every disadvantage. It would have been a good thing to have taken the place, but we had a very limited period to do it in, much too much so for an attack *en règle*. It was worth attempting, and our failing only proves that the place required a more regular attack, for which it is evident we had lost time. It is now free again, and our army has retired, leaving Elvas to its right, and now occupies this place, Campo Mayor, towards Portalegre, and Hill's and Cole's divisions and the heavy cavalry the woods round Torre de Mouro, about 4 miles, half-way between this and Campo Mayor, in which is the 1st Dns. and some P. cavalry, and the 11th Lt. Dns. and 12 hussars are at Elvas and near it, and give that outpost duty.

We dined yesterday with Ld. Wellington at St Vincente, about half-way (5 miles) between this and Elvas, where he has a very pretty Quinta, and after dinner we rode to the Camp (4 miles) and Torre de Mouro, and nearly to Campo Mayor, to look over the positions (4 more), and we had then 8 to ride back to this, which is not a bad afternoon's ride, and it was very late when we got here. This is a little town, and we are pretty well off, notwithstanding its being a good deal crowded with 13th Lt. Dns. and General Castanhos' Hdqrs., who has now no army. He is a good-natured well-meaning man, but not remarkable either for talent or judgement.

I do not think the enemy will advance immediately, though greatly superior to us in number. They must be as anxious as we can be to rest and refit, and can hardly have recovered their defeat at Albuera, though in numbers increased by the junction of Marmont and Drouet with their corps, and he must first besiege and take Elvas, which, (though I have no very high opinion of either its governor, or the principal part of its garrison, and know it to have very weak points,) would I hope at all events delay him some weeks. . . .

The Portuguese Government are wretchedly off for money. Nothing whatever is paid for. The officers have not had a farthing for four months, and when I sent for my pay, the answer was *nao ha dinheiro*. Things cannot long go on so, and I fear all the marshal's exertions hitherto will have been to no avail, and the country go completely to ruin in spite of him and all his zeal and activity, unless some remedy is applied to the horrid mismanagement and almost torpid want of energy in the Government. We want for everything, and have not the means, or are we likely that I can see to have them, for the most trifling occurrences. I feel for the marshal, to whom these disgusts are, I am sure, a great cause of his illness.

No event has given me individually greater pleasure, or will be received by the army in general with more satisfaction than the appointment of the Duke of York, who, notwithstanding the malice of his enemies, and the mischievous revolutionary exertions of a set of low-bred *soi-disant* reformers, was a most excellent commr. in chief, and certainly brought the army to a point of discipline and systematic order that claims from it its utmost gratitude. As to his private amours they are nothing to us, and most indecently brought forward by that set, who perhaps the least ought to have agitated it, from motives most unwarrantable, as we all know. Pray remember me most kindly to General Ferguson and Farrer, and to Ross, Campbell, my friend John Brown, of whom I rejoice to hear such good accounts, and to his brother. With kindest love to all, etc., etc. Ever, my dear father, etc.,

Wm. W.

We have a report of a brilliant victory by Sir C. Cotton in the Mediterranean against 9 sail and 2 frigates of the enemy with 10,000 men for Catalonia from Toulon, but it requires confirmation. Don Josè desires to be remembered to you. Pray make my best respects to his Excellency the Ambassador.

I hear from dear Jacko that he is quite well, amusing himself very pleasantly. The marshal desires to be most kindly remembered to you; pray do also say the same from me to his brother.

St Olaia, June 27, 1811.

My Dearest, Kind Father,

Though I have little to add to what I wrote to you, and my letters to dear Emily and my Uncle William contain all the no news I have to send, I will not delay thanking you for yours of the 5th and 8th and for the newspapers We have been kept very alert lately by a reconnaissance Marshal Soult made on the 22nd on Campo Mayor, with 14 squadrons, pushing at the same time 1000 cavalry and as many infantry close up to Elvas. He *saw nothing*, but I am sorry to say we lost upwards of 100 men and horses, which is a very serious loss to us at present, mostly of the 10th and 2nd German Hussars. It is attributed to some mismanagement in posting our pickets (which I thought very apparent), and by no means the fault of the officers commanding them. Poor Lutyens while retiring from a party which had crossed the Guadiana in his rear, most unfortunately mistook a French body of cavalry for his own reserve, and did not find out his mistake till too late. He then, however, very gallantly attempted to fight his way through them, but was at last overpowered, losing 5 or 7 killed and 20 wounded, and the remainder of 40 taken with himself and another officer. One officer escaped wounded.

We have not since seen anything of the enemy, and it is my opinion that they will not at present attack us, as some think, though it is very difficult to say what those fellows may risk, they are so presumptuous and insolent, though Albuera and the other beatings they have received, must have at least given them prudence and a better opinion of us, and I am unwilling to believe that, now that Badajos is relieved, and he can have no immediate object to gain, he will risk an action which if unsuccessful to him must have the most disastrous consequences, and perhaps decide the fate of the Peninsula, if he should have a war to divide his attention to the North. It is the largest army they have in Spain, and all they can collect from all parts of the South. It would appear to me the height of rashness to venture it at one cast against troops which have just beaten the two corps of which it is composed, and without any positive advantage to gain, for they cannot yet be in a state to advance far into Portugal. I am well aware of the consequences which would attend a defeat of us, against their superior cavalry and numbers, but I feel so confident that this is scarce possible from the state and high spirits of our brave troops, that I have not the least uneasiness about it, and I also am much pleased with our position, which, I think, though not strong by nature, will enable us to bring all our troops into play in the manner best suited to them, and for the use of the bayonet, which in the hands of a British soldier is always decisive. Nor are our brave Portuguese by any means unaware of its utility or backward in applying it with full vigour. The whole army are in the best spirits and most willing to give these boasting miscreants another dressing before we go into quarters, which are, however, very necessary.

I think, when it is decided that the enemy do not mean to attack us, and that they retire from before us, that the marshal will go to Lisbon, which I shall be most glad of for his sake, as I think he requires rest both of body and mind, though, thank God, he is much better than when I first arrived. I quite agree with all you say in his praise. He has indeed deserved all that can be said, and it has been truly gratifying to read the manner in which the thanks of the House were voted to him.

He is of course much pleased and flattered by the approbation of his country, but he is as modest and diffident of what concerns himself as he is brave and clever in the field. We are on the very best terms, and I am as happy as I can be, notwithstanding the heat and turning out at 3 a.m. and then riding all day. We sleep the better for it, and in this respect, I am in great luxury, as I have a little camp bed of Count D'Alva's, with sheets, etc., etc., which I like so well, and so much better than my cloak and bearskin, since he went away, that I intend to buy a camp bed at Lisbon and always carry one in future.

Pray have my newspaper, *The Day*, sent regularly every day; it is a great comfort, and besides enables me to oblige a great many people. Though I sincerely rejoice when anything can be done for my cousins at Rugby, I am extremely sorry that anything should have been asked of Lord Mulgrave, however obligingly granted. I have good reasons for being decidedly against any application whatever being made to him on any account, and do intreat you that you will never allow any; not knowing him, you can have no idea what harm it does, though a very worthy old man, and though we should call and shew him every respect which is his due. I did wish to be under no obligation, and am much vexed that anything should have been asked. It was my intention to have tried by another channel, to have had the boy admitted, but would not have consented to this. It is, however, now too late, and he has behaved very kindly, but for the future pray never think of such a thing.......

(MS. torn, part wanting.)

. . it must have handsome round staff "tawsels" and ribbons at the sides, but must not be gold laced, as the new regulation is, *Deos nos livre*. I suppose our good chiefs do not think our generals or staff get killed off fast enough that they order them cocked hats with gold binding. It must only be meant for Wimbledon. There are no voltigeurs there, and a gold laced cocked hat, though very ugly, is a very harmless thing—not here.

July 1, St. Olaia.

We move tomorrow to Lisbon for a few weeks, which I am not sorry for, as the French are not likely to disturb us, and this place is horribly dull unless we had something to do.

I daresay the whole army will go into quarters during the hottest months. . . .

We are here four in a very small quarter, and not a pane of glass in the whole house, or a wooden floor, which we should not mind at all, if there was anything going on or likely, but the French are as glad, and as likely to be quiet, as we are for the present.

I see I am gazetted as major at last, and the marshal has recommended me for the Portuguese lt.-colonelcy, as I am nearly the eldest major in their army, and several have gone over my head, to whom I am to be antedated.

Lisbon, July 5, 1811.

I am quite well after my very tiresome journey with the hdqrs. baggage, for the marshal has been here these two days and left me to bring the hdqrs. staff. A pretty set to be bear leader to indeed!

Lisbon, August 2nd, 1811.

My Dearest Father,

Nothing can give us greater pleasure than to see you in this country, and I assure you the marshal will also be very happy to see you, and I think your presence may be useful in the north at Porto. I think this country for the present quite safe, and if Russia declares against France, or even continues her threatening posture, so as to occupy a large portion of his force in the north of Germany, things have never looked better in the Peninsula. If not, it is quite impossible to foretell the events of a campaign, or what may happen from one moment to another, particularly if the Spaniards persist in not doing anything.

It is a curious perverseness their dislike to a foreign command, particularly where they confess, they want it, in their armies, and their pride and vain-glory, which one would naturally expect would be the stimulus to anything, in order to avoid subjugation, will probably be the real causes, with the ignorance and treason of their gentry, of their ultimate fall.

As to a battle immediately I do not see the least chance of it. I think the army will shortly make some movement, but as yet I know nothing about it. I pay no attention, and wish you would not, to the nonsense of our wise politicians of London, who speculate mostly, either from very bad information, or as best suits their views.

As to your informant about Ld. Wn. starving the South as well as the North of Portugal, I confess the speech savours as much of roguery as of ignorance, and I should have a very poor opinion of any Englishman who could make such an observation, unless he wishes purposely to discourage the people from continuing this glorious struggle for everything that is dear to man. He shews himself as ignorant of the country as of the means it offers for defence, and of the enemy's decided superiority in numbers, which can only be overcome by drawing him away from his resources, and weakening him before we can strike.

In the action of Mina near Vittoria the French were completely beaten by his guerilla, which for that sort of corps is more organised than usual, and consists of 4 bns. and a regt. of cavalry, from 4000 to 5000 men. They make a good partisan corps, but have neither solidity nor system enough to be much better than a rather more disciplined and subordinate mob, as yet.

The Galicians and Asturians, like the other parts of Spain, I do not think likely to do much at present. Their government gives them no encouragement, and but little hope of any effectual support, and they, poor devils, have felt how inadequate they are alone to resist regular troops.

The fall of Tarragona was a serious disaster, though expected, and may have a bad moral effect upon the mind of the populace, besides giving a handle to the ill-disposed, which order of people I cannot say have increased in Spain, though I fear the indifferents, who are nearly as bad, certainly have. At the same time, I have not a doubt that, where the people are not kept under by force, was there any fair prospect of success, or any disaster to happen to the French, the whole would rise against their oppressors, whom they detest—at least, I think, the whole of the lower orders.

I am much obliged to you for the papers with the vote of thanks from the city to the marshal. They were never better bestowed. He had never heard of them before. I am very glad Le Marchant is coming out, as I think it is what he wished, and I have no doubt that with his extensive theoretical knowledge, and the practice he formerly had, he will be a great acquisition to our army. I hope my friend Johnstone will get leave to come out with him.

I have heard of no disagreement amongst our generals, or that the marshal ever had any idea of going home. We are for the present very quietly settled, and most comfortably, at that lovely place Cintra, where we are likely to remain till some general movement takes place, and something to be done. The air agrees extremely well with the marshal, who is very well. I never was so well for many years. It is very remarkable that the climate of Cintra is as different from Lisbon as London is. We have not had a day of heat, while here they have suffered very much.

The fog morning and evening keeps us, with the number of trees, constantly cool. The rash I had continues, and has increased, but the doctors tell me it is rather beneficial than otherwise, and desire me to do nothing to it. It gives me no inconvenience. They call it "Morphen," and most certainly, notwithstanding, my general health never was better. I came in yesterday on business and return tomorrow. The marshal also. He is at Caxias, nr. St Julians, at the admiral's. . . . I have just heard that a packet is coming in with a mail in 4 days from Falmouth, but have not heard that the bag is landed. . . .

Wm. W.

Cintra, August 17, 1811.

My Dear Father,

I have not written to you by the last packet, as I wrote to some of the family, and had really nothing in particular to communicate. We have been for the last four or five days in Lisbon, as the marshal had a good deal to arrange with the government, who, as usual with the people in power in this country, are the more impracticable in proportion as the danger is removed; and foresight or a liberal policy is not to be expected from people who cannot carry their views beyond the present moment, and though quite impotent in affairs of State, and as ignorant as obstinate, are extremely jealous of the power entrusted to them. Scarce a plan or arrangement, even military, is proposed by the military chiefs, but becomes a subject of discussion, and if not rejected, mostly so delayed that the object is either lost, or rendered far less effective.

It is most disgusting, and if they do not alter, it is quite impossible but the army must go to pieces in spite of even the exertions and firmness of the marshal. The brother (Principal Sousa) to your friend is the worst. Nothing can exceed his vanity and self-sufficiency except his ignorance. (See *Oman*, iii).

The marshal is quite well. The coolness and fine air of this beautiful spot agrees wonderfully with him, and, if we remain a week, or a fortnight longer, I think he will have acquired so much bracing and strength, that he will be fully equal to a campaign, and after next month the heat is not very oppressive. Lord W. has invested Ciudad Rodrigo with his cavalry and light troops, but not quite closely. I hope we shall be more successful in this siege than our last, and have acquired a little more experience. The accounts we have of the number and state of the garrison are very favourable to us, and you know I have not a very great opinion of the strength of the place, but we have but very little experience in this sort of warfare. Hdqrs. are, I believe, at Fuentes Guinaldo. I hope the marshal will have arranged his business and move up in time, as I do not expect we shall break ground for this some time.

Jack is returned from his tour, with which he is much pleased, though it does not seem to have increased his military zeal. He saw some divisions on the march, which has given him *some idea* of the miseries of even a summer campaign, and of the fatigue and inconvenience to which regt. officers and men are exposed. What would he think of one in winter? I think it will do him a great deal of good. I wish a great many more of our English country gentlemen could see a little of real warfare, which they affect to discuss so freely. Jack is quite well, and both Lord Balgonie and he were, I believe, heartily glad to get back to Lisbon again. They had not time to get used to fleas, mosquitoes, and no beds.

I am extremely anxious to hear when you determine upon coming to this country, though I fear it will not be before we leave this and Lisbon, as I was in great hopes you might have contrived. If you are to come, I think it is a pity you should put it off till much later in the year. But pray let me know, and what you wish me to do. Such as they are, I hope you will take my rooms at Cathariz, which I will have prepared for you, though I am afraid that, if we are out of town, a large empty house is not the most pleasant abode. I can make no arrangement for you till I know whether and when you come. It will be most provoking if we should have marched to the army, and therefore pray do not delay longer than indispensable. . . .

The marshal has sent the Brigadier Lemos his military secretary to the Rio de Janeiro on business. He will return almost immediately. As I think it not unlikely the prince may send some honours by him to his officers, it may be a good opportunity to get Dr Ds. (Domingos Antonio de Sousa Contentro, afterwards Conde de Funchal) to write directly to the Count de Linhares (eldest of the Brothers Sousa, Prime Minister at Rio Janeiro) about the *commandos*. As to the other business we spoke of, from what I hear and know of things in this country the idea gives me far more pain than pleasure, and I hope it may never take place. You must be careful that Dr Ds. has not a hint of my extreme dislike to his brothers and their ministry. Yrs., etc.,

Wm. Warre.

Cintra, August 23, 1811.

My Dear Father,

I hope you will not delay your departure for this country till much later in the year, and expect by next packet some further information of your intentions on the subject. I should doubt your finding us here at all events, as I think it very likely we shall join the army again early next month, when the siege of Ciudad Rodrigo will be going on. At present our troops are all around it at a distance, in cantonments, quite quiet, though the place is invested, and for the present the enemy do not show any intention of disturbing us; at least, I have heard of no movement on their part that indicates it. But I cannot think they will quietly allow us to take the place. It is to them well worth risking a battle for, if they intend ever to enter Portugal again. I cannot even guess whether Ld. Wn. will think it worth his while. At this distance I have but general and very imperfect information of the army, and it is dangerous to venture upon conjectures on such a subject.

The Spaniards continue to do nothing, at least on a great scale, and my hopes of any great effort on their part gradually diminish as the accounts arrive of reinforcements entering from France, though it is true in very inconsiderable numbers. We cannot make out that they yet exceed 9,000 to 12,000 men, which is nothing for the Peninsula. I look to Russia with some anxiety, as much must depend upon her conduct in our future operations. Your opinion, I am sorry to observe, is not favourable, though I think it evident there is some great misunderstanding or resistance to the tyrant's will on the part of that emperor, and, from the nature of the man, I should suppose he will not allow him to oppose him long with impunity. In the disordered state in which we understand the Russian finance to be, it is perhaps better, till she can make peace with the Turk, that she should hold her doubtful posture.

I am surprised you have not received a letter I sent you with the *Gazette* containing my Portuguese promotion. For the present, at least, I am lt.-colonel. Except the rank, I have not one advantage pecuniary or otherwise by my brevet majority, but I keep my staff situation, and unless I should get an effective majority of cavalry, it is as good a situation as I can have, and I have not the least inclination to quit that service.

I am vexed that I have been able to get nothing done for Casey, who is well deserving his promotion. I have written several times to Brown, but have no answer, and I know, from my own situation, how very unpleasant it is to be importuned upon these subjects. Perhaps Greenwood could do something for him. The purchase money is, I believe, in Tom's hands.

We have yet no account of the honours conferred by the P. R. of P. on the marshals, and at any rate I do not think them equal to their deserts, and, unless their pensions are better paid than usual in these cases, they will not be much the richer for them. I am glad that you have met the Douglas family. There cannot be a finer fellow or better Officer than he is, and more universally respected and beloved. He is a very great friend of mine. I saw him just before we left St Olaia. He was quite well. General Houston is gone home unwell. Campbell arrived the day before yesterday, and writes that he is quite well.

We are in daily expectation of accounts of the poor king's death, but while I believe every

one must regret the loss of such a sovereign and such a man, considering his sufferings and the present state of the nation, I hardly think it can be a subject of great sorrow to lose him, however much we loved and respected the royal and excellent qualities of such a king.

Your accounts of the internal politics of the country are extremely interesting, but with you I think it is quite impossible to guess the prince regent's intentions, or what his conduct may be after the king's death, and we all naturally look with great anxiety to the first steps of his reign as a criterion to judge of what we are to expect. . . .

Campbell is this moment arrived. I never saw him looking better. He was detained 5 weeks at Portsmouth and nearly a month on his passage. . . . Jack is also here quite well after his trip to Castello Branco, where he saw some divisions marching, and the sight of their hardships, even in a peaceable move distant from the enemy, has not increased his military zeal. It does these English amateurs a vast deal of good to see a little how things are carried on, and what soldiers go through on service, though I think it quite folly for any person, whose duty does not demand it of him, to expose himself as many have, and been laughed at. For after all they but prove what nobody doubted, that they are not afraid of their flesh. . . .

We continue to spend our time very pleasantly. The marshal has a slight cold and lumbago, which will, I hope, soon pass away. He is otherwise very well. . . .

Aug. 24—The marshal is much better today. He desires to be most kindly remembered to you. We have nothing new. The Duke of Leinster, Lords Clare and Delaware, are arrived in Lisbon, and going up to the army. Yrs., etc.,

Wm. Warre.,

The marshal is Count of Francozo, and Lord W. of Vimiero, but they have not yet the regent's permission to accept the titles—which, being compared with Silveira, are not at all flattering to any person but him, and completely marred the p. regent of P.'s intention of obliging them, for though nobody will deny Silveira considerable merit, it is folly to rank him with the other two. Nor has he ever done anything to deserve such a rank.

Poor Baçelar, who commands him, was at least entitled to H. R. H. notice.

Cintra, Sept. 7, 1811

My Dear Father,

I am much disappointed at not hearing from any of you the last two packets, though from my not having any letter at all, I must think it is owing to some mistake either at the Horse Guards, or at the Army Post Office, Lisbon. . . . I hope this will find you preparing to give me the pleasure of seeing you in this country, as I should be extremely sorry, if you intend to come at all, that you should delay it till much later in the year, and I had hoped you might come while we remain at this place or at Lisbon. The marshal does not yet talk of moving, but I should guess we shall not remain longer than this month, as the business that called him to the capital appears now to be nearly concluded.

We continue to amuse ourselves very well, and certainly if we are to be quiet, could not be in pleasanter or better quarters. Jack is with us and very well, and, whenever the time comes, I shall part with him with great regret. I have met few better hearted or more sensible fellows, and he has made himself much liked and esteemed by the whole of our staff.

I do not think the siege of Ciudad Rodrigo is now likely to take place. The supineness of our Spanish neighbours would enable the enemy to collect a force much superior to us for its relief, without any risk to themselves, and Ld. Wn. would fight to a very great disadvantage encumbered with the stores and train necessary for a siege; and, in case of disaster, the loss of them would be serious indeed. In the present demolished state of Almeida, that place could be of no assistance to him. Were it otherwise, the siege might be undertaken, as in case of their advancing in force to relieve it, he could in a few hours place it (the train) in comparative safety, and in case of a defeat, it would enable him to cover his retreat, and get some part of it away. At present Almeida is rather a weight than otherwise to us.

Marmont has moved up part of his corps through the Puerto de Baños, but I do not know that he has advanced himself, though it is not improbable he may draw near our cantonments to observe Ld. W.'s motions. He is not strong enough to prevent his Lordship from undertaking the siege, if he wished it, but I rather suspect that the corps which was collecting at Benevente, whatever its previous destination might have been, will also move to that quarter, in consequence of the advance of the allied army, and perhaps join with him, for I can never suppose that the enemy will allow us to take that town, which is of such importance to them, if they ever intend to enter Portugal again, and which I cannot doubt they will; and, for *many reasons*, notwithstanding the happiness it would be to me to see you, I should recommend, unless your plans are fixed, and that you can come immediately, or that your presence is quite necessary, that you would delay it till the spring, for I think this winter will decide much as to the fate of the Peninsula, which, (this is quite *entre nous*) I fear, if great reinforcements arrive, and that Napoleon's attention is not otherwise diverted, the unaccountable folly of the Spanish Government, and the consequent apathy and acquiescence of the people, has again placed in the balance; and it appears probable we shall have another active winter in this country again.

The Spanish Government have received, I hear, within the last twelvemonths 18 millions of dollars, of which latterly 5 millions; and, notwithstanding, I do not hear that their rabble, called an army, is a bit better provided, or that any effectual step has been taken to organise them, or oppose more effectual resistance to their invaders. It is truly lamentable. It appears that Blake has been defeated at Grenada, and I believe it. It was to be expected, and will always happen where he commands, for I do not believe there was ever a worse general; and these defeats completely destroy even the slight remains of confidence the naturally brave Spaniards had left. They will soon not fight at all, and I am sure it is not to be wondered at.

Genl. Le Marchant has been here for a day or two, and has been quite delighted with the beauty of the place. He is quite well. We have had the Duke of Leinster and Lords Clare and Delaware and Mr Fitzgerald, who left us this morning. They are remarkably unaffected fine young men, and an excellent sample of our young *fidalgos*. Ever yrs., etc.,

Wm. Warre.

Lisbon, 17th Oct. 1811.

My Dearest Father,

I am extremely anxious for the arrival of another packet, which is due, to be able to form some idea of when I may expect you in this country, as I find you still continue your intention of giving us the happiness of a visit.

Things are now quiet on the frontier, and I think may continue so for some time longer. Indeed, I should not suppose anything will be now seriously undertaken by the enemy till the spring. I therefore think the sooner you can come the better, and I certainly would not wait till the season is much further advanced, as what you say about the wine company is true, and nobody feels the tyranny and oppression of this monopolising body more than the inhabitants of this country themselves, you know. But with regard to the fulfilment of treaties with the English, no nation seems to think that necessary, and we are consequently always laughed at. John Bull is a noble beast, and has more good qualities than any other animal in the world, but *en fait de politique* he is generally a great gull.

Witness Sicily, Portugal, Spain, Prussia, Russia, etc., etc., etc., etc. But, as I should not suppose your presence in London necessary to forward its execution, I think it would be a great advantage for you to be here on the spot, and make your own arrangements, which so many others are doing before you. The name alone in the country would have weight, but it must not be allowed to be forgotten if you resolve ever to resume the business, as people will seek other channels for their business, and not be able to disengage themselves for you, even if they wished it. But, as you know all this much better than I do, I hope next mail to hear your decision on the subject.

The marshal, poor fellow, has been very unwell, and that has delayed us much longer here than we expected. We left the Prayas 4 days ago, as the air very much disagreed with him, and are at our old headquarters. He is more comfortable in his own house than anywhere else, and he requires in his present state every indulgence. I have been very anxious indeed about him, but he is now, thank God, much better, though still very weak, and it is therefore uncertain when we may be able to move as there is nothing likely to be doing for the present, and I am very anxious about it, as I think he is as well here as anywhere. His complaint is a low fever and great debility, which has been hanging about him for some months, and which, though it sometimes leaves him for a few days, has never given him time to gain strength; and his constant employment and hard work of mind and body have also greatly retarded his getting well. I should much fear we shall be gone before your arrival notwithstanding, which I shall regret extremely, as it would have been a great comfort and happiness to have seen you while we are quietly settled.

With regard to the honours to officers I can tell you that Forjas (General Miguel Forjaz, see *Oman, iii.)* had nothing whatever to do with the list, or could he send any in without an order from the regency, who are alone to blame. Much has been said upon the subject, and it seems very extraordinary that they should ever have thought of conferring military honours, without reference to the commander in chief of their army, who most certainly is the best judge of who deserves them. But these, like most other things in this country, are ruled by meanness, jealousy, and intrigue, nor can we expect any good and energetical measures while the principal and patriarch, ignorant, bigoted, and presumptuous, and mean enough to have recourse to any dirtiness to attain their ends, are in the regency, and Count Linhares in the Ministry, for he backs his ignorant meddling brother through everything, even in spite of the opinions of the other members. Forjas is often blamed, and most undeservedly so.

I do believe him to be a very honourable and well-intentioned man, and certainly a man of good abilities, and no intrigue and meanness has been neglected to ruin him in Brazil. The P——h hates him, and would willingly, if he dare, replace him by any of his creatures, whom he tries to force into every situation. Quite *entre nous* there never was a more mischievous little animal, or a more treacherous one. And pray be very careful in any opinions you give to Dn.—Ds. that he may suppose from me. He is of the same party and may do a great deal of harm. For they at present rather suppose I never trouble my head about them. As to my own honours, I shall be proud of any *military ones, when they come,* if conformable to my rank. But I put no trust in promises, and quite think with you that your friend knows nothing of the matter. But his strong recommendation to that quarter must have considerable weight. I feel an unconquerable aversion to soliciting any honours, and would not for the world appear to have given any opinion on the subject.

With regard to the representation he made of the poverty of this government, I do not believe it to the extent he says, though they are certainly distressed, and must be, while there is so much mismanagement, and so many useless hangers-on to be satisfied. As to a loan, I quite agree with you, that they must be honest, or, what is not an easy undertaking at present, they must persuade the lenders that they are honest, in their intentions at least.

I should be glad to hear that the Princess Charlotta really again got into power. She is at least energetical, and the changes *you fear* are most desirable from their consequent changes here.

We have no news from the army except an account of Don Julian Sanchez and his guerrilla having taken the general, Governor of Ciudad Rodrigo, Regnioux, while taking his promenade outside the town, and most of the cattle belonging to the garrison. I do not know the particulars, but it appears to have been a neat business enough. We all miss dear Jack very much. Remember me to General Leith, should you see him. I have a great regard for him. He is generally much esteemed. I am not likely to see Douglas for some time. When I do, I will give him your message. Hardinge desires me to thank you most kindly for undertaking his commission of seals. Yrs., etc.,

Wm. Warre.

Lisbon, Nov. 23rd, 1811.

My Dearest Father,

After a very long delay I was at length made very happy by your most kind letter from Cowes.

I quite agree with you about the infamous wine company at Porto, but I think that it cannot stand long, even supposing we are such dupes as to allow the P. Government to infringe so directly on the Treaty. It is a grievous oppression on the farmer, and so generally disliked, that I much doubt, when the terror of French dominion is removed, they will submit either to this or many other oppressions.

O Povo esta mto. desabusado, e seria mto. melhor conceder ehe algums destes privilegios, que em nada contribuem para o bem do estado, mas mto. para o bem de hums poucos de individuos, o menos penso que o que contribue nao sofre o odio de huma tao sega politica.

(The lower classes are greatly undeceived, and it would be much better to concede to them some of these privileges, which in no way contribute to the welfare of the State, but much to the benefit of some few individuals. At least I think that he who takes this course will not incur the odium of such a blind policy.)

I therefore hope to have the happiness of giving you an *abraço* early in the spring, and am not sorry you did not come out at this advanced period of the year, when you would have found very great difficulty in travelling in a country desolate and almost depopulated, in bad weather, and as I could not foresee that our excellent marshal would fall ill again, I had given up all hopes of meeting you in Lisbon, at all events. We were to have moved today, but H. E. has been very unwell, and though now, thank God, much better, our departure cannot take place till the beginning of next month.

He has great confidence in the good effects of a change of air and travelling. I confess I rather dread the effects of any fatigue or cold for him after what happened lately, when a not very long ride quite threw him back. If good wishes, not only from his own family, but from all ranks of the people could avail, he would have been long since well, and it is, and must at all events be, a pleasant reflection to him in illness to see how universally he is regretted, and the fears his illness has raised amongst *almost* the whole nation.

I have not a word of public news to send you. The Prince d'Aremberg, Colonel of the 27th Chasseurs à Cheval, and married to the Empress Josephine's niece, is arrived here, and 1400 prisoners taken at Arroio del Molino by Hill. He is an insignificant looking creature, and not reckoned a great officer. Genl. Bron is not yet arrived. I have dined with the lt.-col. of their 40th Regt. He is a fine intelligent young man, but quite a Frenchman. He lies without the least hesitation. He half cries at times at his misfortune, but, when he has drank a little wine, sings and dances, and seems to forget entirely that he is a prisoner. I am going this morning to take the lt.-col. of 34th F.A. to make some purchases he wants, and then to dine at Hardinge's. I think him steadier a good deal than the other, who is a most amusing companion, and less of a soldier. This man is reserved, but I know what he says is true, and therefore we intend to try what the *bon vin de Bordeaux* will do towards opening his heart, (*cf.* Maxwell's *Life of the Duke of Wellington*, vol. i.) for we often get very interesting information in this way, and, though I hate and despise the fellows, I am rather amused by them now and then.

I think we are likely to remain quiet at Villa Formosa beyond the Coa, where we fix our hdqrs. It was entirely destroyed by the French, but we have had doors and window-shutters put to some of the houses. But I expect we shall *passar m'tos. frios*, and I dread it for the marshal. I do not think the French will make any movement till Ciudad Rodrigo is again distressed for provisions, and then they will probably throw some convoy in which I do not know how we are to prevent, when the Agueda is full and not fordable, unless by a general action beyond it, and that is *most unlikely*, and I therefore do not myself expect that anything more than outpost business perhaps will be done before the spring. The enemy have certainly received great re-inforcements during the course of the year, but even these (say 40,000 men), have not covered the casualties and losses of men in their armies, which are evidently much reduced. I have no reason to alter my opinion about the Spaniards. You know what it is, and I do not expect more from them than I did, and, if Russia does not in the spring declare against Napoleon, the fate of the Peninsula is in my opinion still very doubtful.

As you do not mention anything further in your letters about my business which you said Dr. Domingos wished to be *perfectly secret*, I hope it is given up entirely, and if not, that you will not press it. It would throw me out of the line of my profession, and place me in a situation I do not think I should be fit for, or can like. You however, my dear father, know my situation, and I never willingly have or will act contrary to your opinion or wishes.

A packet is coming in, but I fear we shall not have the letters before the mail for England closes. Yrs., etc., etc.,

Wm. Warre.

Lisbon, Nov. 30, 1811.

My Dearest Father,

I quite agree with you on the subject of the wine company, and do hope we will behave on this occasion with more energy. I hate half measures, and no man in his senses can, I should think, doubt of the ultimate advantage to the country by doing away with this odious and oppressive monopoly, which is only persevered in from the narrow views and interested politics of a few individuals, aided by a little ready money advanced now and then to the government.

Hardinge desires me to thank you in the kindest manner for the seals, and to be also remembered to you.

You really give me credit for more reserve in my letters than I deserve, for I really know nothing, and think we are likely to be quiet for some time. The marshal is, I am happy to say, very much better, though still pale and thin. He is very anxious to move, and I know we shall set out as soon as he prudently can. I suppose in about a week or ten days. . . . Yrs., etc.,

Wm. W.

EXTRACT FROM LETTERS TO HIS SISTERS.

Lisbon, Dec. 6, 1811.

The marshal was to have left this for the army a week ago, and it was his intention to go on Sunday, the day after tomorrow, but a fresh cold will, however, I perceive, detain him some days. He is still very weak and liable to catch cold at the least exposure, which makes me feel quite a horror of his attempting to move at this time of year. But he is very anxious to join the army, and go I see we shall the moment he is able to move. We go to Abrantes first, then Thomar and Coimbra, to inspect the different depots of the recruits, and from thence to the army, to Villa Formoza on the Coa, where we fix our hdqrs. for I daresay the winter.

As I see not the slightest prospect of anything being done, the marshal's health causes my principal anxiety. His loss, or suspension for any time from his duty, would be a very serious misfortune for this country. Everybody feels it and laments his indisposition. It is today very cold, so much so that, as we are not blessed with fireplaces in this country, and have the plague of many doors and windows, all of which require caulking, I can hardly write—and notwithstanding he will go to a review of the Commercial Volunteer Regiment, composed of merchants and gentlemen of Lisbon, who have done all the duties for two years in the town with the greatest zeal and regularity. They are magnificently appointed at their own expense, cavalry and infantry, and upwards of 1300 strong. I wish they were 10 leagues off, that the marshal might not risk a worse cold to pay them a compliment.

We had a most ridiculous hoax here on the 2nd, which put all Lisbon in a ferment. An English officer gave out, and hand bills were spread all over the town, that for a wager of £500 he was to walk across the Tagus, from Belem to the opposite bank, in a pair of cork boots of wonderful construction. The joke took most completely. Everybody was anxious to see this wonderful performance, which was to take place at one o'clock, and even the day before every chaise, mule, horse, donkey, boat or barge, was in requisition, and great prices paid. At an early hour on the 2nd, the beach near Belem was thronged, *grandees* and "little dees," great and small, men, women, and children, of all nations and professions, continued to pour in. The day was very fine and the *coup d'oeil* most beautiful. The river was crowded almost near 1¾ mile with vessels of every description, and the beach and streets with carriages, equestrians, and pedestrians.

At the appointed hour a report was spread that the man could not pass till four on account of the tide, and the mobility and the nobility waited in anxious expectation, though many began to suspect the humbug and plenty retired. I had accidentally got a hint of its being a hoax the day before, and therefore only rode down in the afternoon, and a more laughable or absurd scene I never beheld. The people began to be undeceived, some laughed, some were angry, and meeting in their retreat those who undeceived by the way, went only to laugh at the others, and rallying them most unmercifully made them ten times worse. The Portuguese consoled themselves with the idea that the English were as great fools as themselves. Thinks I to myself, they always are on the subject of wonders. I rode quietly along the pavement and was exceedingly amused with the observations of the people.

I laughed so much that I was hardly able to sit on my horse, and got a little abuse in consequence which I was prepared to answer and laugh at. A great many of my friends were there. To these I bowed respectfully with a malicious smile, and, "how did you like the man with the boots?" Many ladies and gentlemen in order to have a better view took possession of the tower at low water, and were so intent upon the beautiful scene on the river, that they quite forgot that the tide would shut them in, and were obliged to be at the expense of boat hire to take them back to their carriages. Others availed themselves of men's backs, horses, and any conveyance according to their finances, the water being only a few feet deep, but it was really a most ridiculous sight.

Nothing is talked of now in Lisbon but the man with cork boots, and it has given rise to the drollest reports and lies. Some even swear they saw him, and describe his figure, dress, etc. Thinks I to myself, "What a ———." Others say he attempted it and failed. Others that his boots sprung a leak and required caulking. Thinks I to myself, "They all l—." and that is likely, for they have wickedly that vice in this country. . . . We do not move on Sunday, or for some days, as the marshal has again caught a bad cold and is unwell. . . .

Poor Walter has misbehaved, and I have sent him home to his regt. He is a poor devil. His misfortune is to be a great fool.

Lisbon, Dec. 14, 1811.

My Dearest Mother,

The marshal is much better and again talks of leaving Lisbon next Wednesday morning. I hope he will not again relapse, but even if he continues to mend, I am not quite easy about the journey for him at this time of year, and as there is absolutely no prospect of anything being done at present in the way of operations, both armies appearing to have gone very quietly into Winter quarters, I think him very imprudent in venturing, but perhaps the change of air may do him great good.

We go first to Abrantes, Thomar, and Coimbra. I told you I should write a stupid letter, and John Brown is putting all my rhapsodies to flight by his noise. He desires his love to E.'s poodle, and to be remembered to the rest of the family. We are going at 3 o'clock to a grand funeral of Brigadier-General Coleman, who died of fever after suffering a great deal. He is to be buried with military honours. No man ever died more generally or deservedly lamented, and, what is more than anything distressing, is that he leaves his poor father and mother and sisters, who depended on him for support, in rather painful circumstances. His poor old father resigned the office of Sergeant-at-Arms to him *moyennant* a pension, which he loses with his son. I am very sorry for him: what a pity he left the House of Commons to come here at all! ...

I hope the company at Porto's business may be settled to my father's satisfaction, but that he will not come out till the spring, for it is almost impossible to travel in this desolated country in winter. Yrs., etc., etc.,

Wm. W.

CHAPTER 6

1812

During the last three months of the year 1811, Wellington had been secretly preparing for the siege of Ciudad Rodrigo. Almeida was put into a state of defence, and artillery and siege material and stores of all kinds accumulated in that fortress. Meanwhile General Hill to the south by his movements seemed to threaten Badajos, and kept the enemy in expectation of a third attack in that quarter.

On the 1st of January 1812, Wellington, with 35,000 men, moved suddenly upon Ciudad Rodrigo, which was held by the French with a garrison of nearly 2000 men. On the 8th the redoubt on the great Teson was taken by the 52nd Regiment, and on the 19th, two practicable breaches having been made, the assault was ordered, and the town taken by storm—not, however, without loss of men and officers, among whom fell Robert Craufurd, the famous leader of the Light Division.

After securing Ciudad Rodrigo, Wellington lost no time in preparing for the attack on Badajos, which he was determined to take at all cost. A glance at the map shows how with Ciudad Rodrigo and Badajos in the hands of the French, Portugal could not be in any way secure. Before any step could be taken to threaten Madrid, or the northern line of French communications, it was absolutely necessary that both these fortresses should be in the hands of the Allies.

Marshal Beresford, who was now in much better health, reached Elvas on the 6th of March. Within ten days of that date, he had crossed the Guadiana with 15,000 men, and, covered to the east and southeast by the forces under General Hill and General Graham respectively, invested Badajos.

The events of the siege, and the taking of Badajos, are described in the letters, which also are not silent concerning the horrors that followed the assault and capture of the town.

After this success, for which a terrible price had been paid in the loss of nearly 5000 officers and men killed and wounded, no rest was allowed or indeed possible for the Allies. To the south was Soult with nearly 25,000 men, whose advance, however, upon hearing of the fall of Badajos, was checked, and his attention diverted from the allied army, by the movements of Spanish forces in Andalusia and the necessity of saving Seville. To the east was King Joseph with 20,000 men protecting Madrid, from whom, however, there was not for the moment much to fear. But to the north was Marmont with nearly 70,000 men threatening Ciudad Rodrigo. As usual, the movements of the French armies were hampered by the impossibility of finding subsistence in regions already desolated and exhausted by warfare; while combination between them became increasingly difficult, owing to the jealousies and dissensions which reigned among their chiefs. The emperor himself was now far away, and fully occupied with his designs upon Russia.

Upon hearing that Marmont was moving westwards, Wellington hastened from Badajos by forced marches to the north, securing his right flank by the destruction of the bridge over the Tagus at Almaraz, which was effected by General Hill on the 18th of May.

It was now the turn of the Allies to take the offensive in the field, and Wellington determined to attack the so-called army of Portugal under Marmont, whose forces, however, were at the time greater than he supposed.

Accordingly, on the 13th of June, the allied army entered Castile, with Salamanca as its objective.

Marshal Marmont, who was expecting reinforcements, retired before the Allies, and on the 16th of June evacuated Salamanca, leaving, however, some forts, the guns of which commanded the bridge over the Tormes, garrisoned by about 800 men. As the letters show, the strength of these forts was much underrated by the Allies, and they were a cause of considerable annoyance. Their reduction was not effected till the 27th of June.

After this Marmont retired behind the Douro, across which he desired to draw Wellington. The manoeuvres which followed are difficult to describe, or indeed to understand. The armies marched and countermarched, till at last by a skilful manoeuvre Marmont was able to throw his force across the Tormes and to threaten Wellington's line of retreat upon Ciudad Rodrigo. This attempt culminated on the afternoon of 22nd July in the Battle of Salamanca. At the moment when Marmont pushed forward his left under Thomières to gain the high ground, which would enable him to command the road leading to the south-west through Miranda, Wellington, detecting his mistake, launched his attack on the French Army. The battle, which is graphically described in the letters, resulted in the total defeat of the French, with the loss of guns and eagles, and colours, and many generals. Marmont himself was badly wounded, and lost 6000 men killed and wounded, besides 7000 prisoners.

Nor was the loss of the Allies other than severe. General le Marchant was killed, and five generals, including Beresford, wounded, while the death-roll included 41 officers and 658 men, and the other casualties amounted to 253 officers and 4273 men wounded or missing.

When his marshal was wounded, his *A.D.C.* remained and carried him off the field, and with some difficulty conveyed him to Salamanca, where he nursed him through his illness, and accompanied him when convalescent to Lisbon.

With the Battle of Salamanca, the letters come to a conclusion. Major Warre returned to England, and, having received a Staff appointment at the Cape, proceeded thither in 1813.

Letters

Torres Novas, Jany. 4, 1812.

My Dear Father,

We are at length clear of Lisbon, and thus far on our journey to the army. We were to have gone to Abrantes, but the heavy rain has prevented us, and we must therefore make the best of our very indifferent quarters, which are perhaps better than we shall often have, and at least the marshal has a fire in his room. He is much better, and, so long as he is comfortable, we cannot mind how we *A.D.C.'s* are off. We are pretty well used to rough it, and must expect hereafter seldom to meet with even such quarters as these. I am very well in health.

Coimbra, 10th Jany., 1812.

Dearest Mother,

We arrived here the day before yesterday after a tolerably pleasant journey, though we had a good deal of rain the first days. Latterly the weather though very cold has been very fine. And, as we came by the route by which the enemy retreated last year, and the marshal was very communicative and pointed everything out to us, it was extremely interesting. But it was impossible to pass through a country so completely devastated without feelings of horror and pity for suffering humanity. Nothing can exceed the wanton cruelty and barbarity of those wretches. We passed many formerly fine towns nearly entirely burnt or destroyed, and scarcely saw a house or village but shewed evident proofs of their barbarous wanton cruelty and destruction. It is quite impossible to give people in England an adequate idea of the sufferings of these unhappy people. We even at this period saw many people and children absolutely starving and living upon nettles and herbs they gathered in the fields.

We leave this the day, and are to go by the route the French turned our position at Busaco, before, last year, which with the marshal will be highly interesting. The siege of Ciudad Rodrigo is determined upon and will begin about this time. It will be a very instructive lesson to us, and will, I hope, be managed better than that of Badajos. We want experience in these matters, and I am very glad we shall have something to do. If we can succeed in making the French assemble their army at this season and distressed as they are for provisions and transport, we shall gain a great point, as we shall draw them off from the Asturias, Aragon, the neighbourhood of Madrid, and Estremadura, which will be a great diversion in favour of the Spaniards, and as the loss to the enemy must be very great, even if we are obliged to retreat, and to raise the siege, we shall have gained a great deal, and if they let us take the place, which I do not expect, the advantage is evident, as it secures that frontier and gives us an entrance into Castile. According as they collect a greater or less number, we shall fight them, I suppose, or not, and in my humble opinion the whole of this movement is highly judicious, as well as Hill's advance into Estremadura, which will draw off, I trust, Soult's attention from Ballasteros.

We are all quite well, and I think the journey has done the marshal good, as he is in high spirits. The fine weather seems likely to continue, and that we shall join the army without any more wettings, which, though they have done us no harm, are not pleasant, as the weather is very cold.

Wm. W.

Gallegos, Jany. 20, 1812.

My Dearest Father,

I have only just time to tell you that Ciudad Rodrigo is ours. It was taken by storm yesterday evening at 7 o'clock. The batteries had been firing away from 30 24-pounders since the morning of the 14th, and before yesterday evening two breaches, one a very extensive one, and a lesser, were deemed practicable, and the 3rd (Picton's) and the Light Divn. (Craufurd's) were ordered to storm, supported by an attack on the opposite side of the town from Pack's Portuguese Brigade, who were to escalade the wall and take the enemy in the rear.

They were quite prepared, but nothing could resist the ardour and impetuosity of our Troops, and in 20 minutes after the storm began, they were in full possession of the town, and in less than ¼ of an hour Lord Wn. and the marshal were in it in perfect safety from the enemy's *resistance*. Indeed, no part of their staff were much exposed during the whole time, and we are all safe and perfectly well. The regts. employed were the 52nd, 45th, 74th, 88th, 43rd, 95th, and some more British, which I cannot now recollect, the 1st, 2nd, 3rd, 4th, Caçadores, and 16th and 1st Portuguese Infantry.

Our loss in men has been less than we could possibly have expected, had the garrison made a more vigorous *resistance*, but the proportion of officers has been very great. Poor Genl. M'Minnon was killed by the blowing up of a magazine, which killed a great many of our men, and young Beresford of the 88th, the marshal's nephew, is wounded by it, but not dangerously. General Craufurd is wounded, I fear, very badly. General Vandeleur not dangerously, Col. Colborne (52nd) severely, and poor George Napier (52nd), who commanded their storming party, and has been wounded in every action, has lost an arm, but is doing very well. Pray send word to Mrs Gibbs that Gibbs is quite well. Dobbs, poor fellow, is killed.

Ewart, young Dawson, and Royds are quite well. Pray send word to their friends. I am so much hurried and fagged I can hardly write, but I do not wish Major Gordon to go without writing a few lines. I remained in Ciudad Rodrigo last night, and it would have been impossible even for me to form an idea of the horrors and misery of a town taken by storm. It was on fire in several places. It was quite impossible to prevent its being plundered. It was quite dreadful, and the scene which presented itself this morning on the breaches, and the streets, beyond my pen to describe. Another magazine blew up today and destroyed about 50 of the prisoners and a few of our men. It is quite out of my power to do justice to the heroism and gallantry of our troops both British and Portuguese. It is not easy to express my admiration. They seemed to surpass their wonted bravery and intrepid contempt of danger. Nor can I describe the awful feelings of suspense and anxiety before or during the storm. There cannot be a grander or more impressive sight, and I had full time to experience the fulness of these feelings as I was little exposed, or was there indeed time for any danger except to the storming parties, as they drove everything before them, and we scarce thought the business begun when the hurrahs announced their glorious and well-earned victory. The whole siege has been a most interesting and grand sight; and even the French prisoners this morning cannot help expressing their admiration of the gallantry of our artillery and troops. The 88th and 45th have suffered most.

Pack's Portuguese had escaladed the walls, and were in the town, when they heard the hurrahs of the others. There never was a better planned enterprise or more completely successful. Marmont and Dorsenne were collecting to relieve the place, and would arrive 3 days hence, but it is impossible to guess what they will do, now that the place is taken. They cannot be equal to us, and I do not expect they will attempt to disturb us. If they do, I am sure they will repent it. I have not a doubt of the result.

I am perfectly well, though much harassed and tired, but a night's rest will set that to rights. I will certainly write again by packet. Yrs., etc.

Wm. W.

I am so bewildered yet that I cannot collect my ideas. Do not therefore pray shew my letter, and excuse such an incoherent scrawl.

EXTRACTS FROM LETTERS TO SISTERS.

Elvas, March 6, 1812.

I avail myself of the departure of an extra courier for Lisbon to thank you for your letter. . . . We arrived here about an hour ago, all quite well, and think we shall remain for some time, or till the siege of Badajos is over. We came by Villa Viçosa and visited the palace of the P. R. which is without doors or windows, which the soldiers of all parties have gradually burnt. It is a pity, as in one room there are really some fine pictures, painted on the ceiling, of the Dukes of Braganza, which will be quite spoiled. The park is very handsome in their way. We should call it rather a forest, and there are a great many deer, which looked very pretty, but the wild boars, being of a more contemplative, solitary turn, kept themselves concealed, for which want of respect one is ordered to be shot for our table. He had better have made his appearance at once, and had the honour of being shot by a marshal or *a.d.c.*

The weather is very fine and dry, but rather too warm. We have been since the 2nd coming, and had a tolerably pleasant journey, being received everywhere with the greatest honours, bells ringing, guards of honour, illuminations, etc., and never exceeding 5 leagues a day, except the first, so that we were never fatigued, or our horses, and had plenty of time to look about us, and make our observations, and, being with the marshal, we are at least sure of always having plenty to eat. If I could be in good spirits, I should have perhaps enjoyed this mode of travelling through a country in state very much.

As it is, it was rather a bore, and I am glad we are likely to be quiet for a short time anywhere, though a large fortified city full of troops is not exactly the place I should have chosen. The beautiful *quinta* we had here last year is pulled down, house and all, when the suburbs were destroyed for being too near the body of the place, which is now very much improved and strengthened by some very fine new works in front of the town, and which makes it highly respectable, but I could not look at the remains of our beautiful shady walks and fountains without great regret.

Ld. Wn. will not, I believe, arrive for a day or two. The army are on their march, but will not arrive to assemble on this frontier till the 10th or 12th, when I suppose poor old Badajos will be serenaded again. If we succeed as well as we did at Ciudad Rodrigo, we shall do well enough, but a protracted siege is to me the most tiresome thing in the world, and two have quite satisfied my curiosity as far as that goes.

John Campbell is here, very well, but quite disfigured by having his face all covered with his mustachios and whiskers. He is full colonel in the P. service, and desires to be most kindly remembered to you all. He is a very excellent fellow. I wrote yesterday a very hasty scrawl, and thought I should not have any time to write any more as the courier went off, but today Mr Stuart the Envoy, who is here, is sending off one express, and I will therefore not omit to tell you I am in health quite well.

I have just got a note from young Cowell of the guards, who wants me to obtain leave for him to shoot deer, etc., in the Prince's Park at Villa Viçosa, *a pretty modest request*, which I am sorry I cannot comply with, as I cannot obtain leave even for myself.

The style and writing of my letter will shew you the bustle and hurry I am writing in. Every officer in the garrison, and all the authorities, civil and military, have been here to be presented and make their bows, I suppose some hundreds, which, added to a long ride in a hot day, has condensed my powers of composition and made me stupider than usual.

Elvas, March 18, 1812.

My Dear Father,

I did not receive your long and kind letter of the 10th Feby. till the 16th inst., the same day on which I received yours of the 8th of March. I have intended thanking you for both for the last two days, but, as the investment of Badajos was begun on the 16th and completed yesterday, I had not a moment's time, having been almost constantly on horseback. I could wish to have written you a long letter, but I find that at present it is impossible, for though I have remained at home today on purpose, I am a good deal fagged and hurried. . . .

I am very much obliged to you for your most interesting ideas and communications on the politics of the day with you. They are to me most interesting, and I am happy to think that generally on these subjects our sentiments are exactly the same. But I have not now time to enter on the subject. I regret Lord Wellesley's going out, as I have a very high opinion of his talents, and am quite convinced that the surest means of keeping the war ultimately from our own shores, is to persecute it vigorously on the Peninsula, where everything has hitherto been as successful as brilliant both to our interests and national glory. And I fear by his removal from office these exertions may be relaxed, and our brave general not seconded with the zeal he deserves, for I never considered Ld. Castlereagh as a decided public character. . . .

With regard to ——'s letter, I can only say that I should be very sorry to allow any officer to *purchase* the majority over my head, if I could afford to purchase it. If not, it is no use saying anything on the subject. But if I could, ever so well, I do not think it would be worth my while to enter into Colonel ——'s exorbitant demands, and as I do not wish to be like the dog in the manger, I shall not prevent him from making what arrangements he pleases with —— by exchanges, etc. But could I afford it I most decidedly think that, should such a thing offer as direct purchase, I should do very wrong in not taking it, and trusting to my interest to avoid joining.

At present I am literally no more than captn., and must become an effective major before I can either purchase or get a lt.-colonelcy, except by brevet, which I assure you is most improbable, and at all events I could exchange to infantry as major, if by that means I could remain in the country to the end of the campaign. I shall answer —— that he may do as he pleases, as it is not worth my while to give so much, beyond the regulation, for the majority. But, if you can afford to do it, I should be very sorry that he purchased over my head, should —— from length of service be allowed to sell his commission, which from the style of ——'s letter I rather suspect may be the case. *But certainly, even if I had the money, I would not give more than the regulation, or allow any officer to do it over my head,* by informing the agents that I was ready to purchase at the regulation. But if —— chooses to make any bargain with —— by exchanges, etc., I have no objection.

With regard to any place of emolument, or settled situation in this country, I must frankly tell you that there is no rank that they could give me in their service which would induce me to remain *permanently* in it, or beyond the campaign, during which I do not think I can quit it with propriety.

My next situation will probably be the command of some regiment when, by the obtaining my effective majority, the marshal may not be able to keep me on his personal staff. In that, as in every other situation, I shall endeavour to do my duty to this country with zeal and assiduity, while I think my services are required, but no longer than that we are on service, and that there is an English Army in the country, and, while that is the case, I shall use all my interest to remain, however otherwise unpleasant to me. But you may rely on it that, the moment the law of necessity is removed, there will be but little credit and no pleasure to be gained in the Portuguese service under such a government.

The siege of Badajos commenced on the 16th, when the place was partly invested by the marshal, as Ld. Wellington was rather unwell. We had a little skirmishing but of no consequence, and the place was civil enough to fire very little at us, and the lateness of the time the columns arrived prevented the place from being completely invested. Ld. Wn., who is quite well again, thank God, did so yesterday without loss, and yesterday evening they commenced breaking ground in front of the Picorina, a small work in advance of the town, on the other side of the Guadiana, on which side all our attacks seem to be directed and not against St Christopher, which, as well as the town generally, the enemy have greatly improved, and have built a strong redoubt, where our batteries were against St Christopher last year.

The firing this morning has been pretty brisk notwithstanding the heavy rain, which came on last night, and is rather unfortunate for our poor fellows, most of whom, however, have tents. Both hdqrs. were to have encamped yesterday, but by some accident or other, it is put off till tomorrow, when I hope the weather will moderate. Our Hdqrs. Camp is about a mile ½ from the town, and quite out of sight under a little hill, where we shall be snug enough if the weather holds up. If not, we must have *paciencia*, and make the best of it. I have a very good tent. I remained at home today in order to write to you, but I will add to my letter before the courier sets off, and let you know how things go on. I have no doubt that, with the great means we have, we shall take the place, if the enemy give us fair time. But in my opinion a general action is almost certain. I do not for a moment doubt the result, but on it the fate of Badajos will probably depend.

Our battering train is very complete. We have 16 24-lbers. 20 18-lbs. 16 5½-inch. or 24-lb. Howitzers, with 10 18-lbs. in reserve at Evora. The 3rd, 4th, and Light Divisions and the Algarve Brigade, with the necessary artillery and engineers, and 14th Lt. Dns. and 3rd P. Cavalry, are the *Armée de Siege*, and Graham and Hill, the two worthy new knights, command the

Army of Observation, which consists of the 1st, 2nd, 9th, 7th, divisions and some cavalry regts., and occupy from Caçeres by Merida, Almendralejo, Los Santos, Zafra, towards Frejenal, having on their right in the Condado de Niebla the Spanish general Morilho, with about 4000 men, in observation.

Marmont, it is said, is collecting on the Tagus, and I also expect Soult will move up as many troops as they can bring together from all parts for the relief of the town. But, I think, we shall have near 60,000 bayonets, and that is quite enough to beat any force they can collect in a month. The 5th division is on its march up, but I do not know whether it will join the Army of Observation or the siege. The 14th Lt. Dns. arrive here tomorrow, and will, with the 3rd P. Cavalry, take the siege duties.

The only casualties today are 6 or 7 killed or wounded and 1 French officer killed. The trench is as much advanced as can be expected, considering the constant heavy rain which had set in and is very unfortunate for our poor fellows.

Both hdqrs. encamp near Badajos tomorrow.

Lord Wellington will be much obliged to you if you would have the pipe of wine bottled for him, marked with his name, and taken care of for him in a good place till his return, as he wishes to keep it as a *bonne bouche!* I saw young Cowell the day before yesterday. He was quite well, and is a fine gentlemanly fellow as possible, and seems to like the business very much.

General Leith is very well, and on his march here with his division, the 5th. Pray carefully avoid mentioning the probability of a general action, or the badness of the weather, to my mother. I have merely told her that we were encamped at a distance from Badajos to facilitate our communications, which so far is true, and I think my dear sisters also need know nothing about the matter. . . .

Camp before Badajos, 20th.

We have had most dismal weather since we began the siege. It has rained incessantly. It however goes on very well, and our loss in the trenches not very great.

The enemy made a sortie yesterday about 11 to 12 a.m., with about 2500 men, but were repulsed with loss it is supposed of about 300 men. We have also lost some men, but I do not know exactly how many. Poor Capt. Cuthbert, *A.D.C.* to General

173

Picton, was killed by a cannon shot. Lt.-Col. Fletcher, chief engineer, wounded slightly, and some more officers. I hear we had 80 men killed. Some of their dragoons galloped into our Engineer Camp, but of 4, 3 paid the price of their temerity. Hill has taken 4 officers and some few men at Merida, and, if the weather would but hold up, we should go on famously here. The prisoners yesterday say that General Verlet commanded the sortie, and I have also heard that they had two officers killed on 16th. They are keeping up at this moment a brisk fire from the town, which I hope in a few days we shall be able to answer. Our trench runs very near the Fort Picorina. From both parties a pretty brisk fire of musquetry is kept up.

I enclose my answer to —— which, if you approve of, you can deliver; if not, as you know my sentiments on the subject, you can answer for me.

Lord Wellington came into camp yesterday, but we were not able to move till this morning, and have escaped a most boisterous night. I am quite well in health notwithstanding our hard work, and, if the weather would moderate, should be rather glad to be encamped, as it will save some very fatiguing rides. I will send you a return of our forces by my next. At present I have not time, nor after such a long epistle would you wish me to enter into the other subjects of your letter, but I am most happy to find our politics are exactly the same. I am very sorry for poor Farmer's death. Poor Vesey's is melancholy indeed for his family. *C'est la fortune de la guerre.* We never allow people's deaths, who are not nearly connected with us, to disturb us much, or we should always be unhappy. . . . Yrs., etc.,

Wm. W.

It is not easy to write connectedly with such a noisy serenade, but as we are out of danger, we shall soon be accustomed to the noise. You shall hear from me constantly.

EXTRACTS FROM LETTERS TO SISTERS

Camp before Badajos,
March 29, 1812.

I am amused with your complaining of the noise the parrot makes, which prevents, your writing, when I am at this moment, and constantly since the siege began, serenaded by the roar of cannons and musquetry of both sides. We are out of danger, but have all the advantage of the noise, and if I was to write only when we are quiet, my friends would have reason to complain of me, but habit reconciles us to everything, and we sleep as sound in the uproar now as if in Lisbon. They sometimes disturb us at daybreak when the fire is always heavier, and tomorrow and the next day, when the breaching Batteries open, we shall have an additional bass of near 30 great violoncellos.

Pray give my love to Aunt Jane. She would think ill, though I don't, of her own countrymen, if she had seen how coolly Pat put all the "Frinch to dith" in the fort the other night. The Connaughts (88th) have declared that "they will patronise Ld. Welln. no longer if he accepts any 'Campititation' from the governor, for sure, if they can but get a cavity in the wall, they will get in every bit of them"!

You must not quiz my spelling or writing, as, please remember, I am writing in a tent on my bed, and that those varlets the French are making more noise than the parrot. It is really impertinent of them, but they do not know that I am writing to you.

April 3rd.—Quite well.

Camp before Badajos, April 2nd, 1812.

My Dear Father,

Since I wrote to you on the 27th the siege has gone on very well indeed, and the weather has been fine though rather too hot, which has in a great measure made up for the very bad weather we had at the commencement, which certainly retarded us two full days. Our men have worked very hard, notwithstanding the very heavy fire from the place, which the enemy have kept up at times, and which our ricochet batteries did not prevent much, and some of them even suffered very considerably themselves, particularly No. 5, and No. 6, which is a howitzer battery. They are most to our right, and exposed to a commanding fire from the castle.

Though our loss has not hitherto been very great considering, we have to lament that of some very valuable officers, amongst others that of Capt. Mulcaster of the engineers, Lt. Connell of the artillery, two most promising young men and universally esteemed. On the 29th poor Major Thomson, the commg. officer of the 88th, was killed by my side in the 8-gun breaching

175

battery. We had been walking together in the trenches and went down to see how far the battery was advanced, and when it would be ready. The enemy kept up a heavy fire of musquetry on it, as it was only 150 yards from their covered way. We were standing up with Major M'Lean of the 1st Caçadores when they fired at us and hit poor Thomson through the head, and M'Lean had his watch broke. I fortunately jumped down in time and escaped, as they hit instead the sandbag I was leaning against, which did quite as well.

These escapes are not at all extraordinary in our trenches, as our 2nd parallel is nowhere more than 400 yards from the covered way of the town, and in many (places) much less. The 6-gun breaching battery is only 200, and a new one, which is constructing, and will be ready tomorrow morning, much less. But notwithstanding the enemy's fire of shot, shells, grape and musquetry, it is astonishing the little damage they do, or how few men comparatively are hit. The 8-gun breaching battery opened on the 30th against the flank of the bastion of St Maria, with considerable effects, but it drew upon it the whole fire of the place, and suffered a good deal itself.

On the 31st the 12-gun battery of 24-prs. and the 6-gun battery of 18-prs. opened against the right face of the bastion of La Trinidad, with excellent effect, and though it has proved a very tough one, the old wall is now coming down very fast, and as it is more forward a great deal than that on the flank of St Maria, the 6-gun battery was also this morning turned against it, and I have great hopes that on the 4th or 5th at furthest it will be ready for the general assault. It will be a glorious night, and I have not a doubt, though there are great disadvantages to overcome, that we shall take the town, and the enemy will probably retire into the castle, which is an old Moorish or Gothic one, and from whence they will be forced to capitulate, as well as the adjacent forts.

Our artillerymen, both British and Portuguese, have fired extremely well indeed, much better than the enemy, whose fire, though at times very brisk, is very ill directed, and their shells do very little harm, though tolerably well thrown, on account of some mismanagement in their fuses. They either burst too soon, or so late that everybody has time to get out of their way. Yesterday and the day before their fire was heavier than I ever have seen it before in the siege, but today it has been very slack indeed on their side. We have lost two very good Portuguese artillery officers, Captn. Julio Caesar D'Amoral and Barceiros, both very gallant good officers, and Capt. Dundas of the British artillery, and Lieut. Grimes, badly wounded. The former has lost an arm. Major M'Leod of the engineers is doing well. He is a very zealous and good officer.

The conduct of the Portuguese troops during the whole siege, and under very trying circumstances, has been most exemplary, particularly their artillery, which is really very good. It is difficult to say which troops, the British or Portuguese, are the most indifferent to danger. In both it is quite remarkable. But John goes to work more steadily and sullenly, while the Portuguese must be well led, and have his joke. They are great wits in their way, and, without the resolution and impenetrable *sang froid* of the British, which no danger can disturb, they have more patience and subordination under greater privations and hardship. But the Portuguese has not the bodily strength of the former, is naturally lazy, and is not used to our pickaxes and shovels. Therefore, on the working parties the British do their work better in half the time. But both seem equally careless of danger. They agree perfectly well together, and amongst the men there is scarce an instance of disagreement or disturbance.

On the evening of the 30th the enemy made a small sortie with 200 or 300 men against a working party of 200 men of the Algarve Brigade who were constructing a small redoubt, on the other side of the Guadiana opposite St Christopher's Fort Napoleon, and who allowed them to come close up to them, gave them a volley, and drove them in a moment back into their works, leaving their commanding officer and some men dead on the field, since which they have never ventured to molest them, though they are only 2600 men, Portuguese, and part of the 3rd P. Cavalry without a British regiment, the 5th Divn. (Leith's) having marched to Valverde to be ready to join Graham, should it be necessary, which I much doubt, for I hope we shall be in the place before either Soult or Marmont can possibly arrive to relieve it.

With regard to what they are about, we have so many reports, and so different, that I do not know exactly what to believe, but do not think they can collect a sufficient force in time. I think by the 4th or 5th the breaches will be ready for a general assault. We shall lose a great many men, but I have not a doubt we shall take the place.

General Graham's expedition against Drouet did not succeed. The enemy had too good information, or were too vigilant, and they could only come up with their rear-guard of cavalry, and there was a little skirmishing.

Ewart is getting on quite well. His wound was slight through the fleshy part of the arm. All our other friends are well. You will of course, my dear father, not show this letter to ―――― or mention my being exposed at all. There is no occasion for them to know that I have anything to do with the trenches or batteries.

April 3rd.

Our new 6-gun battery (opened) against St Pedro curtain, but I have not yet heard with what effect. An attempt was made last night to blow up the dam which confines the water in the inundation and ditch of the place, but though our fine fellows, Captn. Douglas and Robert Campbell, with their companies, contrived to creep unperceived to the place which is behind the ravelin and St Roque, and about 50 yards from the wall of the town, the explosion had not the desired effect, but we had not a man hurt.

General Graham has returned to Villa Franca. Yrs., etc.,

Wm. Warre.

We have a pretty little spot for our hdqrs. opposite the English *Troupe D'Orée*, under a little hill, which just conceals us from the town, whence they have never molested us, though they sometimes fire along the road 40 yards to our left, and, if we are quite safe, we have at all events all the advantage of the noise, which is at intervals like the rolling of thunder.

Badajos Camp,
April 7.

My Dear Father,

I have the happiness of communicating to you the capture of Badajos by assault last night after a most obstinate resistance, and with, I am grieved to add, as a painful counterpoise to the exaltation of victory, very severe loss.

Since I wrote to you on the 3rd the breaches have become

daily more practicable, and the day before yesterday a new one, which was begun between the two others, was also very forward and yesterday practicable. It was intended to have stormed the day before, but the enemy's defences were considered in too perfect a state, and the fire of most of our batteries was directed for the last two days against the new breach, and to silence and dismount their guns.

The attack took place last night at 10 o'clock. The Light Division was to storm the breach in the flank of the Bastion of St Maria. This consists of 43rd, 52nd, 95th, 1st, and 3rd, P. Caçadores.

The 4th Division (Genl. Colville's), the 7th, 23rd, 48th, 40th, and 27th, were to storm the main breach, while the 3rd Division (Picton's), the 5th, 45th, 88th, 74th, 94th, 77th, with 9 and 21 Portuguese, attacked the castle by escalade, and General Leith's (the 5th Div.), consisting of the 4th, 9th, 1st, 44th, 30th, 38th, were partly in reserve, and partly escaladed a weak part of the town near the Guadiana.

The advances to the breaches were found much more difficult than was expected, having to descend before the main ditch into a very deep *avant fossé*, and the enemy perfectly prepared to receive them with mines, shells, entrenchments, in short, a most excellent system of defence. Our brave fellows did all that men could do, but they were mown down by hundreds, and their officers mostly killed or wounded, and, after losing a great many men, they were repulsed, but fortunately the two attacks which were the least probable, by escalade, having succeeded, Picton having got into the old Moorish castle, which commands the town, and part of Leith's people (General Walker's brigade) on the left, another rush was made at the breaches by part of the light division, and, about daybreak, the town and its adjacent forts were in our possession, with Philippon the governor, a General Weyland, a great many officers, and about 3500 prisoners.

I dare not enter into the detail of our loss. The papers will too soon publish the painful news. Of all my friends Dawson is the only one I can say is safe, and Hunt. The remainder I know nothing of for certain, but that the loss of 52nd, and of that whole division, very great indeed, as well as of the 4th, Generals Bowes, Colville, and Walker, wounded, and poor Gibbs. Merry

52nd Regt. wounded, but not very badly. Jones, Poole, Madden, killed. I am, thank God, quite well, though very much tired and fagged. I was on horseback all yesterday, (and the weather is dreadfully hot,) and all night, or on foot, and such a night, I think, I never spent of suspense, horror, and expectation. I was sent before daybreak, as soon as our men were in the town, to endeavour to establish a communication, across the bridge and *tête de pont*, with Genl. Bowes, who was on that side. I met Lord Fitzroy Somerset, who was going on nearly the same duty, and at the *tête de pont* we found an officer and 40 men, and in Fort St Christopher, whither we heard he had retreated, the Governor Genl. Philippon, General Weyland, and a great many officers, all of whom surrendered immediately, on our summoning them, and the chiefs we conducted to Lord Wellington.

It is most extraordinary that, notwithstanding the obstinate defence, and causes of animosity which our men had, and all their previous determinations, they gave quarter to almost every Frenchman, and I really believe their loss in killed and wounded must be comparatively very small to ours. The marshal and everybody belonging to this hdqrs. escaped unhurt, and are well, as also all Lord Wellington's staff. My friends of the 4th Regt. have suffered very much indeed. There was scarce a regiment engaged that has not, for the fire at the breaches was immense, and from the depth of the ditches, and accumulated means of defence, it appears to me that it was almost impossible for our brave fellows to force them, and it was most fortunate that the side attacks succeeded at the castle and at the bastion of St Vincente. I am so tired I can say no more. God Almighty bless you all. My kindest love. Your most affectionate Son,

Wm. Warre.

(Written across the above)

8th April.

My Dearest Father,

I avail myself of the delay of the officer, who is to carry the despatches, to tell you that I am quite well, notwithstanding the fatigue of the other night which I have nearly got over. I think I never was more completely fagged in my life than I was till I got to bed last night, for mind and body had been on the constant stretch for 36 hours incessantly.

I am just returned from the town, to which I had not been

since the night of the storm. The breaches and advance to them present a dreadful spectacle even now that the wounded are removed. Our loss was very great indeed, particularly in officers. I think, including the losses during the siege, we have upwards of 3000 killed and wounded. Many regiments (had) almost all their officers hit in some way or other, though I do not think the proportion of killed equal to that of the wounded. The town also has suffered much from the effect of three sieges within a year, and being taken by assault, when it was almost impossible to restrain the avarice and licentiousness of the soldiery, which so greatly sullies the brilliancy of their conduct and victory, and forces their officers to blush for the excesses of the very men they before admired as heroes.

Fortunately, a greater part of the inhabitants had quitted the place previously. Those that remained have paid dearly for their folly, and have but little reason to rejoice in the victory of their friends. However, it is perhaps impossible entirely to prevent these excesses, when the place is taken in the manner this was. And it is also as prudent to hold our tongues, and shut our eyes on miseries it is out of our power to prevent, but must deeply feel, and our hearts and wishes naturally but longingly turn to dear, dear old England, and those beloved friends it contains, as we pray Almighty God to preserve them from the horrid scourge of war as the greatest of human miseries.

The enemy's defence was admirably prepared at all points, and does great honour to the talents of the chief engineer, as well as the great improvements he has made in the works of the place since the last siege. Everything bespeaks of great activity and talent, and in a few months hence the conquest would have been much more difficult. Could one forget what rascals these fellows are, one would admire their gallantry and military abilities as they deserve, but they do nothing from laudable motives, and we are forced from many circumstances to attribute even this obstinate defence rather to fear of their relentless Tyrant, than to any motives of honour and proper military spirit.

Their entrenchments behind the breaches, *chevaux de frise* of sword blades, etc., were very formidable, and, added to the difficulty of access to the breaches from heavy fire, made it almost impossible to force them, had not our escalading parties fortunately succeeded. Generals Colville, Walker, Harvey, P. Bowes, and Kemp, are wounded. I had written General Picton, but it was only a contusion from a spent ball and not worth mentioning.

Soult was advancing, but I believe with not sufficient force, to endeavour to relieve the place, and perhaps, in conjunction with Marmont, to have fought us, if necessary, but I now have little doubt that he will retire again towards Seville. His advance was at Villa Franca, but I fear has retired again. We are yet unable to foresee Soult's intentions. He is within 8 leagues of us, his advance guard. But he has not more than 30,000 to 35,000 men, and we could fight nearly double that number. I wish to God he would advance.

Marmont was between the Agueda and Coa threatening Almeida and Ciudad Rodrigo, but I trust he will now be forced to retreat. The latter place is but ill provided with provisions, but Spaniards require little, and it would hold out some time. Unless he retreats, I suspect part of our army will march again towards the north. Marmont, however, cannot at all events subsist there long.

Camp before Badajos,
April 10th, 1812.

My Dear Father,

Though very much pressed for time I will not let the mail go without adding a few lines to what I wrote you the day before yesterday, particularly as I shall be unable tomorrow to wish you many happy returns of your birthday, as I shall go into Elvas.

Our people are now busily employed in filling up the trenches and destroying our batteries. By yesterday evening most of the dead were buried, though from the unavoidable confusion on such occasions and their great number, it was delayed till the spectacle became more horrid than can easily be conceived.

The inhabitants also are beginning to return. Most of them had left at the beginning of the siege, and many to fly from the horror of a storm on the morning that we entered, so that since order was restored on the morning of the 8th, and most of our people except the garrison turned out, the town looks quite deserted, and in many parts is nothing but a miserable heap of ruins. Great pains are taking to clean the streets and clear away the rubbish, which will, I hope, prevent any great sickness from ensuing, and the weather has fortunately become much cooler. Soult had advanced to Villa Franca with about 30,000 men, but hearing that the place was taken, and that Ballasteros had entered Seville, he yesterday morning commenced his retreat again rapidly towards the Sierra Morena, to prevent Ballasteros from attacking the *cartucha* where the French have huge magazines of stores of all kinds. I hope he will in the first place destroy the arsenal and foundry, for he can hardly expect to hold it, if the French were to return in force, which was most probable, and these have been of the greatest use to them. Soult's communication with Victor now and Cadiz must be very difficult.

Marmont also, with about 17,000 men, was between the Agueda and Coa, and threatened Ciudad Rodrigo and Almeida, towards which latter place he had sent about 4000 men to attempt to take it by escalade, but they were repulsed most gallantly by the militia under Trant and Colonel Le Mesurier the governor. Yrs., etc.,

Wm. Warre.

The marshal, Hardinge, etc., are quite well. Gibb's wound is, I hope, not bad. Merry (52nd) is dead of his.

Nava, on the Road between
Sabugal and Alfaiates,
April 24, 1812.

My Dearest Father,

Having just heard that the mail is detained I will not miss telling you that I am well. I wrote yesterday to Jack, but in such a hurry that I had not even time to read my letter over, and fear he will have much difficulty in reading and making sense of my letter, as I was obliged to write standing on an old broken chest at Malcato, and am now using the same description of table, though with the luxury of an old broken chair. It is impossible to give you an adequate idea of the misery in every village into which the enemy have entered, as they have destroyed everything that they could not carry away, and in my present habitation a considerable part of the floor has been torn up, and the windows, doors, and furniture burnt, except my old chair and chest, which appear to have placed the flames at defiance. Hunger and famine surround us in all directions among the unhappy peasantry, and our charity to some few has now completely exhausted our means. Money is of little use where nothing is to be bought. All our forage for our horses, for the last two days, consists in what we can cut in the fields, which even have not escaped the rapacity of the enemy.

Marmont has retreated across the Agueda, and is I believe in full march to Salamanca. We have communicated with both Almeida and Ciudad Rodrigo. I do not myself think that Ld. Wn. can pursue them much farther as the country is a desert, and our supplies very distant, owing to his rapid and long march of 200 miles since the 14th inst. As far as Castello Branco we had most wretched weather, but latterly it has been fine, though cold.

Thus, has ended Marshal Marmont's grand diversion with his whole army. He advanced to Castello Branco, Covilhao, and Fundao, plundered the already often plundered places between them and the Frontier, and drove away some cattle. He blockaded Ciudad Rodrigo, and threatened Almeida, but was warmly received on a reconnaissance he made there, and never made any further attempt.

His army has suffered dreadfully from want. The prisoners and deserters describe it as equal to when they retired from the Lines, and the few cattle he could catch in this mountainous country could afford him a very scanty and precarious supply. The moment we crossed the Tagus he fell back, the division on his left upon Peña Maior and Sabugal, and we were in hopes for a day or two that he would wait for us, but that soon vanished, for as we advanced, he fell back, and finally across the Agueda without waiting even to see our advance guard. Had Badajos held out some time longer this diversion might have been of some consequence, as Ciudad Rodrigo would have been much distressed for provisions, and Almeida not in the safest state of defence. As it is, all he has got has been his trouble for his pains, great sufferings to his army, and a hasty retreat before an army but very little superior in numbers to his own.

Lord Wn.'s rapid movement appears to have astonished him a good deal, and hitherto the army has suffered no privations. Those we do are owing to the ignorance and obstinate indolence of the Portuguese commissariat. I am perfectly ignorant of Ld. Wn.'s intentions, but should not imagine we should advance much further for the present. Tomorrow we move to Fuente Guinaldo, 4 leagues. We were to have gone there today, but the enemy was still with their advances too near for hdqrs., or rather were supposed to be, for it appears they retired last night.

Our approaches at Badajos have been filled up and levelled and the breaches put in some temporary state of defence. We have therefore nothing to fear from that quarter, as Soult is fully occupied in keeping Andalusia. Had Badajos not fallen, and that he had persevered in advancing, he would have got a famous licking, as we should have been equal at least to him, leaving 10,000 men to carry on the siege. But Ballasteros' advance to Seville embarrassed him very much, and a defeat would be ruinous to him, or Marmont, who to the great disappointment of our army seems determined not to risk it.

I am perfectly well, though we have all had a good deal of fatigue and knocking about in this wretched Beira. I fear our horses will suffer most, which annoys me more than anything, and a person must be more hardened than I am to warfare to be either very happy, or in good spirits, surrounded as we are by scenes of misery and distress beyond what we can give our happy countrymen in England an idea of. I do not think it by any means improbable that we shall return to the Alemtejo, and that the active scenes of this campaign, which is far from being over, will be in Spanish Estremadura. But this is mere conjecture. The present object is to revictual Ciudad Rodrigo and Almeida, and place them in a respectable state of defence. I hear very well of the Spanish garrison of the former.

All our wounded at Badajos are, I understand, doing extremely well. This change of weather from great heat to cool and rain has been quite providential and saved many lives.

The marshal, Hardinge, Arbuthnot, etc., are quite well. Hardinge got a shot through his coat at the assault, and as usual behaved with great zeal and courage. Sewell is, poor fellow, ill again and must return to England. I fear much that his is a bad case. Yrs., etc.,

Wm. Warre.

Ld. Wn.'s Hdqrs. are at Alfaiates today, as badly off as we are. Tomorrow he will be at Fuente Guinaldo.

P.S.—I have written on two half sheets for the best reason in the world!

Fuente Guinaldo, May 20, 1812.

I must begin in order to prepare you for the worst by telling you that this is a very stupid place, that I am very stupid, and that I have nothing to say, and therefore you must receive a very stupid letter.

I am quite well, though we are all heartily tired of Fuente Guinaldo where our only amusement is hunting. Yesterday we went out to a grand *chassé au sanglier*, but the only bore we got was a great wetting, for it rained incessantly after we were posted behind trees and rocks, and while a great many peasants were driving the woods towards us, and not a single boar or wolf made its appearance. We were so completely wet through that when I tried to fire at a fox which passed close to me, my gun missed fire, being quite wet, and we returned home two leagues in despair. It would have been a very pretty scene if the weather had been fine, as we went out a large party, and a great many peasants, and all in great glee.

We should have found some wild animals, as there are a great many, particularly wolves, who have had the impudence to walk away with several mules and horses from this place, but it rained so heavily, that both the wolves and boars remained at home, and were not to be seen, and we became cold geese for going to see them in such weather. We hope before we leave this to have another hunting party, as it must be a very gay and fine spectacle in fine weather. The peasantry are obliged by law to go out on these occasions, as the destruction of these animals is beneficial to the whole community. The people that are armed are placed behind trees or rocks, or hid in the brushwood forming a sort of chain round a particular part of the mountain, and the remainder go in with dogs, and by their shouts and noise drive the animals towards you. . . .

We do not know when we are to leave this place, or in what direction we are to move. It is so great a secret and so well kept that I cannot even guess it, but I am sure I shall have no great regret for Guinaldo whichever way we go. . . . I can hardly write at all, and to add to my misfortunes they have just been trying a poor devil of a commissary at the same table, and I wonder I have not entered some minutes of his examination.

My Dear Father,

I had yesterday the pleasure to receive your very affectionate and kind letter, and with all my soul I thank you for all the solicitude you express about me, and congratulations on my escape at Badajos. I have hitherto been very fortunate, and have much cause to be grateful to Almighty God for his infinite goodness in protecting me. It appears to mortals almost a lottery. Some are never hit, while others less exposed never go into action without.

I felt painfully the loss of so many friends, but in this profession, we dare not long indulge or admit such feelings. It would but ensure continued misery, and such is the force of habit or prejudice that one scarcely feels for the death of a friend in action, whose death if from illness or other cause would be a source of real affliction; and fortunate it is that it is so. We are all quite well here (barring a broken shin I got from a stone, which has confined me for a day or two, but is now getting well) and all most anxious for a move, though it is yet a secret which way it is to be. As far as conjecture goes, I do not think we shall recross the Tagus, for the present at all events, and probably move forward towards Salamanca.

Sir Rowland Hill's success at Almaraz has put us all in great spirits, and must have puzzled the enemy a good deal as to Lord Wellington's plans. This affair has been conducted with his usual judgement and gallantry. The general had arrived by a rapid march in front of the enemy's works at Mirabete, which is a strong pass over the mountains leading to the bridge at Almaraz, and about a league distant from it, but he was delayed here a few days, as he found the works were not to be carried by a *coup de main*, nor could he while they were in the enemy's possession get his artillery over the steep rocky mountains in order to attack the forts, which protected more immediately the enemy's arsenal, barracks, bridge, etc.

He therefore left it behind, and a corps to observe the fort, and made his infantry scramble over the mountains with nothing but their fire-locks, and immediately attacked with the greatest gallantry the enemy's works on the other side of the river, and carried them, turning their fire on those which they had over the bridge on this side, which they were forced to abandon, and he got possession of the whole, except those at Mirabete, with the loss of only two captns. killed, about 9 officers wounded, 25 men killed, and 120 or 130 wounded. I have not seen the return. The enemy lost 300 taken prisoners, and 200 were drowned by the bridge giving way, or killed. 300 cars of different descriptions, the bridge, arsenal, and barracks they had constructed, a large depot of stores and provisions, all the works, and two large pontoons they had on the stocks, completely destroyed, and the communication the most direct between the north of Spain and Castile cut off, which must annoy the French very much, and force them to communicate by the bridge of Arçobispo, which is considerably about. Major Currie, *A.D.C.* to Sir R. Hill, goes home with the account, but as he goes by the packet, which has been detained, I think it the surest way to send this in the mail.

The enemy on hearing of this affair have evacuated Ledesma, and only left a very small garrison to take care of their sick at Salamanca, which shows that they do not think of opposing us should we move on in that direction.

Hill had moved again towards Medellin and Don Benito, which will force the enemy to withdraw the small parties they have in that neighbourhood, or advance in force, which I do not think they are likely to do.

Lord Wellington has adopted a new plan in order to derive a more effectual assistance from the Spaniards. Each British regiment, except the guards and dragoons, are allowed to enlist ten men per company of a certain stature, 5 ft. 6 inches, who are to be in every respect treated as British soldiers, to serve as long as the army remains in the Peninsula, and then to have a month's pay to take them to their homes. I think it is a most excellent plan, and I have very little doubt we shall very soon get the whole number, 5000, and they will make excellent recruits, for in point of activity and fineness of appearance the Spanish peasantry are certainly inferior to none, and this measure may hereafter serve as a foundation for a more regular Spanish Army, and Napoleon will be greatly annoyed at our having adopted this measure of filling up our casualties, without draining England, and with recruits little inferior to our own in appearance or physical strength.

I went yesterday to a review of the Light Division, 43rd, 52nd, 95th, 1 and 3 Caçadores, and a troop of R. Artillery. It was a most animating sight, and they moved very well. Ld. Wn. was apparently much satisfied with them. They are getting very strong again in numbers, nearly 3000 in the field, but very weak in officers from the losses at Cd. Rodrigo and Badajos.

(Remainder of letter wanting)

(On a small sheet separate.)

May 30th.

The mail has been detained, and I therefore open my letter to add that Hill has returned to his old positions after resting his troops a few days at Truxillo. Graham has also returned to his cantonments at Port Alegre, having advanced to Caçeres and Albuquerque to support Hamilton's division, in case Drouet had thought proper to assault it in Hill's absence. Everything is quiet in our front. I am laid up with my broken shin, but more from prudence than necessity. As we are likely to move soon, I thought it best to get it well while I could, for fear that by moving in the heat is might give me a great deal of trouble. It was deep and, on the bone, and I sillily neglected it at first. It is now getting much better. The marshal is quite well. Poor Sewell has left us and gone home ill, I fear very seriously so, whether from his liver or consumption. . . .

Pray see about the places I mentioned, what can be done about them. They are highly desirable in every point of view, and there are several of the same description abroad, but I have no great fancy to go to the West Indies or further East than the Cape, though should such a situation be offered me in the East, I scarce think I could refuse it. . . .

Salamanca, June 17, 1812.

My Dearest Mother,

I have hesitated whether I should write to you to thank you for yours of 30th of May, or to my father for his of 21st and 27th. . .

. . . We arrived here yesterday, the enemy having retired towards the River Douro, only leaving a small garrison in a fort they have made in the town round the convent of St Vicente, and round which they have pulled down all the houses. It is, however, a very bad fortification and was not finished. I have therefore no idea that it can stand a day, when our battery opens, which will be tomorrow morning. We are quite out of danger in this part of the town and very comfortably quartered.

The army crossed the Agueda in 3 columns on the 13th. The right, commanded by Sir J. Graham, marched by Tamames; the centre, by General Leith, marched by San Meñios; and the left, by General Picton, by St Espiritu and Martin d'El Rio. These roads run parallel very near to each other, so that the army was nearly assembled every night. On the 13th the River Yettes, the 14th the Huebra, and the 15th the Valmaza. We saw nothing of the enemy till the 15th. When about two leagues from this the advance guard fell in with some cavalry, about 5 regts. supported by 1500 infantry, near the town, with which our cavalry skirmished with very little loss, and as our columns advanced gradually drove them back upon the city, within two miles of which our posts were established. They took from the enemy an officer and about 20 men. Our loss is 3 officers wounded slightly, and about 7 men wounded and some horses.

Yesterday at 1 a.m. Marmont left this, with his cavalry, taking the road to Toro, and only leaving a garrison in the fort or convent, which appears to me sacrificed, for they cannot hold out. Our cavalry passed the Tormes without opposition and occupied the town, avoiding the streets which lead to the fort, and the left column and advance guard moving to the villages in front of this, and the greater part of the cavalry.

The enemy attacked the cavalry picquets in the evening, but were immediately driven back, and today, when we rode out at daybreak, we could only see them at a great distance, where I suppose they will watch our movements, but most probably retire as we advance towards the Douro, which appears to be Ld. Wn.'s plan, and the French have yet no force to meet our army. But I do not suppose Ld. Wellington will himself advance further than that, but he keeps his plans a profound secret, and the whole army follow him with confidence and affection wherever he chooses to lead us.

We have been everywhere received with the greatest cordiality and joy by the Spaniards as their deliverers from the oppressive tyranny of the French, much more than ever I saw before. At this place yesterday it was quite affecting to see the joy of the inhabitants. Many absolutely cried for joy, and we were embraced, or had to shake hands with everybody we met. One old woman hugged and kissed Ld. Wn. to his great annoyance, and one man literally kissed my horse as I rode into the town. We were followed through the streets with cheers and *vivas*, which have annoyed the Frenchmen a good deal, and they revenged themselves by firing at everyone they saw in the cross streets leading to their works. They have pulled down a considerable part of the town to lay open the space round them, and down to the bridge, over which nobody can as yet pass safely. But in two days I hope they must surrender, or be taken by storm. It is such an insignificant place that nobody except the troops immediately employed in making the battery or covering the workmen, seem to trouble their heads about them, and walk about the streets, men, women, and children, in perfect safety and with the greatest unconcern.

I am perfectly well though a little fagged, as we have for the last few days had an active life both for mind and body. We generally get up at 3 o'clock and ride till 11 or 12, and sometimes again in the evening. Everything is done to avoid the heat of the day, which, however, has not been very great, as we are very high above the sea in this part of the country. There is almost always a breeze, and at this moment the Bejar mountains, which are at no great distance, are covered with snow.

Parts of this fine city have suffered very much from the enemy, who have destroyed part of it to make their fort, and yesterday burnt a suburb that was near it, but notwithstanding there are some beautiful buildings left, particularly the cathedral, which is magnificent. But the monsters fired at the steeple yesterday and knocked away a very beautiful buttress, and nobody is allowed to go there, to avoid drawing their attention in that direction at all. I quite agree with you about the state of the country (*sc.* England). It is most lamentable though most disgraceful at the time, that in the middle of peace our worthless manufacturers, excited by still more worthless because wiser politicians, are killing and rioting amongst themselves.

In this town, yesterday evening, the people were, in the very centre of warfare, dancing and gay in almost every street. Such are the dispensations of Providence. There is no accounting for such things, and it shows how little people know when they ought to be happy and contented, and how unjust to repine at whatever our fate may be. But it is human nature, and I blush to think that I must cease to consider the British the high-minded generous people they used to be. It can hardly be believed that Englishmen could glory in the most cowardly of all revenge, that of assassination, with which they have so often rebuked other nations.

Your countrymen (*sc.* the Irish) have behaved very well, and most sincerely I wish them the reward they deserve, and every civil liberty which is compatible with the Constitution of the State. I have written a very stupid and hurried letter, which pray excuse as I have been up since 3 o'clock, and did not go to bed till past 11, besides a long ride, but I never was in better health in my life, and so are the whole army. Yrs., etc.,

Wm. Warre.

I am so tired I can hardly write, so pray excuse my stupid letter to my dear father.

Salamanca, 25th June 1812.

My Dearest Father,

I have been too constantly occupied since the 17th to write even a few lines to anybody. I gave in my letter of that date some account of our advance to this place. . . .

We have had a most interesting though harassing time of it since I wrote. On the 18th we began to fire at the fort, from a convent near it, with field-pieces, and next day, finding it much stronger than was expected, 4 iron 18-prs. were mounted, which knocked down very soon one end of the convent, but the works, which we found to be by no means so easily forced, were not at all injured, and the enemy seemed determined to make a gallant resistance.

On the 19th, in the morning, accounts arrived that Marmont and his whole army were advancing in sight. The 6th Division under Clinton was therefore left to carry on the attack of the forts, and the rest of the army assembled in a position tolerably strong for an army of equal strength, the left near St Christoval de la Cuesta extending in rear of Castillejos de Morisco and Morisco towards the Tormes, from which our right, however, was some distance, though the ground is strong and we could easily move to it if all attacked in that direction. The Spanish corps of about 3000 men under Don Carlos d'Espanha, and 800 cavalry guerrillas under Dn. Julian Sanchez, were on our left on some strong ground in continuation of our line.

On arriving there we distinctly saw the French Army advancing towards us from Toro, by Aldea Nueva, Archidiacono, etc., etc., in heavy columns of infantry with a strong advance guard, and about 3000 cavalry.

The day was very unfavourable, as we had heavy rains and thunderstorms, which however have cooled the air, and since been of great use to us. During the night of the 20th the enemy advanced, and occupied the ground within cannon range of our position, and the villages of Castillejos and Morisco, concealing their numbers by the inequalities of the ground, and certainly giving us every occasion to believe they had come down determined to fight, which everybody was glad of, as it would save a great deal of trouble in going after them, away from our resources, and which we could not do till we had taken the fort in the town, which completely commands and prevents our making any use of the bridge.

Nothing, however, was done on the 20th, except a pretty brisk cannonade towards evening on both sides, though it did not last long. We lost a few horses of the heavy dragoons, and there was some skirmishing on the right with the 11th Lt. Dns. and 1st German Hussars.

On the 21st the enemy continued all day to receive very strong reinforcements. We were so close, and overlooked their position so completely, that we could see everything that entered their lines and every movement they made.

Everybody expected that they would have attacked next morning, as it was known that Marmont had received every succour he could, except Bonnet's division from the Asturias, which was not expected to be coming up, but we were again disappointed. They only occupied a small hill on our right near Morisco, which overlooked our position, but from which they were driven by part of the 7th division, which cost about 60 or 70 killed and wounded, but the enemy's cavalry and infantry must have suffered a good deal from our cannonade and musquetry, as they were very close to each other.

The enemy seemed jealous of their left flank, which was not at all secure, and moved the greater part of his cavalry, and a column of infantry to strengthen it, but nothing more was done, except that our cavalry chased Marmont, who had advanced a good way to our left to reconnoitre, but he had some Infantry with him and they could do nothing against it. The enemy fired a few cannon shot at them, which did very little harm.

The next morning, to our great surprise, we found the enemy had retired, and when the day broke saw them moving off at a short distance towards our right, and then halted on some heights, about 6 miles in front of our position. The cavalry was sent forward to pursue them, and took up a line of vedettes very near them. Lord Wellington and the marshal rode out to reconnoitre them, but I do not think anybody could make out anything of their intentions. We were very close to them, and they appeared to be halted near Aldea Rubia, and Morréra, to allow their baggage to move off to the rear, which, however, does not seem to have been the case, for they are still there.

We thought this morning that they had retired further, in consequence of which we returned early to this place and the baggage was ordered up, but I have just heard that they are still near the same ground.

Marmont yesterday crossed the Tormes with about 5000 men, cavalry and infantry, to manoeuvre to get Lord Wn. from his position, I suppose, or to endeavour to get off the garrison of the fort, which still holds out. But not succeeding they returned in the evening, having contented themselves with cannonading the heavy cavalry of the German Legion, who behaved with great steadiness and gallantry and have received Ld. Wn's. thanks. Several divisions were moved to our right, ready to cross, and the 1st div. was at the ford of Sta. Martha. The 7th went over to prevent any attempt towards the bridge of the town and to support our cavalry. The whole day was spent in manoeuvring. After the unaccountable movements of the enemy lately, it is impossible even to guess the probable result of all these movements. I think a general action probable. Till they retired, I thought it was inevitable. For I suppose there was scarcely ever such a thing heard of as two hostile armies being without any obstacle between them, the lines within cannon shot of one another, and the advanced vedettes short musket shot, without a battle.

Marmont, I think, certainly intended to fight, but his courage failed him. Our position is tolerable but very extensive, and we have thrown up some parapets to cover the artillery. From the enemy's lines they could not see our force, and could have but little idea either of its strength or disposition. I have not a doubt that we should have beat him, and shall now, whenever he chooses to fight us, even though joined by Bonnet from the Asturias, which an officer of theirs, who deserted this morning, says they expect would be in two days, and that he was at Valladolid yesterday. But this is not believed generally, and he certainly shows no inclination to fight until he arrives.

Some people say that it is a pity Lord Wn. did not attack him on the 20th before his reinforcements arrived, and when he was so near us.

But I think Ld. Wn. knows what is right to do. He must to have attacked him given up the advantage of his position, and advanced along a plain a very great distance, without any cover, exposed to a heavy fire. He must have forced two villages, and his loss would be much greater than by waiting for the enemy, and a very great victory to his army would almost be a defeat. For if this army gets crippled very much it cannot continue the operations. For my own part I feel perfect confidence in anything he decides upon, though I shall be glad of anything that will give us a few days' rest, and I think we had better fight them here than further on.

Our mode of life has been latterly extremely harassing. On the march up we turned out at 3 a.m. and only marched part of the day. Latterly, as the marshal has generally returned 5 or 6 miles to town, we usually rise at 1 a.m. and often, after either riding all day, or broiling in the sun, on a position, which has not a twig to defend us from the sun, or a drop of water but at a distance, we do not get anything to eat, or home till 9 or 10 at night, and rise again at one, so that we are all completely tired, and our faces so burnt that we cannot bear to touch them. The weather, however, has been very favourable, as there has always been a breeze. The mornings are very cold, but the whole army are extremely healthy, and I am quite well. I had hoped these vagabonds were off, and that we should have had a good night's sleep instead of 3 hours, but I suspect that we shall move as usual at one, and therefore took a nap this morning.

The fort still holds out. Some 24-lb howitzers have fired with the 10-prs. against it, and a large part of the building of the convent was knocked down, but the works are otherwise unimpaired. It was attempted to be stormed on the night of the 23rd but failed. We lost some officers and about 150 men killed and wounded. Poor General Bowes, who was wounded at Badajos, is killed, I believe, and Sir George Colquhoun of the Queen's. The *commandant* had been previously summoned to surrender, but, while the flag of truce was up, he answered that he had had a communication from his army, and would listen to no proposals. I hope he will now be given no terms. He deserves to be cut to pieces with his garrison, not for his obstinate defence of the fort, that is right enough, but for his wanton and cruel barbarity in firing upon the town and killing or wounding several people, or for firing and defacing the beautiful cathedral, one of the most magnificent works in Europe, without a shadow of utility, and from mere love of mischief. We have been obliged to desist from firing for want of ammunition, but I hope the day after tomorrow we shall have enough in, and, unless Mr Marmont can beat us before that, I think we shall knock the place about his ears.

Their loss inside has already been very great we know, and if the fellow had only defended himself like a gentleman, everybody would have admired his defence.

There seem great doubts whether or not Bonnet is coming up from the Asturias to join Marmont, though the deserters say he is, but, whether or no, I think we need be under no alarm for the result of a battle. Soult is said to be advancing from the South, and Hill has taken up his old position at Albuera. . . .

The enemy in the villages they have entered have proceeded with their usual barbarity, unroofed and quite destroyed them *de fond en comble*, (from top to bottom). I could never give you an idea of the scenes we witness of misery and suffering, nor do I wish to attempt it. . . .

Of your domestic news in England I say nothing. The Ministry, and a country, showing that they have lost that noble, generous spirit for which they were so remarkable, are not very cheering topics, and I am too much fagged to dwell on anything so disgusting. I wish we had some of the *soi-disant* patriots here for a month. Yrs., etc.,

Wm. Warre.

The marshal is, thank God, perfectly well, and so is Ld. Wn., which, considering all his mind and body go through, is wonderful.

My Dearest Father,

Since I wrote to you on the 25th from Salamanca a very hasty letter, our military situation has altered very much, and you will see by the map that we are already two marches in advance. The forts at Salamanca, which had given us more trouble than was at first expected, were taken on the morning of the 27th. On the evening of the 26th, our reserve ammunition having arrived, a battery was opened against the rear of the advanced fort of St Catano with excellent effect, and the convent of St Vicente, in the principal Fort, was set on fire by red hot shot, but as night came on, and the breach in St Catano was not practicable, the firing ceased from the Batteries till morning. The enemy kept up their fire with great briskness the whole evening, but we lost very few men.

In the morning the firing was renewed, and when we returned from the position with Ld. Welln., it was found that the breach in the outwork was practicable, and the convent in a famous blaze. The garrison appeared cowed and in considerable confusion and fired very little. The morning had been rainy and unpleasant, but towards 10 o'clock it cleared and everything was ready for the assault, when the enemy sent out several flags of truce, but it appeared that they only wanted to gain time and perhaps put out the fire. They asked 3 hours to consider it, but as we had no time to lose, the fort was attacked, and surrendered with very little resistance, and was taken possession of by our troops. We had only one man killed, and 5 or 6 wounded, even at the points assaulted, and our people behaved with their usual humanity to the enemy.

We found these forts a great deal stronger than we had any idea of, with deep ditches, the whole faced with strong masonry, the stones for which they took from about a 3rd of the town and some of the most beautiful buildings which they had pulled down to make an esplanade round their works. They also had excellent casements and splinter proofs, and but for the circumstance of the place being on fire, they did not appear to have any more reason to surrender now, as far as their works went, than the first day.

The enemy had between 500 and 600 men in them, and the

commandant who did his duty very well, and is a fine young man enough, told me they had 3 officers killed, 11 wounded, 40 men killed and about 140 wounded during the siege. They had mounted 29 guns and 7 howitzers; a large quantity of ammunition and stores of all descriptions for their whole army, clothing, provisions, etc.

The flames gained so fast that it was impossible to extinguish them, and it was feared that the magazine would blow up. The wounded were therefore removed as quickly as possible, and some of the stores that evening, and nobody allowed to go near it. It, however, fortunately did not explode, and all that was not burnt has been removed, and proper officers have been left completely to demolish the forts.

The capture of these forts was of the greatest consequence, as they most completely commanded the bridge over the Tormes, and gave the enemy, in case of any accident, a nearer way to cross than we had by the fords; besides opening a direct and easier communication for our provisions, etc.

On the 27th, next morning as the day broke, we found that Marmont had retired, and on advancing about two leagues to reconnoitre him with the cavalry, we came up with his rearguard near Pitiegna, who retired on our approach. The enemy seemed to take the road to Valladolid, retiring rapidly. Yesterday our whole army advanced in three columns, the advance guard to Aldea Nueva de Figueroa and Parada de Rubiales, and the army to near the little stream of Orbada, at which place were Ld. Wellington's Hdqrs., and ours at Pajares.

Today the army has again advanced to the River Guarena, the left at Fuente Sanco, and advance at Guaratte.

Ld. Wn.'s Hdqrs. are at Fuenta da Capeña, the right of the army near Castrillo, and our hdqrs. at this place.

The whole army continue healthy and in high spirits. We have only seen the enemy's posts at a distance, and their army, it appears to have crossed the Douro, over which they have destroyed all the bridges except those of Toro and Zamorra. It is impossible to know what Ld. Wn.'s intentions are. The position at Toro is very strong, and 6 leagues from hence.

General D'Urban with about 1000 P. cavalry are manoeuvring in rear of the enemy, and the Galician Army under Santo Cildes is also at Astorga trying to take the French fort, or advanced on their rear. He has, I believe, about 15,000 men.

Mina and Longa's guerillas and Mendizabels corps are near Burgos or Valladolid. Therefore, the enemy will find himself *assez reserré* (pretty tight), but whether Lord W. intends to force his position, or to manoeuvre to make him quit it without an action, it is, I believe, known to himself, the marshal, and Sir T. Graham alone. We feel quite confident in what he may think proper, and a day or two will show. I do not think he will fight if he can do without. But if he does, I have no doubt we shall beat them most completely.

In Estremadura Drouet, finding General Hill steady, has retired from Villa Franca, and our people have moved forward to Sta. Martha, etc., etc. Nothing can exceed the joy of all classes of the people of this country at their delivery from their insolent oppressors. For two nights after the fort was taken, they were dancing and singing all night in almost every street (which were illuminated), nothing was heard but the tabor and pipe and castanets. Next morning there was a grand *Te Deum* in the cathedral, and the town gave a ball in the evening, to which, however, not many officers went, as it began at 10, and we were to march at half past 3, and had not had 4 hours' sleep (at least staff officers) any night since the 19th, so that we were very glad to get some rest.

I amongst others did not go. I never was in better health in my life notwithstanding the really harassing, fatiguing time we have had latterly for mind and body. The weather has fortunately not been very hot, and we have had a constant breeze, or I scarce know what we should have done on that scorching hill all day without shelter of any description, or water. . . .

I hear Admiral Martin is coming to Lisbon to supersede the Berkeleys. I think you know him, or that my uncles do. He can be sometimes very useful to me, and I therefore wish you would continue to have me strongly recommended to him. The old administration continuing in has astonished us not a little. I should hardly think it could stand. Yrs., etc.,

Wm. Warre.

We look anxiously towards Russia, and I hope they will not fight a general action but retire and draw the tyrant on. If they fight, they will be beat, I fear.

The marshal and Lord Wn. are perfectly well, which I wonder

at, for they have scarce a moment's rest for mind and body. Sir T. Graham has equally not had a moment quiet, and I am sorry to say had a painful disorder in one of his eyes. He is one of the most excellent, worthy men I know anywhere, and like Hill beloved by everybody. Ferguson is arrived at Lisbon, and I am sorry to say has been unwell. I saw Genl. Leith today quite well. He desired to be most kindly remembered to you, as do Le Marchant, Hardinge, Douglas, and the marshal.

La Seca, Province of Valladolid,
July 7th, 1812.

My Dear Father,

Since I wrote to you on the 30th from Villa Escusa the enemy have gradually retired, and the Allied Army have occupied on the 1st a bivouac on the River Trabancos with headquarters at Alaejos, and on the 2nd it moved towards the River Zapardiel, with the right at Medina del Campo, and the left extending towards Torrecilla, while Lord Wellington moved himself with the cavalry light division and Pack's Portuguese brigade, supported by the 3rd divn. and the Spanish Infantry and Bradford's P. bge., on Rueda, to induce the enemy to cross the Douro at Tordesillas, while the main body of the army moved parallel to it so as to threaten their communication with Madrid.

At Rueda we came up with the enemy's rear-guard, and a sharp skirmish and cannonade took place in which the enemy lost considerably owing to not bringing up their guns till very late in the day, and our loss was only a few horses. They gradually retired, and as we gained the high ground between Rueda and Tordesillas, we could distinctly see the greater part of the enemy's army formed in large massive columns covered by their cavalry preparing to cross the river, which they did in the course of the day without Ld. Welln. being able to interrupt them, as he had only his cavalry and advance guard up. In the evening he took up his hdqrs. at Villa Verde, and the marshal at Nava del Rey.

The army has been nearly in the same positions ever since, but on the 4th he moved to Rueda and the marshal to this place (La Seca). The troops are placed so as to watch the different fords of the Douro, and be ready to move at once in any direction circumstances may require, and are extremely healthy and in high spirits.

The 3rd division and Spaniards under Don Carlos d'Espanhana are near Polios on the Douro watching the fords.

On the 3rd Ld.Wn. and the marshal made a reconnaissance on them with some cavalry and that division. The enemy had 5 battns. and some cavalry, which on being cannonaded retired to the heights behind the Fords, and some of our people got over and have since established themselves on the other side. They returned our fire very briskly but with no effect, as their shot all fell short, and we have very few men hurt by the skirmishing.

The enemy appear to have concentrated their force on Valladolid, leaving some strong corps on the Douro to watch us, and sometimes patrolling to about 2 leagues from this on the River Adaja. I do not think they are yet in force to undertake anything against us, and Ld. Welln.'s plans are too well kept to himself for it to be possible for anyone to guess what they may be. I think, if we advance, the enemy will fight us.

I have not a doubt of the result, in the state of their army, whose morale appears gone. But how far Ld. W. may think right to risk an action is quite another question. Though the harvest is extremely abundant this year, it is not yet ready. Deserters report that they are much distressed for provisions at Valladolid. If this is true (which I doubt), Lord Wn. perhaps intends to force them back by waiting patiently till they have exhausted what they have. But these are all speculations without much data, and Ld.Welln.'s despatch may give you better grounds to conjecture upon than I can.

The country, through which we have marched from Salamanca, is extremely fertile and well cultivated, producing abundance of corn of all descriptions, sometimes in one year for the consumption of three, and this year the crops are remarkably fine, though much has been consumed and more destroyed uselessly by both armies. The country on this side of Villa Escusa produces mostly wine, and the whole face of the country is covered with vineyards, which give it a very rich appearance in general. The country is flat and quite open, almost totally without trees, and not much water. From the want of the two latter our troops have suffered considerably, for the weather, though far from so hot as Portugal, has been hot to people marching and obliged to be always exposed to it.

We have had a very harassing, fatiguing life of it since we left Guinaldo, and are much the better for the few days' rest we have had here. The towns in this part of Spain are generally very large, clean, and populous. The houses particularly neat. Nothing can exceed the joy and acclamations with which the army is everywhere received by all classes. That there are many traitors I believe, but that the joy of the greater part is sincere it is impossible to doubt. Nothing can have been more oppressive or insolent than the conduct of the French for the last 4 years. They levied enormous and repeated contributions upon the people, at the same time that they deprived them in kind of the means of paying them. Military executions and coercion followed of course, and all its miseries. It will scarcely be believed that even at this moment they have several of the principal *ladies* and inhabitants of this large town prisoners at Tordesillas as hostages for the payment of some of their requisitions.

While writing, Mr Bertie of the 12th Lt. Dns. has brought me a letter of introduction from you, and on every account, both as the Admiral's son and from your letter, I shall be most happy to have it in my power to show him any kindness or civility. He is a very fine lad and quite well. We yesterday received letters and papers to the 19th. . . .

From circumstances that have occurred I am no longer so anxious about the majority of infantry, unless with the certainty of returning to the cavalry. The other situations are indeed desirable, if not beyond my reach, but many considerations have now determined me otherwise to remain in the cavalry. Lt.-Genl. Sir T. Graham left the army yesterday for England to consult the best advice about a disorder in one of his eyes. I fear it is a bad case. He is regretted by everybody and the army as a most excellent zealous soldier, and a most amiable worthy man. I know none I have a higher respect and veneration for. Yrs., etc.,

Wm. Warre.

EXTRACT FROM LETTER TO SISTER.

La Seca, July 10, 1812.

It is a terrible thing to be tanned by the sun. I have been half grilled for the last month, which has cost my nose and lips a great deal of flesh. It is expensive on the score of skin, but it is in a good cause, and my nose suffers like a martyr. It has completely spoiled all complexions, and made us like hideous creatures. I shall not burn your letters—if my baggage should be taken, the French will derive great amusement from them, and being of political importance we shall have them in the *Moniteur* with notes! I have no news to tell you of the army. The French are on one side of the river, and we are on the other. Both parties are very civil to each other, and both seem on the *qui vive* for fear the other should cross and attack him. It is comical enough to see hostile troops quietly watering their horses, or washing, within 30 or 40 yards of each other, like perfect good friends. We are forbid to talk to them for fear of spoiling our French, and are therefore highly profuse in bows and dumbshow. I hate the very sight of the villains, but it is no use for either party to annoy the other when nothing is to be gained by it.

We are quartered in a very nice town, about two leagues from the river, where the people are very civil to us. I am quite well, though much thinner for our marching, and I do not believe that anybody is sorry for the week's quiet halt we have had.

La Seca, July 13, 1812.

My Dear Father,

I have to thank you for your letter of the 17 *ultmo.* and your very interesting communications on the domestic politics of the country, and also for the printed correspondence. Your letter, etc., did not arrive till by last packet, and should have done so by the former, and I therefore had seen all these discussions between parties in the newspapers, and the only conclusion I have drawn is that there is no public spirit in any party. Each acts from its own particular prejudice, or party spirit, and they care little about the country, unless they can serve it exactly in their own way. I am glad of anything that saves us from a Grenville administration, and am therefore not sorry the present Ministry have been continued, though I have not much confidence in them, and should have preferred one that included Ld. Wellesley.

The first measures of this administration plainly say, we have not strength to act up to our own principles in certain leading questions. We will therefore act contrary to our principles to keep our places. This appears to be the real state of the case, though as to the measures themselves to which I refer, except with regard to the Americans, I hope great good from them, but though most decidedly for the admission of the Catholics to all rights we possess ourselves, I am not for granting them one bit more. Their Church in temporal matters must be subordinate to the king. The king's rights with regard to the rejection or nomination of their bishops must be the same as our own, and which is nearly the same as in Portugal, Spain, France (formerly), and almost every other Roman Catholic country. None of those countries ever thought of a clergy independent of the crown, or that the Pope had any power whatever in the temporal arrangements of any kingdom.

The consistory (Claustro) assembled at Salamanca on this very subject of Irish emancipation in, I think, 1789, declared that any country which admitted such a principle would be a traitor to itself, of whatever sect the sovereign might be, Protestant or Catholic. If therefore the R. C. of Ireland insist on greater rights and liberties, in their religious liberty, than the rest of their fellow subjects possess, or object to the veto (at least) in the king, I shall strongly suspect that they have other purposes in their discontent, and shall think any concession dangerous.

We continue here much in the same state as when I wrote to you last week. Since then the enemy have been joined by Bonnet from the Asturias with about 4000 to 5000 men, but do not show at present any disposition to attack us. They have manoeuvred a good deal. Indeed, they seem to keep their people in constant motion. Till lately they seemed to be drawing everything to their right towards Toro, and the position of our troops was altered from perpendicular to parallel to the Douro, the 5 and 6 Dns. moving to Nava del Rey, the 4th to Foncastin. The 3rd and Spaniards continue at Polios, and the 1st and 7th at Medina del Campo, the advance guard and lt. cavalry at Rueda and this place, and our picquets watch the fords of the Douro and of the Adaja.

Yesterday morning we saw a large column of about 4000 returning towards Tordesillas, from whence they had marched the evening before towards the fords at Herreros and Torresilla de la Abadessa, but to what end all this marching and countermarching of theirs can be, I cannot guess. If they mean to harass us, they do not succeed, for though we narrowly watch every movement they make, Ld. Wn. is not easily humbugged, and lets them wear out their shoes as much they please without disturbing his army.

The enemy's hdqrs. are, I believe, at Tordesillas, where they have one or two divisions, 1 at Simancas, 1 opposite Polios and Herreros, 1 at Toro. In short, they extend along the river from Simancas to Toro, and have their reserves and depot at Valladolid. As to the exact disposition of their troops it is impossible to say, as they are continually moving.

I believe the whole army would rejoice if they would cross the river and attack us, as I am quite confident, we should beat them, though they have 80 pieces of cannon. Their cavalry is much inferior to ours in every respect, and they have such want of horses that they have taken all the infantry officers' horses to mount their cavalry, and which has given great disgust, and would, I should think, benefit them very little.

What Lord Wn.'s plans are I cannot even guess. He is best informed and best able to decide what is best. We must therefore quietly wait the event, and, in the healthy state and high spirits of the army, we have little to fear for the I result.

I do not doubt much that he is waiting for Santo Cildes with the Galician Army, who are besieging the fort at Astorga, to advance and co-operate with him previous to any movement on our part. But this is only guess. I am surprised that the French, who have, I believe, nearly equal numbers, do not attack us before this co-operation can take place, particularly as they do not seem to expect any further reinforcements.

Our posts on the river continue very near each other, very amicably, and literally nothing has been done by posts of any consequence since I wrote to you. The account I sent you was of the Portuguese Army only, and it has since rather increased, as we have left sick and wounded.

The enemy have also some posts at Villa Nueva and Puente de Douro and on the River Adaja.

With regard to the purchase of the majority of infantry, as I had purchased my troop, the purchase of a majority of infantry required no advance. On the contrary, by the regulation there would be a surplus of £500, and my intention was to have remained in the infantry for some time at least. But other considerations have since decided me not to go into the infantry at all, except I got a permanent staff situation, or was quite sure of returning to the cavalry immediately. I do not quite agree that the command of a Portuguese battn. would be much less eligible than my present situation, as far as the means of distinguishing myself goes, as I should then have a positive command and responsibility, and now have, nor can have, neither, and it must at last come to that, or to my joining my British regiment. . . .Yrs., etc.,

Wm. Warre.

A very dreadful accident happened at Salamanca since we left it. A very large quantity of powder which had been taken in the fort and was deposited in the town caught fire and blew up, in consequence of the folly of a Spanish officer, who was guarding it, smoking. Two streets were, I hear, almost totally destroyed. The whole guard and upwards of 100 Spaniards (inhabitants) killed and wounded, and some soldiers. The town was otherwise very much damaged and all the windows broke, and in the greatest confusion, as everybody fled into the country, many *en chemise*, it having happened at 8 o'clock in the morning. It happened very near one of our hospitals, but fortunately killed very few of our sick or wounded. The weather has latterly been exceedingly hot, and it is very fortunate that we have not been moving, as our people are suffering a good deal from want of wood and water.

July 14th.—By an intercepted mail from Paris to Madrid which was taken by Longa, who killed the 400 men who escorted it except 12, who, he says, did not show so strong an inclination to leave their bodies there, we have *Moniteurs* to the 24th, by which it appears that Boney was arrived at Konigsberg. Amongst a great many letters, amatory, friendly, etc., there is one from the Spanish Ambassador at St Petersburg, who describes the state of the Russian Armies as very formidable and in excellent order—both on the frontiers of Poland and Turkey. The emperor and Romanzow without any boasting, he says, are quietly determined to try the event. They wish to settle matters with Napoleon amicably if possible, but will not even hear of the commercial system. All the letters complain of not hearing from their friends in Spain, and of the frequent interception of the mails by the guerillas. *Adieu*—we have nothing new with this army. I am well.

My Dear Father,

I have very, very great pleasure in communicating to you one of the most decisive and complete victories that was ever gained by the valour and intrepidity of our brave troops, but alas! my exultation and joy are not without great diminution, for our brave and excellent marshal is severely wounded, as well as a great many of our brave generals, but for none of course can I feel as I do for our worthy marshal. It is, however, though painful and severe, *not* certainly a dangerous wound, and this country, as well as his own, will, I trust, be only temporarily deprived of his most necessary services and example.

We have been terribly harassed since the 16th, day and night, owing to Marmont having crossed the Douro by a skilful movement upon Toro, at which place he sent a force across, and drew our army to that neighbourhood, and then by a forced march returned and crossed at Tordesillas, and immediately commenced his manoeuvres to turn the right flank of our army, which forced Lord Wellington gradually to fall back successively behind the Guarena and Tormes.

On the 18th our army made a forward movement towards Alaejos and Nava again, but the lt. division coming up with the enemy at Castrejon, a sharp cannonade and skirmishing took place, and the direction of the army was altered to the direction of Torrecilla de la Orden, as the enemy seemed determined to move round our flank. (It is necessary to observe that we had retired the night before to Fuente La Pena, Castrello, and Canizal, in consequence of the enemy having crossed at Toro, and were at this time advancing, having heard that he had recrossed again and was at Nava and Alaejos.) Several divisions were ordered up, and all the cavalry to support the lt. division, but finding the enemy in great force and the ground offering no position, we were forced to retire under a heavy cannonade, which they renewed again as they gained the heights above the River Guarena. But our loss was very trifling indeed considering.

Towards evening the enemy endeavoured to move round our left flank with two divisions, and sent a brigade to attack a height on which our left rested, but they were charged most gallantly by the 27th and 40th, supported by the 11th and 23rd Portuguese, and completely routed, paying us with great interest for our losses. They lost upwards of 500 men, of which we took 130 prisoners. The marshal was at this time slightly wounded by a grape shot in the thigh, but very slightly, and we had one officer killed and about 150 to 160 men killed and wounded. I do not know what our loss was in the whole day.

On the evening of the 19th we saw the whole of the enemy's army in march to turn our right apparently, and the disposition of our army was altered to La Vallesa, where the next day both armies were at daybreak close together, and a battle seemed inevitable. Lord Wellington began to form on a perfect plan to receive them, and they never had a finer opportunity, but though their whole force seemed to threaten destruction to our right, they suddenly moved off by their left along some heights, and Lord Wellington moved his army, in order of battle, in two lines, along the plain and halted at night between Cabeça Vellozo and Pitiegna, our people much harassed and fatigued, as the heat was incessant, and no water hardly to be found. But I suppose there never was a more interesting or beautiful sight than that of two hostile armies of upwards of 35,000 men each moving parallel within a mile and a half of each other and often within cannon range.

On the 21st our army was forced to cross the Tormes, by Marmont's moving round it, and took up a position at night to cover Salamanca, our left to the Tormes, our right to some isolated heights in rear of Calbaraza de Ariba and beyond Na. Senora de la Peña, the enemy moving to the woods nearly half way between Alva de Tormes and Calbarasa, having crossed at Ençina. During all these days there was a great deal of skirmishing and cannonading on both sides, and we were all greatly harassed and fatigued, having scarce time to rest or eat, and on horseback all day long, and the troops suffered much from the excessive heat and almost incessant marching.

On the forever glorious 22nd we found the enemy at daybreak in our front, but at a distance, and some skirmishing took place about a hill they had got in our front, which it was as well that we should have. It was, however, strongly supported by them, and Lord Welln. did not think it worthwhile to lose many lives in retaking it, and our people were ordered to withdraw.

As the morning advanced the enemy got possession, before our people could, of a very strong and commanding height which was on our right, and as they continued to move in that direction the position of our army was altered, and we every instant expected to be attacked, as the enemy had the finest opportunity during this change of position. But it was ordained otherwise by that great and merciful Disposer of all events, and we remained quiet till a little before 4 in the evening, when the enemy opened a most tremendous cannonade upon our whole line from, I should guess, upwards of 50 pieces of cannon, and soon after pushed forward a crowd of sharpshooters, it should appear, however, only to insult our army, as they were not supported, and the heavy columns they had on the hills did not move forward. I suppose that Monr. Marmont, with French insolence, thought, because we had not attacked him before, and had moved back to counter manoeuvre him and to avoid being turned, that we were afraid of him, and that he could thus insult us with impunity, but retribution was at hand, and before sunset he was doomed to pay most dearly for his impertinence by the entire ruin of his army and loss of at least half of it.

About 5 o'clock Lord Wellington ordered our lines to advance, having previously detailed the 3rd division and all our cavalry to turn the enemy's left.

The army moved forward most gallantly under a heavy cannonade to the attack of the heights on which the enemy was posted, at the same time that Major General Pakenham with the 3rd div. attacked the height on their left and succeeded in forcing it notwithstanding the enemy's obstinate *resistance*, and afterwards advanced along their line, completely doubling it up, as the rest of the army advanced in its front. As we came near, they kept up a most galling fire of grape and musquetry on our line, and in many places stood most gallantly, but it was impossible to resist the steady though impetuous advance of our brave troops, which no loss can make waver or delay, and they were soon driven from their first position to a second behind the right of it, which, our troops being reformed, was successively attacked, and at last carried, notwithstanding our people being sometimes repulsed by the gallant charges of the enemy and the heavy fire of artillery to which they were exposed in advancing. It was near sunset, and in endeavouring to make a Portuguese brigade charge the enemy, (who were driving the 4th division back with 5 bns.) in flank, that our excellent marshal was wounded, while exerting himself, as he always does with the greatest zeal and gallantry, and by his noble example, to cover the 4th divn. by this flank charge. But they soon rallied and regained the ground they had lost by the sudden attack of the enemy, and the heights were retaken just as the marshal was hit. I was obliged to quit the field with him, and with some difficulty got him to the rear, and to this place at 11 at night, after having his wounds dressed on the road.

The battle, however, continued with unabated fury till late in the evening, and the enemy fought at last from despair, but pursued with undiminished ardour by our troops, notwithstanding the fatigue they had gone through. They at last broke and fled in all directions in the most complete confusion and dismay, followed by our people, who only halted for the night at two leagues beyond the field in which the battle commenced, and next day, yesterday, Lord Wellington continued the pursuit with 10,000 men to near Peñazanda, where the enemy had taken up a position. Several partial engagements have taken place since, in which both our cavalry and infantry have constantly routed the enemy, who now desert to us in hundreds every hour.

Marmont is said to have died of his wound. We know he had lost an arm.

The enemy have left upwards, I hear, of 5000 dead on the field on these three days. We have taken 1 general, 2 eagles, 2 standards, 20 guns, and near 6000 prisoners, but this as well as our loss, which is computed at 3000 killed and wounded, (but a very large proportion of general officers) I tell you from hearsay, as I have not been able to leave the marshal since, and the *Gazette* will tell you better, but I believe it to be nearly true. Of the prisoners, 4000 and odd hundred have been sent off from hence to the rear, and 1500 were taken in one bunch by the 4th Dragoons, or Heavy Germans, yesterday evening, and I should think I do not exaggerate at all in stating the loss of the French at from 15,000 to 16,000 men. There never was a more complete rout. They are flying in all directions, and either come or are brought in in hundreds at a time. I am much annoyed at being here at such a moment, but more a thousand times at the cause.

I need say nothing in praise of the allied troops: their conduct and the event speaks stronger in their favour than any words of mine could. Our cavalry constantly charged their infantry and cavalry, and upset everything that opposed them. I am very sorry indeed to tell you that poor General Le Marchant was killed charging at the head of his brigade with his usual gallantry and judgment. He is universally regretted, and in him the service has lost one of its best cavalry officers. I feel very much for his unfortunate young family now left without father or mother.

Generals Leith, Cole, Sir Stapleton Cotton, are also here wounded but not dangerously, and Maj-.General Victor Allen badly. We hear that Marmont is dead of his wounds. It is, I believe, certain that he lost an arm, which makes this likely. Nearly the whole of the enemy's baggage was taken by the Portuguese 3 regts. of cavalry under D'Urban, who behaved very well indeed, and twice charged the enemy's infantry, and once their cavalry, with complete success, and the general speaks in the highest terms of them.

I mentioned that we remained quiet all day nearly till 4 o'clock, but it was not so, as there was a great deal of skirmishing and cannonading at times. The battle made me forget, I suppose, all the rest.

I am very well. I was nearly knocked up by the constant fatigue and exposure to the sun, but the victory set me nearly right again, and the rest we have had here the last two days entirely so. I cannot be enough grateful to Almighty God for his infinite goodness and protection for the last fortnight, and particularly during the hard-fought battle, but I escaped very well with two shots on my sword scabbard, and one thro' my holster, which is as near as I ever wish to have them.

The marshal is quite free from fever, and doing as well as possible. The ball entered the side below the left breast, and, slanting round the external part of the ribs, was cut out at the back about 4 inches below. The bone is not supposed to be injured at all, and it is thought that the ball went round it through the muscles. His wound in the thigh, which was very slight, is nearly quite well.

Being separated from hdqrs. we find great difficulty in sending our letters, and I much fear may miss the officer who is to carry the despatches . . . I wrote a few lines to —— and sent them off yesterday to take their chance of finding him still at hdqrs. I should also have written to you, but that I have not been able to leave the marshal a moment, and am now writing close to him, and constantly interrupted, which will, I hope, excuse this incoherent epistle.

General Leith is doing very well indeed, and it is now found that the ball has not hurt the elbow joint. Of all our other friends I dare say nothing, for all I know is from hearsay, and may be wrong, and of those that are hurt the *Gazette* will too soon give the distressing account.

I saw Ferguson the 21st. He was quite well. I have not heard of him since, but I hope that he is not hurt. The guards have, I hear, lost very few officers. I only know of a Mr White of the 3rd Guards Lt. Company being wounded.

25th.—The marshal continues to go on as well as possible and has no fever. Generals Leith, Cotton, Cole, also are doing well. Yrs., etc.,

Wm. Warre.

Lord Wellington is continuing the pursuit of the enemy, who are retiring in great confusion. He was shot through his cloak and holsters during the action, but, thank God, not hurt.

Salamanca, July 27, 1812.

My Dear Father,

I wrote to you on the 24th an account of the most glorious and decisive battle of the 22nd, and also telling you of our worthy marshal being severely wounded. I am now most happy to be able to assure you that he is very much better, and doing as well as possible, is quite free from fever, and has kept very well. The ball does not appear to have touched the ribs, but to have gone round the muscles of the side. Lord Wellington has continued the pursuit of the enemy, who has retired in great confusion, and His Lordship was yesterday at Aldea Seca. Joseph Buon-aparte had advanced to reinforce Marmont, but hearing of his disaster had retired, not before we had taken one of his picquets. I have not yet seen any return of the loss on either side. I believe ours to be between 3000 and 4000 killed and wounded. Poor Le Marchant, whose son has just left me to return to England, was killed charging most gallantly at the head of his brigade, and is a great loss to the service (as he was an excellent officer), and to his numerous family, who are now without father or mother. I pity them from my soul. Sir Stapleton Cotton, Genls.

Leith, Cole, and Victor Allen, who are here, are doing very well. Leith's wound is a severe one through his arm obliquely, but it has not broken the bone. His nephew Leith Hay is wounded, not badly, through the leg. The town is full of wounded officers, who are mostly doing very well indeed. Poor Antonio de Lacerda's son died, and he is himself here wounded. The son was a remarkably fine gallant lad, and the poor father is in great affliction.

The enemy continue their retreat towards Madrid. We calculate their total loss at 15,000. We have 2 generals, 2 eagles, 2 standards, 19 guns, and upwards of 6000 prisoners, and from the appearance of the field of battle, I should suppose they had left 1500 to 2000 dead on the field besides what they lost after they retired from their last position, and in the subsequent pursuit, in which they have been followed up very close, and completely routed whenever our advance has been able to come up with their rear-guard. Marmont, Bonnet, Clauzel, Thornier, are said to be badly wounded, besides Carrière and Gravier wounded and taken. The latter, I believe, is dead since.

Owing to the army having advanced and the few means of transport, many of the wounded, particularly of the French, have suffered horribly, for, three days after, I saw a great many still lying, who had received no assistance or were likely to till next day, and had lain scorching in the sun without a drop of water or the least shade. It was a most dreadful sight. These are the horrid miseries of war. No person who has not witnessed them can possibly form any idea of what they are. Humanity shudders at the very idea, and we turn with detestation and disgust to the sole author of such miseries.

What punishment can be sufficient for him! Many of the poor wretches have crawled to this. Many made crutches of the barrels of the firelocks and their shoes. Cruel and villainous as they are themselves, and even were during the action to our people, one cannot help feeling for them and longing to be able to assist them. But our own people have suffered almost as much, and they are our first care.

I am very well and have quite recovered the fatigue we went through for several days, but I am most happy that the marshal is doing so well. During the action I escaped quite providentially, as I have a shot through my holster and two on my sword scabbard, but as long as they keep at that distance, I shall be very well satisfied.

I think we shall remain here quietly for some weeks. Indeed, I do not think Ld. Wn. can pursue them much further, as they are moving back upon their reinforcements, and have the strong passes of Guadalajara in their rear, and, besides that, our troops must have some rest, having been so much harassed lately.

What may be the consequences of this splendid victory it is not easy to say. They must be very great, for we have never gained a more decisive or more complete one, or followed it up so rapidly. I think it must bring Soult up from the South and raise the siege of Cadiz. Marmont's army is quite crippled for a time, having lost all its baggage and so many guns and men. They were joined by about 1500 cavalry and some guns the evening of the action, which were beat next day.

Young Cowell is here unwell, but not wounded, and is getting well fast. I shall take care of him. The guards were scarcely engaged and have lost few men and no officer that I have heard of. My friend Jackson is quite well. Pray, if any officer should be coming to the army, send me 2 lb. of good black tea. It will be a great treat. Yrs., etc.,

Wm. Warre.

Molloy was taken for a minute by the French cavalry, but got off. I am very anxious to hear if you have done anything about the appointment I mentioned to the Cape. This action has confirmed my opinion that we may be shot at all day and exert ourselves as much as we please, but according to the proverb, *It is a bad thing to be second fiddles to a second fiddle.*

EXTRACT FROM LETTER TO SISTER

Salamanca, Aug. 19th, 1812.

While you were amusing yourself with quizzing your brother Wm. and abusing him for not being in love with honour and glory, I was straining my arms to reach one little leaf of the laurel tree, which, to a fanciful imagination, is considered a sort of introduction to those gentlemen. Lo! while you and —— were trembling at the rolling of the thunderstorm, and . . . thinking of honour and glory, I was amused by an equally loud though less innocent storm from about 70 pieces of cannon, of which 50 belonged to the adverse gods who fulminated us for 7 hours, as hard as they could, and with malice prepense, but with very little effect except the effect of the sublime, of which there was a good deal, for I think it combined so much of beauty and grandeur and *awe* that certainly Edmund Burke would have classed it with the sublime. As for beauty, *ça va sans dire*. You cannot think how beautiful it is to be cannonaded all day, being very tired and hungry, and at 5 p.m. instead of setting to to eat a good dinner, to set to to give the French a good beating in a very strong position, which, however, is the best part of the whole *divertissement*, and though Ld. Welln. naturally got all the laurels, it was a most glorious business, and would almost put even me in conceit with honour and glory. . . .

Since then we have been very peaceably settled here, and the marshal recovering very fast from the delightful effects of honour and glory. I rather expect in a few days we shall leave this for Lisbon by Oporto. It will be an exceedingly interesting journey as, not being able yet to ride, he goes in a carriage as far as San Joao da Pesqueira (*vide* the map), and from thence down the Douro, which is beautiful, to Oporto, and from thence in some ship of war to Lisbon. The only thing I am sorry for is not seeing Segovia or Madrid.

EXTRACT FROM LETTER TO SISTER.

(?) Salamanca, Sept. 2nd, 1812.

We leave this tomorrow morning for Porto on our way to Lisbon. We go down the Douro, which at this time of year is quite beautiful, and I think altogether this jaunt promises to be very pleasant, and, if the sea voyage agrees with me, and that the marshal remains any time at Lisbon, you must not be astonished if I pay you a visit for three weeks or a month, but this is a great secret yet. Say nothing about it to anybody, till I see how things are, when we arrive at Lisbon, as everything must depend upon that. The marshal and myself are again upon excellent terms. We have great battles sometimes, but they never last very long. . . .

Of public news I have not a word to send you. The enemy have evacuated Zamora, and are preparing to retire again on any motion of Lord Wellington's towards Burgos.

Of the six divisions which formerly composed that army of Portugal (Marmont's) it has now only 3 divns. commanded by Foy, Maucune, and Clausel. The latter commands *ad interim* till

MAP OF
SPAIN & PORTUGAL
TO ILLUSTRATE THE PENINSULAR WAR

Miles

Bonnet recovers from his wounds. Marmont has asked for leave to return to France for the recovery of his health. His wounds are of a very bad nature. The whole army is of about 15,000 men (out of 42,000) and about 1700 cavalry, and do not seem at all inclined to fight against English honour and glory again. King Joseph is at Valencia. Lord William Bentinck at Madrid, but some of our divisions have moved towards the Douro to drive the enemy further back. They will retire, I am sure, as soon as these seem to advance in earnest. We are in hourly expectation of hearing that the enemy have raised the siege of Cadiz and have abandoned Andalusia. Everything seemed to indicate their intention of doing so. And we have a proclamation of Soult's, in which he avows it, and endeavours to *console* the Spaniards for his absence, and promises to return *as soon as he can*, good natured soul!

I have just seen the garrison of Guadalaxara marched in. About 800 men, a great part renegade Spaniards, and in most miserable plight, as their better countrymen have plundered them of everything, and I don't pity them. I hate a traitor worse than a Frenchman. There is a general with them and some field officers, etc., etc.